IMAGES
of Aviation

AVIATION *in* HAMPTON ROADS

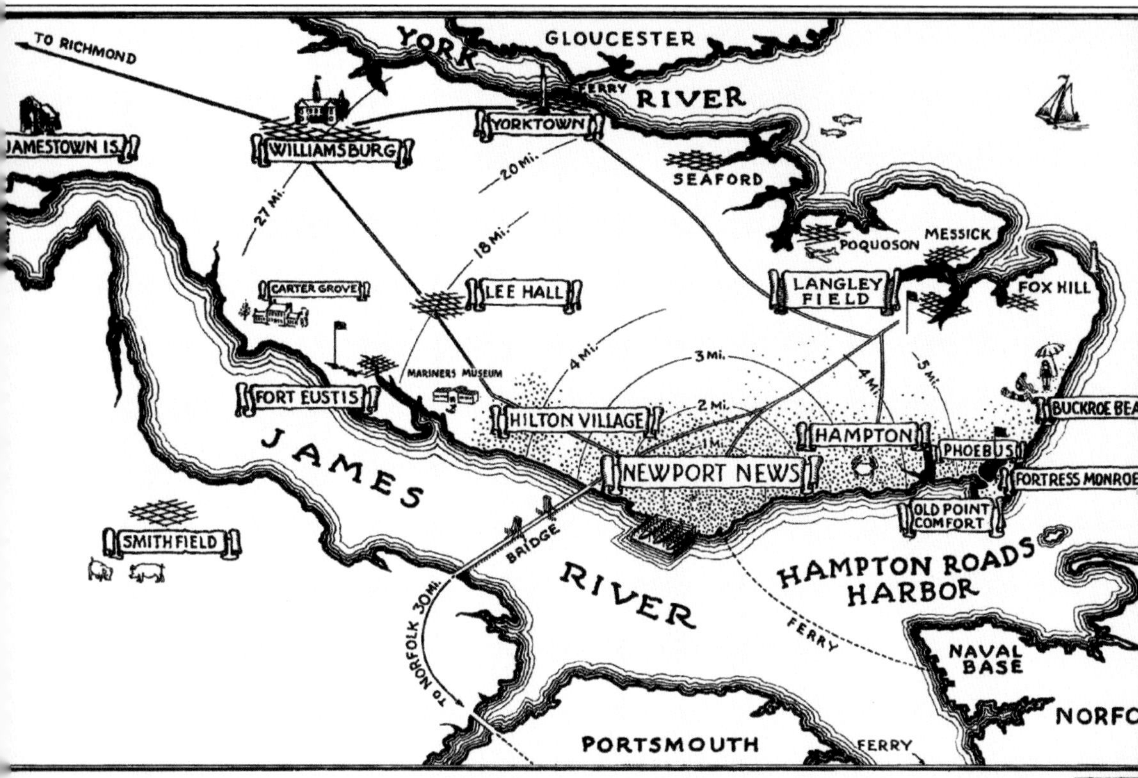

HAMPTON ROADS, VIRGINIA. The Gateway to Southeastern Virginia, Hampton Roads (also known as Tidewater) includes 16 municipalities; the region contains such cities as Chesapeake, Hampton, Newport News, Norfolk, Portsmouth, Suffolk, Virginia Beach, and Williamsburg. It is a metropolitan area with a combined population of more than 1.5 million. The original name, Southampton Roadstead, was given in the 17th century for the royal governor, who was formerly of Southampton, England. The nautical term "roadstead" means "safe anchorage," referring to the myriad of harbors, rivers, bays, and inlets in the region. Also dotting the area are a number of civilian, commercial, and military airports; in fact, there are two airports with scheduled air service, two large naval bases with very active runways, and an Air Force base. This Langley Memorial Aeronautical Laboratory map from the late 1930s shows Langley Field in the center, which today is Langley Air Force Base. (NASA.)

On the Cover: **EUGENE B. ELY.** Eugene Bruton Ely, born in Iowa in 1886, was an early, self-taught aviator. He pioneered military aviation by piloting a Curtiss biplane off the deck of a ship anchored in Hampton Roads and landing on shore. In this photograph, he is shown with his wife, Mabel. Ely died in 1911 in a plane crash in Georgia. (HRNM.)

IMAGES
of Aviation

AVIATION *in* HAMPTON ROADS

Patrick Evans-Hylton

ARCADIA
PUBLISHING

ISBN 978-0-7385-1820-6

Published by Arcadia Publishing
Charleston, South Carolina

Printed in the United States of America

Library of Congress Catalog Card Number: 2005922731

For all general information contact Arcadia Publishing at:
Telephone 843-853-2070
Fax 843-853-0044
E-mail sales@arcadiapublishing.com
For customer service and orders:
Toll-Free 1-888-313-2665

Visit us on the Internet at www.arcadiapublishing.com

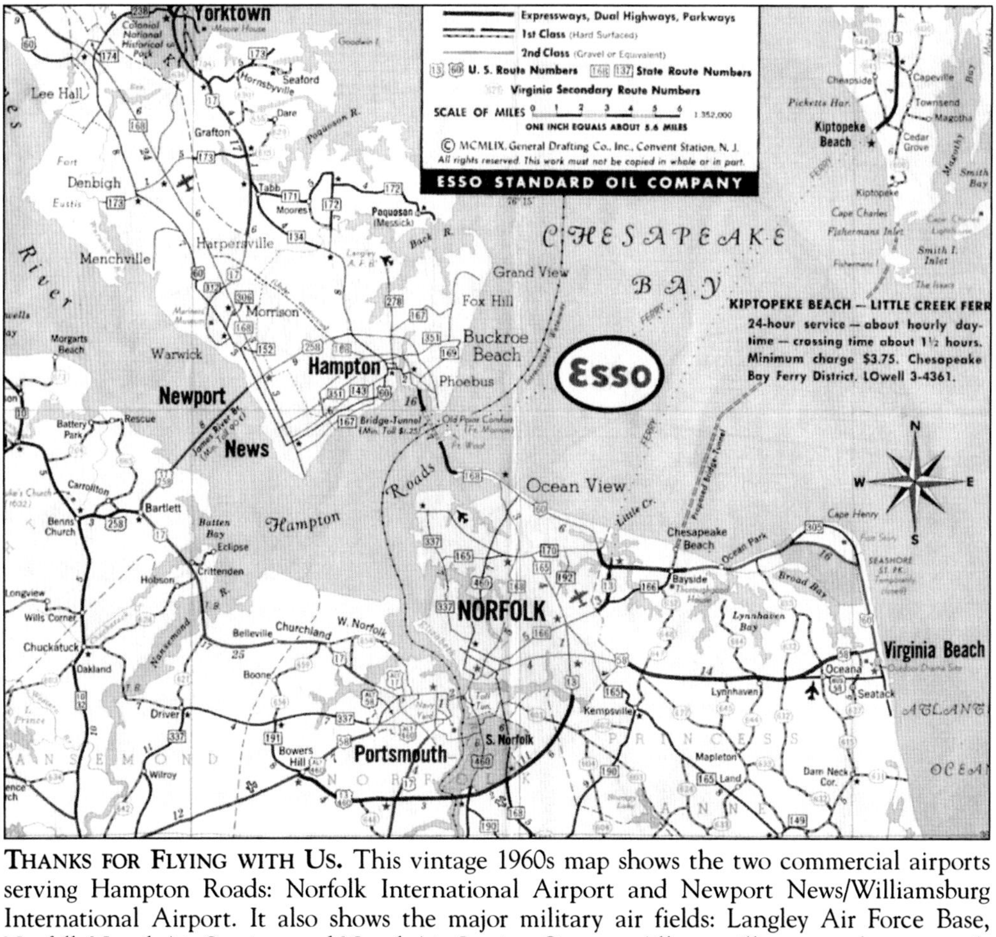

THANKS FOR FLYING WITH US. This vintage 1960s map shows the two commercial airports serving Hampton Roads: Norfolk International Airport and Newport News/Williamsburg International Airport. It also shows the major military air fields: Langley Air Force Base, Norfolk Naval Air Station, and Naval Air Station Oceana. All are still open and active with hundreds of daily flights. (PEH.)

Contents

ACKNOWLEDGMENTS

Compiling information and photographs that chronicle the rich commercial and military aviation history in Hampton Roads, Virginia, was no small task. It was only possible because of the assistance and expertise of many giving and gifted individuals. To everyone who lent their time, talent, and support in this effort, I thank you.

I would like to personally thank the following individuals who went above and beyond in their assistance and support: Kathryn Korfonta of Arcadia Publishing, Wayne Shank of Norfolk International Airport, Sarah Sager of Newport News/Williamsburg International Airport, Peggy Haile McPhillips and Robert Hitchings of Norfolk's Kirn Memorial Library, Megan Steele of the Virginia Air and Space Center, Troy Snead of Naval Air Station Oceana, Fielding Tyler and Julie Pouliot of the Old Coast Guard Station Museum, and Joe Judge of the Hampton Roads Naval Museum.

Thank you, also, to my grandmother, Barbara Evans, for all those trips to see the jets at the Atlanta International Airport while I was growing up, and to my aunt, Brenda Evans-Potter, a flight attendant with United Airlines for 35 years, for getting me interested in aviation in the first place.

Special thanks for moral support and encouragement is due to the rest of my family and my friends, especially Wayne.

INTRODUCTION

Just a little more than 100 years ago, the nation was passionate for flight.

There was something in the air—literally—that drew the attention of young and old. The nation was familiar with lighter-than-air craft; the first hot-air balloon flew in 1783. In fact, they were seen often over Hampton Roads in the 19th century, particularly during the Civil War, as reconnaissance aircraft.

But the drive for heavier-than-air flight was in its heyday.

This was the Victorian era, and the idea of soaring in the skies in a flying machine was a very romantic notion. The country watched as daring aeronauts crafted contraptions from wood and canvas and tossed their dreams to the wind.

There were, of course, limited successes . . . at first.

In Hampton Roads, Virginia, the intoxicating concept of flight was strong, too. Flight has forever thrilled, but it took two brothers on wind-swept dunes just south of the region to do what no one had before.

Or at least what no one had proven. There is still dispute as to whether Orville and Wilbur Wright were indeed the first in powered flight. In fact, some 30 years before, right in Hampton Roads' backyard, James Henry Gatling built an "aeroplane" named the "Turkey Buzzard" out of wood and powered by paddle wheels, which reportedly flew up to 100 feet before crashing into a tree.

But regardless, the claim goes to the Wright brothers, who did have a revolutionary concept and made it work, successfully. After their first flight on December 17, 1903, they telegraphed the news home. An alert reporter at Norfolk's *Virginian-Pilot* newspaper heard about the flight and broke the story to the world.

The seeds of the fledgling aviation industry, planted in Hampton Roads, took root and grew.

On November 14, 1910, naval aviation was born in Hampton Roads when pilot Eugene B. Ely took off in a Curtiss biplane from the deck of the cruiser USS *Birmingham* at anchor off Old Point Comfort. He flew two miles to Willoughby Spit and landed on the beach, clearing the way for the modern aircraft carrier.

The daring young men in their flying machines also put on shows for thousands of folks. When an aviator came to town, the whole town turned out, as indicated in a front-page story in Norfolk's *Ledger-Dispatch* on December 21, 1910. "M'Curdy Will Fly Over Norfolk Tomorrow, Weather Permitting," ran the headline. The story took top billing over another reporting a fire that destroyed an entire town in West Virginia.

In less than 20 years, Norfolk would have commercial airline service, with daily flights to Washington, D.C., and Philadelphia, Pennsylvania. There would be a succession of airport terminals over the years: one off Granby Street, one in the Glenrock neighborhood, and three at the current site near the Norfolk Botanical Gardens.

In the late 1940s, the peninsula would get airline service, too, on the site of the former Camp Patrick Henry in Newport News.

Aviation pioneers came to the region, like Glenn H. Curtiss, who operated the Atlantic Coast Aeronautical Station from 1915 until 1922 on a 20-acre tract east of Newport News. The school was an important part of American history; some of the country's first aviation heroes got their start here.

Following the legacy of Eugene Ely, military aviation would grow exponentially in Hampton Roads.

Langley Field, named for aviation pioneer Samuel Pierpont Langley, was established in 1917. The base grew and included facilities for studying flight; Langley Memorial Aeronautical Laboratory (now NASA Langley Research Center) was the nation's first civilian aeronautics lab.

Later, the laboratory would be instrumental in the establishment of manned space flight. Adjacent Langley Air Force Base is today one of the oldest continuous operating military aviation bases in the world.

Norfolk Naval Air Station began life as Naval Operating Base (NOB) Norfolk in World War I, when the government established the base at the abandoned 1907 Jamestown Exposition site.

When World War II broke out, NOB was 236 acres with two small operating areas, Chambers Field and West Landing Field. The space doubled and is even bigger now: the station is the world's largest naval base.

Also during World War II, Oceana Auxiliary Landing Field (ALF) was created to relieve some of the traffic from NOB. What started as a series of small landing strips in the middle of a farm in rural Virginia Beach has grown to the world's largest naval air station and is designated a Master Jet Base. Naval Air Station Oceana today has almost a quarter-million flights from its four runways.

What is the future of aviation in Hampton Roads? The sky's the limit.

PHOTOGRAPH LEGEND:

HRNM: From the archives of the Hampton Roads Naval Museum
NASO: From the archives of Naval Air Station Oceana.
NIA: From the archives of Norfolk International Airport.
NNWI: From the archives of Newport News/Williamsburg International Airport.
NPL: From the archives of Norfolk Public Library.
VASC: From the archives of the Virginia Air and Space Center.
OCGS: From the archives of the Old Coast Guard Station.
USCG: From the U.S. Coast Guard Historian Office.
PEH: From the personal collection of Patrick Evans-Hylton.
All other photographs individually credited.

One

First Flights

It is hard to imagine a time when flight was new, when the possibility of breaking earth's grasp of gravity was magical and not a common occurrence. But little more than 100 years ago, that was the case.

Balloon flight had been possible since 1783; balloons, in fact, were seen often over Hampton Roads in the 19th century, particularly during the Civil War, when they were used as reconnaissance craft.

However, motorized, controllable flight remained elusive until the turn of the last century.

Heavier-than-air flight began in Hampton Roads' backyard; experiments in motorized flying machines took place in Murfreesboro, North Carolina, with a contraption named the Turkey Buzzard but, most famously, with Orville and Wilbur Wright and their flyer of canvas and wood on North Carolina's Outer Banks in 1903.

In fact, it was Hampton Roads that first told the story of that historic event—since the flight was reported by members of the Life Saving Station at Kitty Hawk, North Carolina, the message was relayed by telegraph up the coast, through Virginia Beach and into Norfolk and then out to the world.

The news caught the attention of the local paper, the *Virginian-Pilot*, and the story broke here. It, along with other stories of aviation firsts in the region, continues to be told.

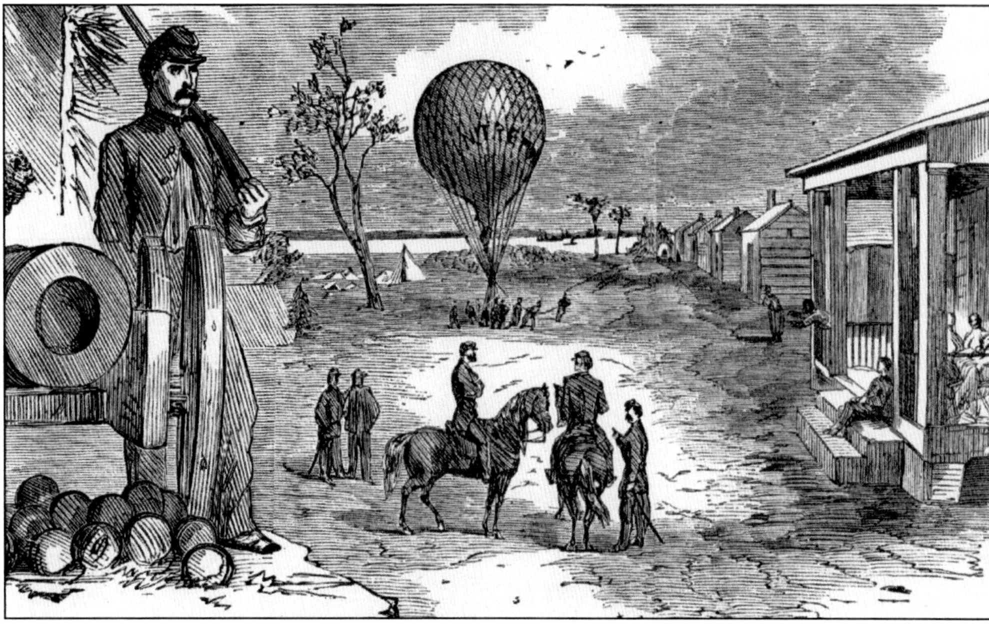

TAKING TO THE AIR. By the 1860s, ballooning was not a new thing in Virginia; in 1801, three students at the College of William and Mary launched, after three tries, an unmanned hot-air balloon from the courthouse green in Williamsburg. This was the first recorded aeronautical event in Virginia history. Beginning in 1861, both Union and Confederate armies used balloons in Virginia as surveillance platforms to gather intelligence on each other. These vintage sketches from news magazines of the time show how hot-air balloons, usually tethered, would be launched either by Union or Confederate forces to gather information about troop size, movements, and the like. Even after the Civil War, balloons had military uses: in 1902, a year before the Wright brothers' flight, the army organized a balloon detachment at Fort Myer in Arlington. (HRNM.)

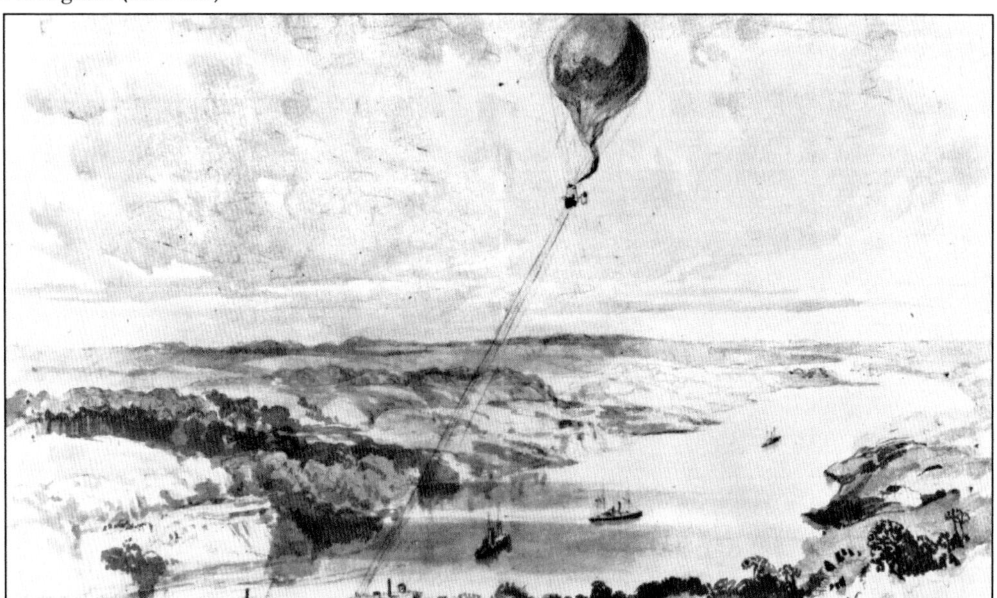

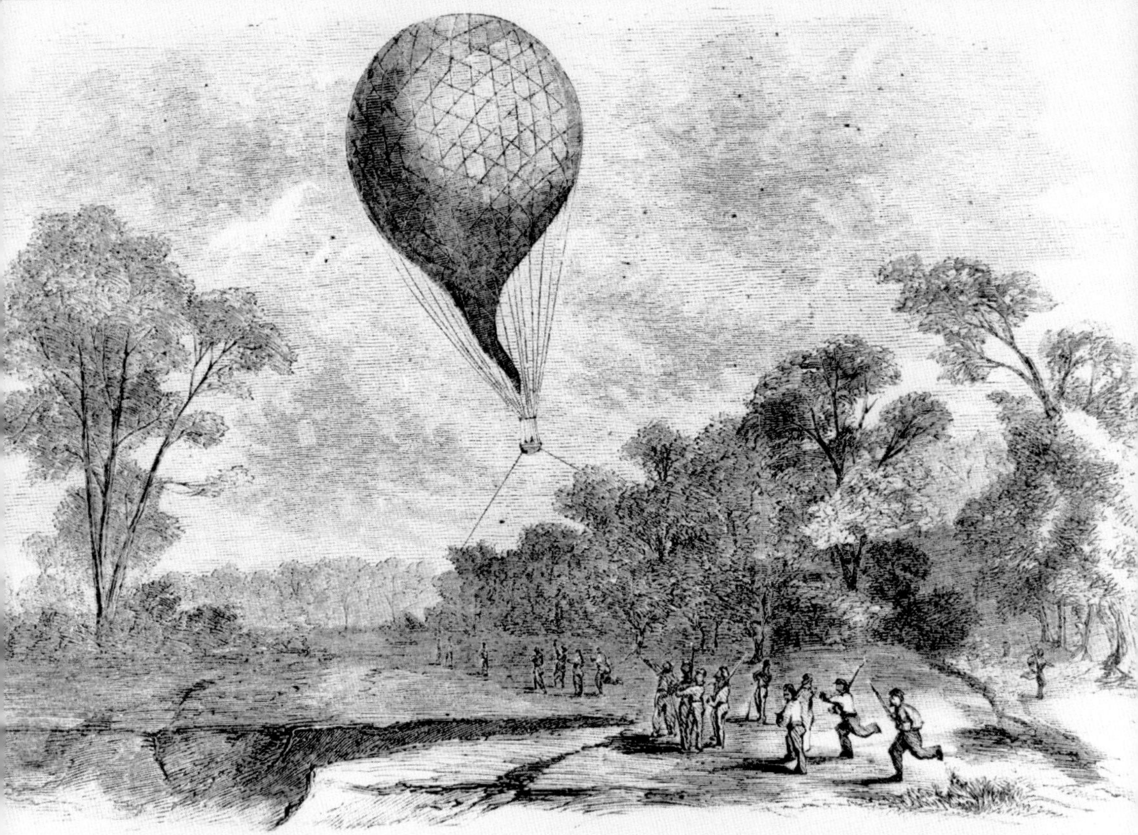

PROFESSOR LA MOUNTAIN, THE AERONAUT, RECONNOITREING THE REBEL POSITIONS NEAR FORTRESS MONROE.—FROM A SKETCH BY OUR SPECIAL ARTIST.

UP, UP, AND AWAY. The above image caption from *Frank Leslie's Illustrated Newspaper* reads, "Professor [John] LaMountain, the aeronaut, reconnoitering the rebel positions near Fortress Monroe." LaMountain was hired by the commander of the Union forces at Fort Monroe (in Hampton), Maj. Gen. Benjamin F. Butler. During a demonstration flight in 1861, LaMountain said he could view Confederate encampments as far as Newport News. His employment only lasted, however, until 1862. Although the use of balloons provided intelligence, the corps was disbanded in 1863 after one of its supporters, Gen. George McClellan, was relieved of his duties. The Confederates used balloons on a smaller scale but did have some success.

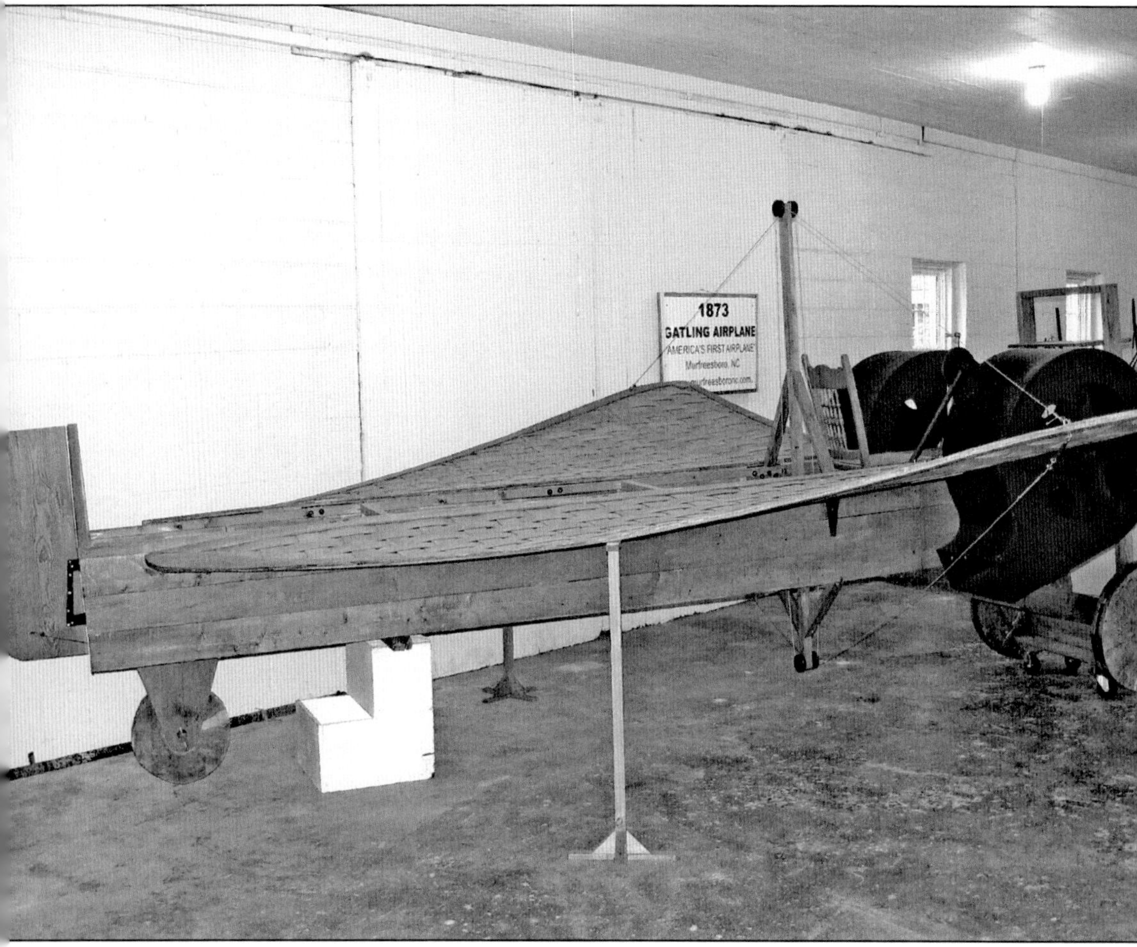

THE TURKEY BUZZARD. "The desire to fly is an idea handed down to us by our ancestors," wrote Wilbur Wright. For hundreds of years, there were dreams of powered flight, as evidenced in drawings by Leonardo da Vinci as early as the 1480s. One of those dreamers was James Henry Gatling of Murfreesboro, North Carolina, located just southwest of Hampton Roads. Gatling, older brother of Richard Gatling, inventor of the Gatling Machine Gun, is reported to have flown a heavier-than-air machine on his family farm in 1873. A replica of that "aeroplane," shown in this photograph, is on display at the Murfreesboro Historical Association. According to witnesses, Gatling took flight on a Sunday afternoon, powered by twin blowers under each wing. Folks report he flew up to 100 feet before crashing into a tree. While in flight, the name "Turkey Buzzard" was given to the machine because of the way it resembled a bird of that name. After the crash, the damaged machine was stored in a barn, which later caught fire before repairs could be made, and the craft was destroyed. (PEH.)

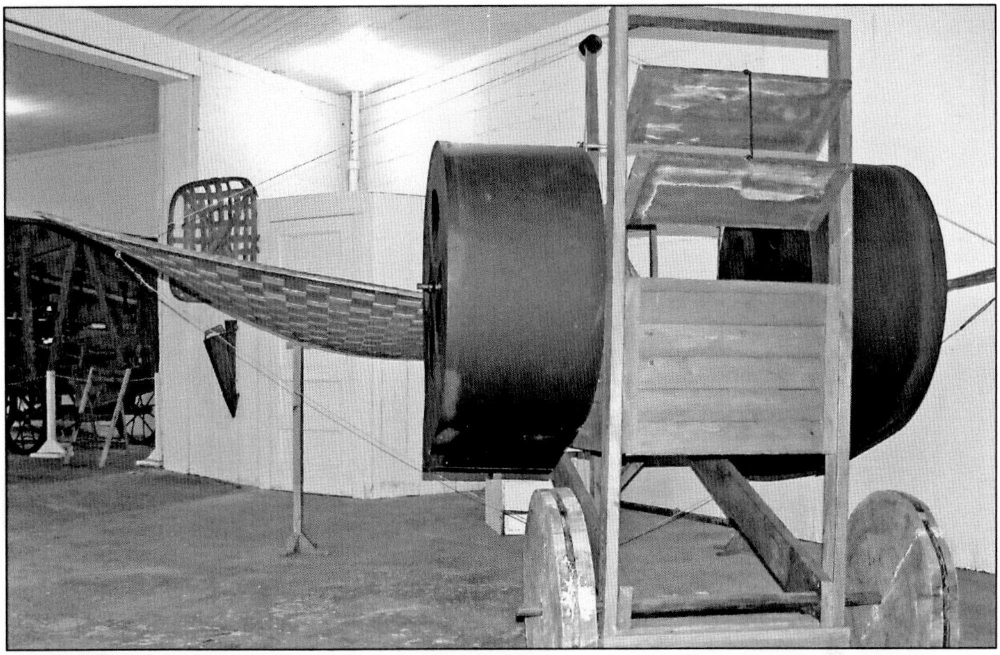

An Obscure Footnote in History. Few people have heard of James Henry Gatling or his Turkey Buzzard airplane, but the Murfreesboro native reportedly flew his heavier-than-air craft in 1873, some 30 years before the Wright brothers. Very closely resembling a modern aircraft, the machine, made of light poplar wood, was 18 feet long and had a wingspan of 14 feet. It had an elevator in front for vertical control and a tail in the rear for yawl control; both connected to a lever in the cockpit, where the pilot sat on a wooden kitchen chair. Twin blowers under each delta-shaped wing were muscle-powered by the pilot. They drew air into curved blower casings and out under each wing for lift. The fuselage rested on a tricycle landing gear. (PEH.)

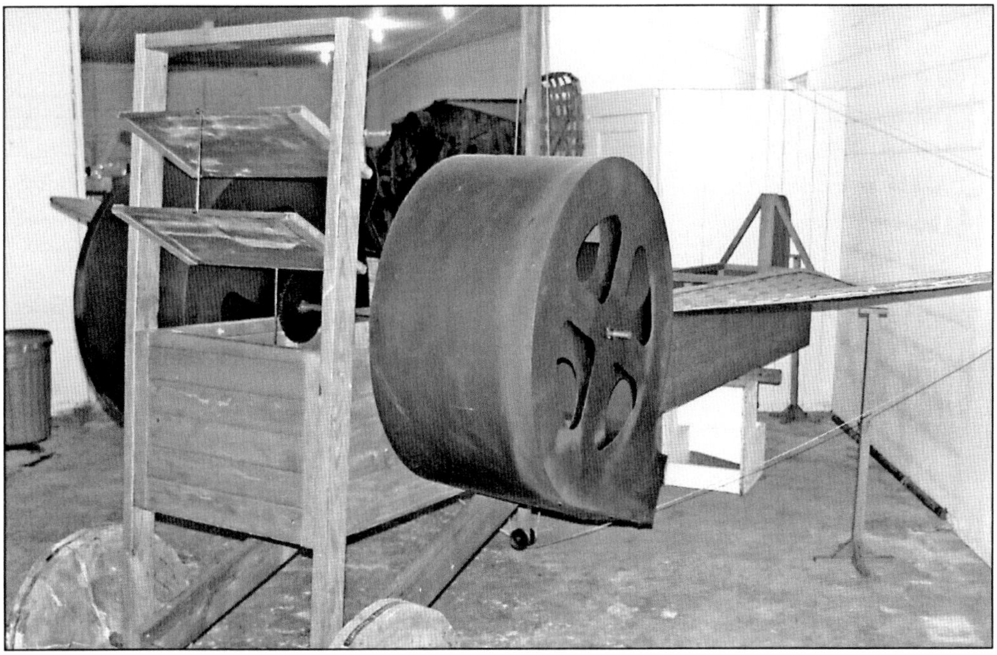

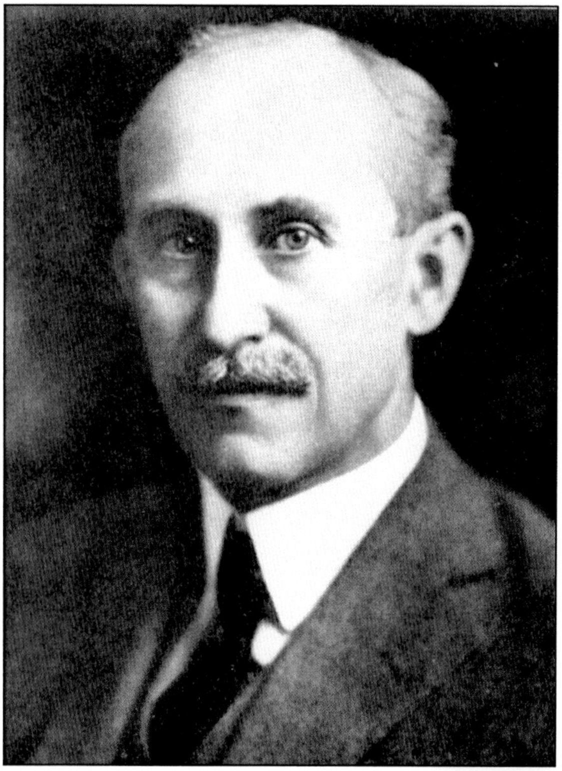

ORVILLE WRIGHT. Born in 1871 in Dayton, Ohio, Orville, along with his brother, Wilbur, is generally credited with the design and construction of the first practical heavier-than-air craft. The brothers grew up in Dayton, where they opened a bicycle repair, design, and manufacturing company. With a keen interest in flight, they began mechanical aeronautical experiments in 1899. Orville died in 1948. (USCG.)

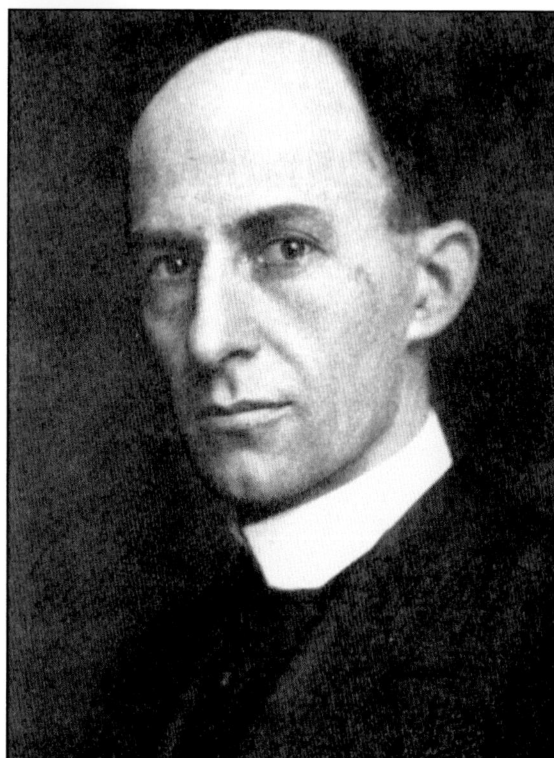

WILBUR WRIGHT. Born in 1871 in Millville, Indiana, Wilbur, like his brother, received a high-school education but no diploma. With an eye towards navigational control in addition to lift and propulsion, the brothers made successful flights in gliders before their famous powered flight. Wilbur died in 1912. The brothers' mother, Susan Catherine Koemer, was born in Hillsboro, Virginia. (USCG.)

A COASTIE CONNECTION. Few folks realize the significant role the U.S. Life Saving Service (a forerunner of the U.S. Coast Guard) played in the Wrights' first flight. Located near the brother's encampment, the crew at Life Saving Station No. 6 provided temperature and wind velocity for the experiments at Kill Devil Hill. On the day of the flight, four lifesavers and a boy from the village were present; lifesaver John T. Daniels took the famous photograph as the 705-pound machine of wood, wire, and canvas lifted off the windswept dune with the aid of its 12-horsepower engine. Today, the structure shown in these photographs is the Black Pelican Oceanfront Café (http://www.blackpelican.com/). (USCG.)

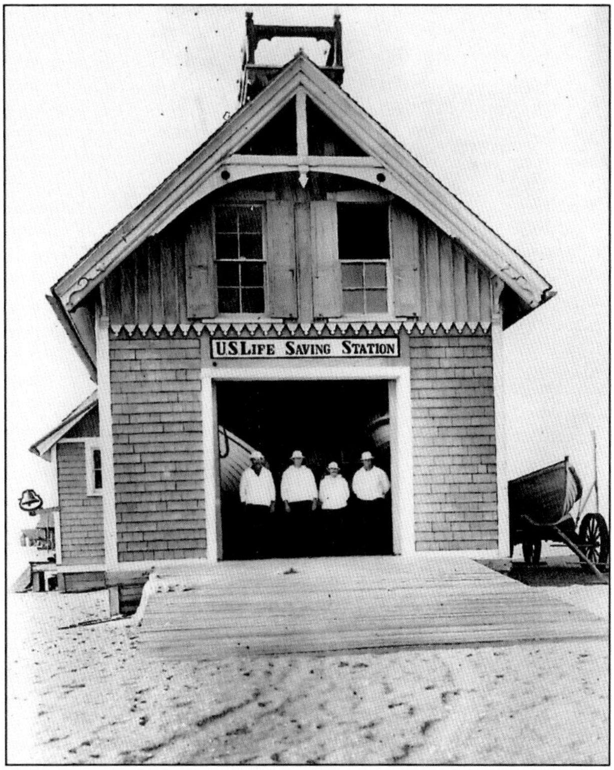

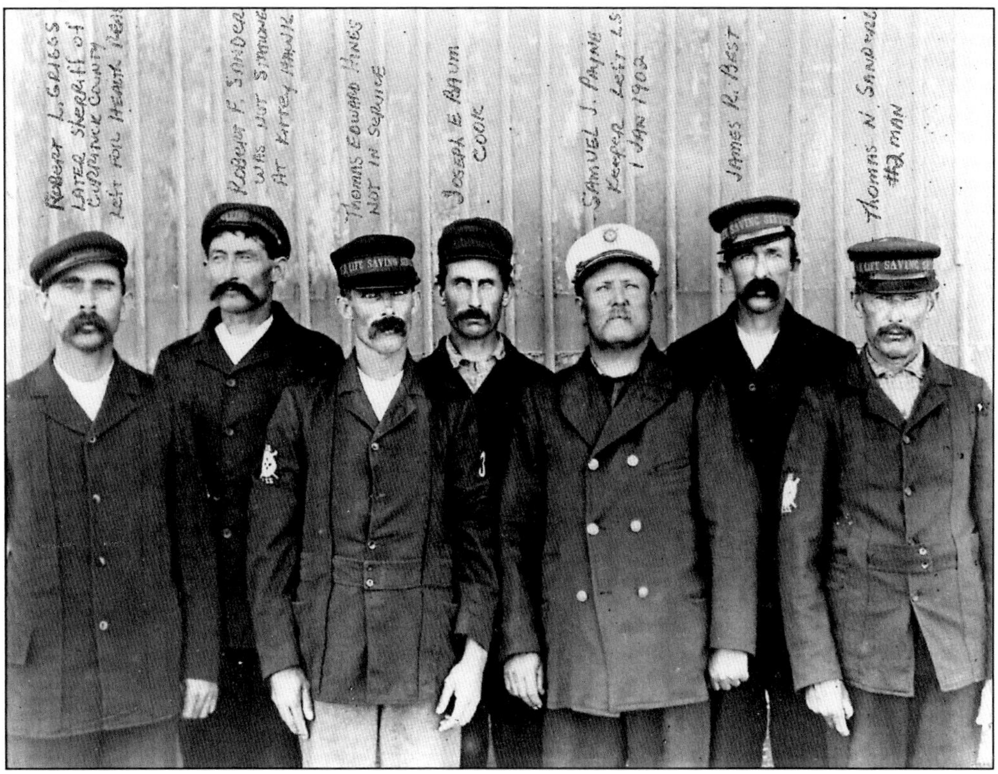

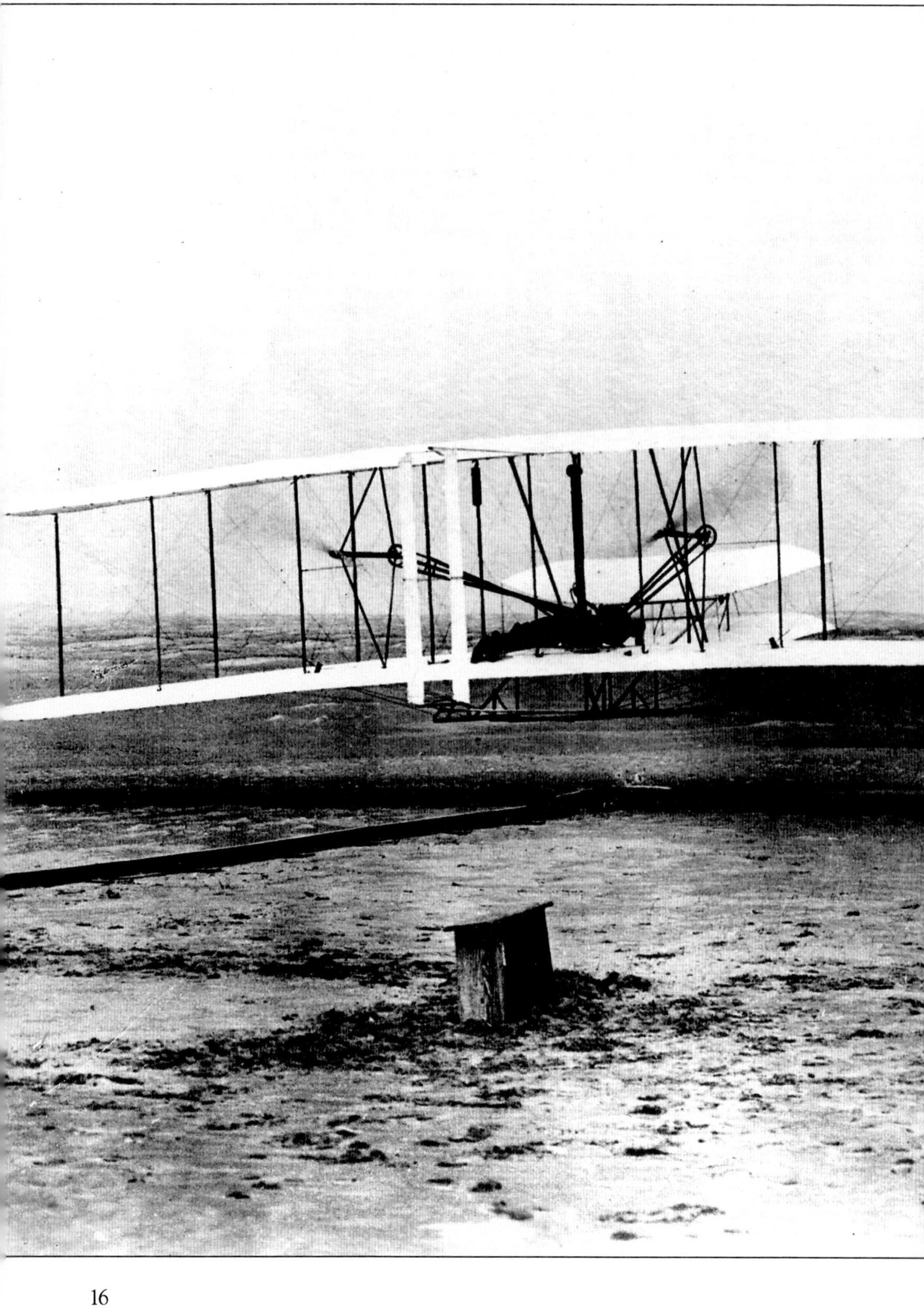

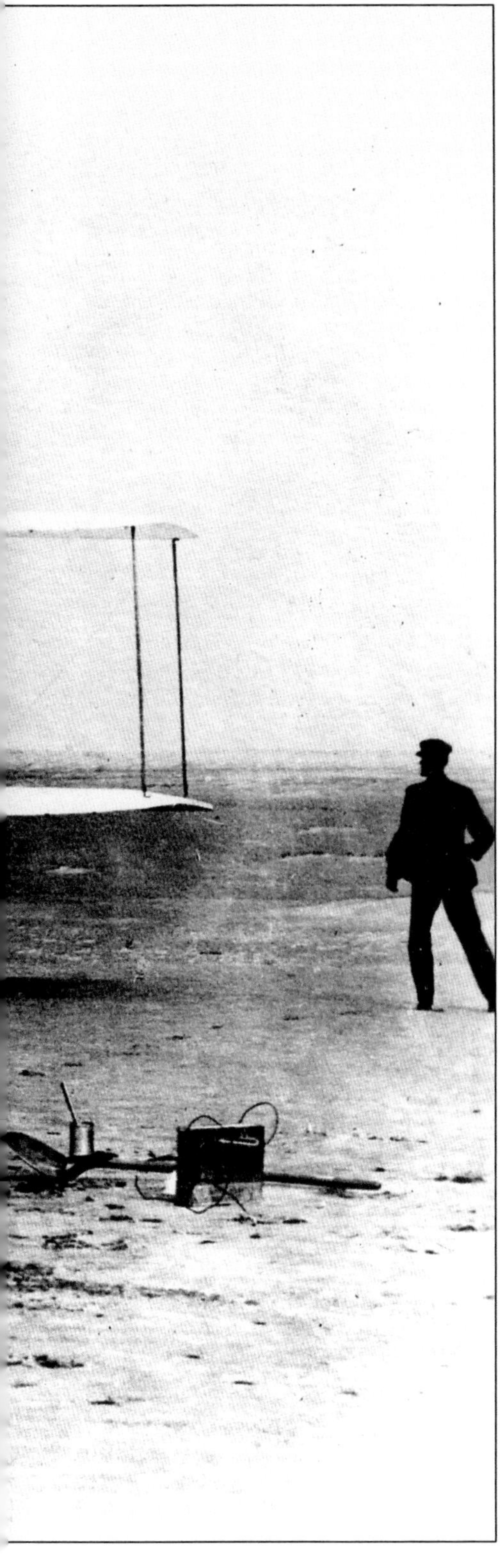

FIRST FLIGHT. The biplane *Kitty Hawk*, piloted by Orville Wright, has just taken off from the monorail on a field at Kitty Hawk, North Carolina, on the icy, windy morning of December 17, 1903, as shown in this historic photograph. Wilbur Wright ran alongside the craft and held the wing to balance the machine until it left the rail. This is the only photograph of the first flight, snapped for the Wright brothers by U.S. Life Saving Serviceman John T. Daniels, one of the crew of the nearby Kill Devil Hills Life Saving Station. The first flight lasted only 12 seconds but was significant because the machine was able to raise itself to flight by its own power, sail forward on a level course without reduction of speed, and land without crashing. (USCG.)

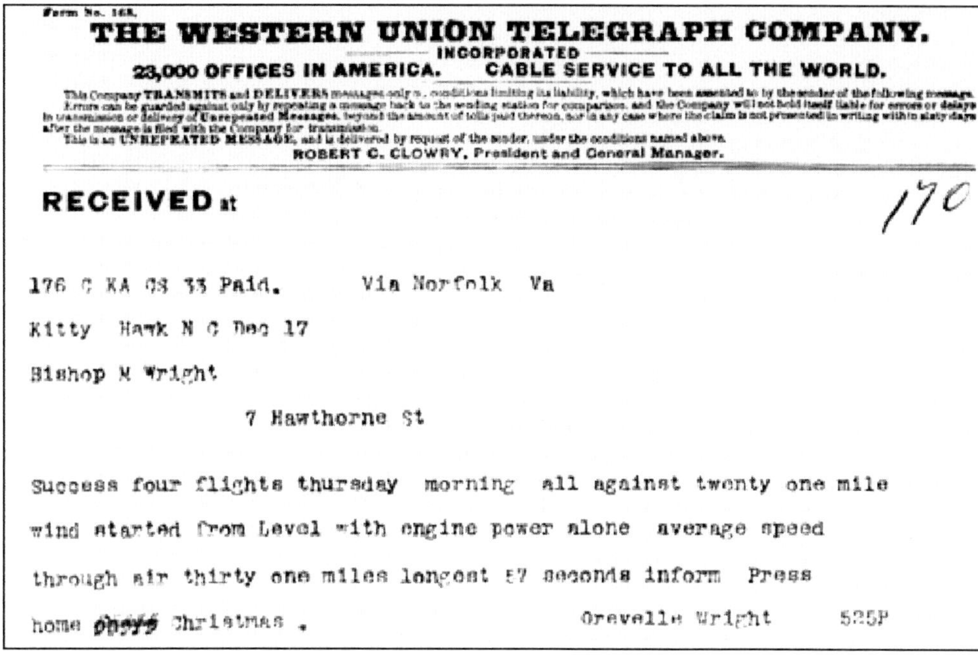

Form No. 168.

THE WESTERN UNION TELEGRAPH COMPANY.

INCORPORATED

23,000 OFFICES IN AMERICA. CABLE SERVICE TO ALL THE WORLD.

This Company TRANSMITS and DELIVERS messages only on conditions limiting its liability, which have been assented to by the sender of the following message. Errors can be guarded against only by repeating a message back to the sending station for comparison, and the Company will not hold itself liable for errors or delays in transmission or delivery of Unrepeated Messages, beyond the amount of tolls paid thereon, nor in any case where the claim is not presented in writing within sixty days after the message is filed with the Company for transmission.
This is an UNREPEATED MESSAGE, and is delivered by request of the sender, under the conditions named above.

ROBERT C. CLOWRY, President and General Manager.

RECEIVED at 170

176 C KA CS 33 Paid. Via Norfolk Va

Kitty Hawk N C Dec 17

Bishop M Wright

7 Hawthorne St

Success four flights thursday morning all against twenty one mile wind started from Level with engine power alone average speed through air thirty one miles longest 57 seconds inform Press home Christmas .

Orevelle Wright 525P

SUCCESS FOUR FLIGHTS THURSDAY MORNING. That is how the telegraph began when Orville sent word home to his father, Milton Wright, that aviation history had been made. When the message was wired through Norfolk, on its way to Dayton, Ohio, the local telegraph operator shared the story with a reporter friend at the *Virginian-Pilot* newspaper, and headlines were made. (USCG.)

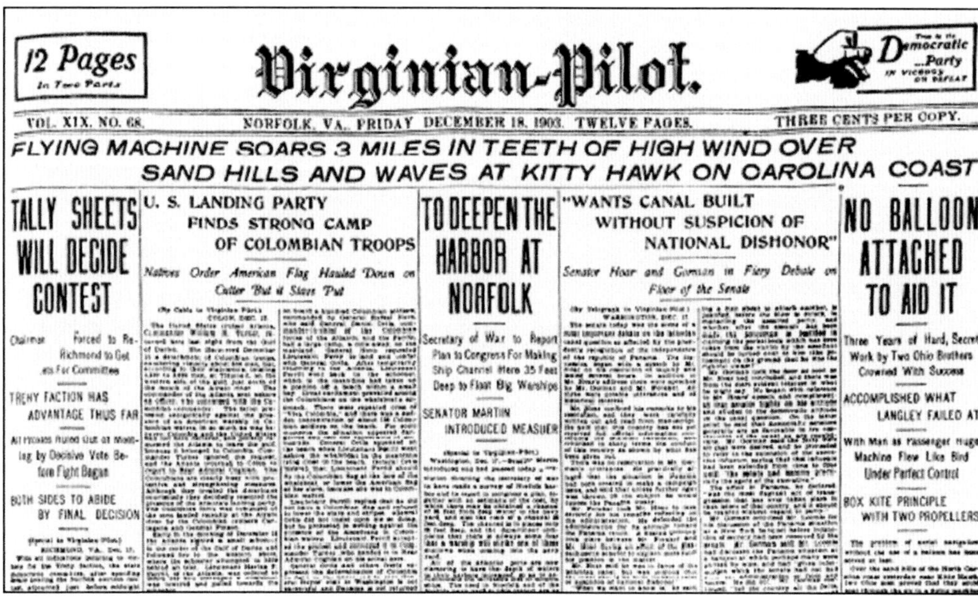

12 Pages In Two Parts

Virginian-Pilot.

Democratic Party

VOL. XIX. NO. 68. NORFOLK, VA., FRIDAY DECEMBER 18, 1903. TWELVE PAGES. THREE CENTS PER COPY.

FLYING MACHINE SOARS 3 MILES IN TEETH OF HIGH WIND OVER SAND HILLS AND WAVES AT KITTY HAWK ON CAROLINA COAST

TALLY SHEETS WILL DECIDE CONTEST

U. S. LANDING PARTY FINDS STRONG CAMP OF COLOMBIAN TROOPS

TO DEEPEN THE HARBOR AT NORFOLK

"WANTS CANAL BUILT WITHOUT SUSPICION OF NATIONAL DISHONOR"

NO BALLOON ATTACHED TO AID IT

Three Years of Hard, Secret Work by Two Ohio Brothers Crowned With Success

ACCOMPLISHED WHAT LANGLEY FAILED AT

With Man as Passenger Huge Machine Flew Like Bird Under Perfect Control

BOX KITE PRINCIPLE WITH TWO PROPELLERS

FLYING MACHINE SOARS. The headline of the December 18, 1903, *Virginian-Pilot* told the story, although somewhat inaccurately (they flew only 852 feet, not 3 miles). Regardless, it was the scoop of the century. The Wright brothers were a little miffed at the leak of the story, wanting the Dayton press to pick up it up first and afraid their pending patent would be encroached. (USCG.)

AFTERGLOW. Following his brother's successful flights on December 17, 1903, Wilbur Wright, standing in front of the *Kitty Hawk* flyer, gestures with his right hand while discussing with others the historical first flight of the biplane. They chose North Carolina's Outer Banks because of the sustained winds and the privacy the isolated beach offered. (USCG.)

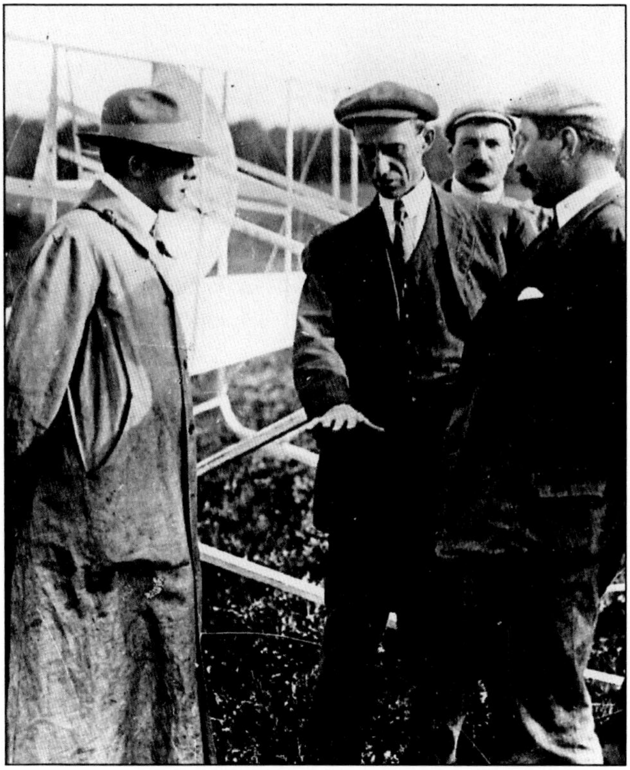

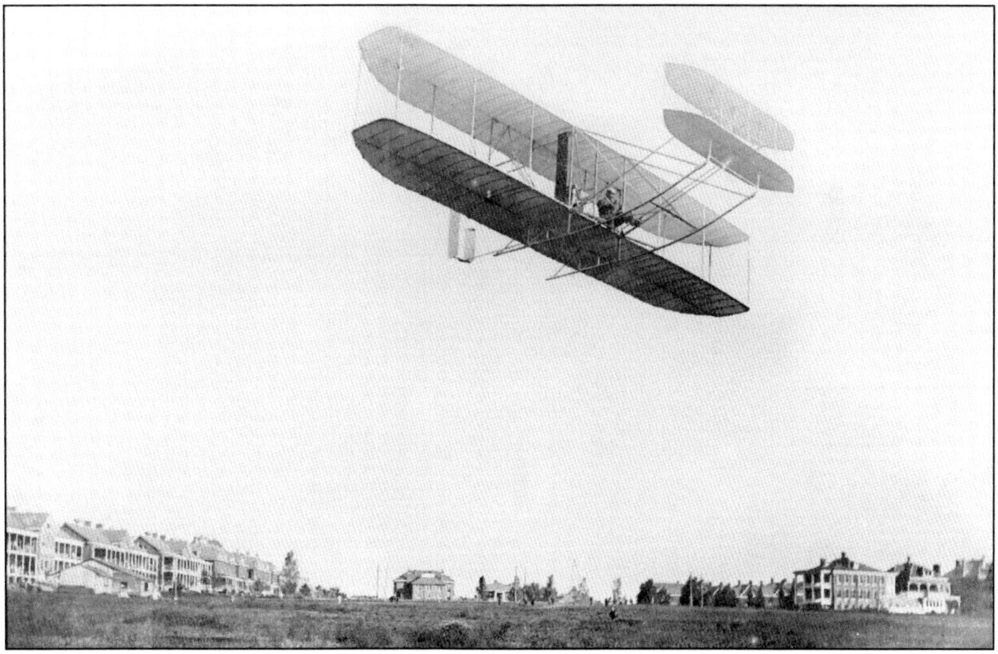

THE WRIGHT STUFF. Orville Wright pilots a Wright Type A flyer undergoing military trials at Fort Myer on September 9, 1908. With reconnaissance in mind, the army specifically wanted a plan that could carry two people, fly 40 miles per hour, and fly for up to one hour. The Wrights met the criteria, and the Signal Corps Airplane No. 1 was delivered in 1909. (USCG.)

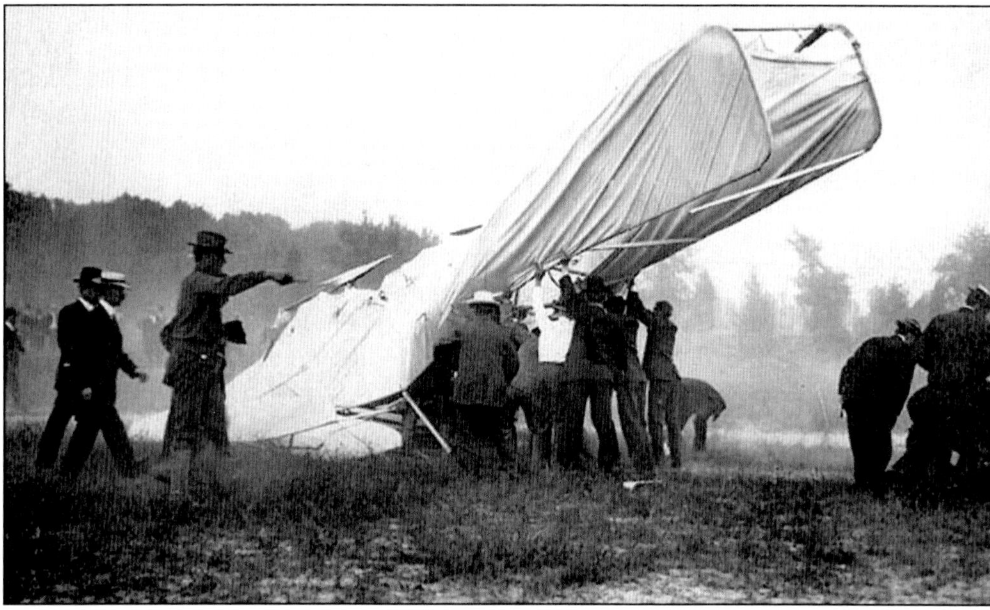

First Fatality. The world's first airplane fatality happened September 17, 1908, at Fort Myer, when an airplane piloted by Orville crashed during a demonstration flight, killing the passenger, army lieutenant Thomas Selfridge. Even so, the military saw the useful application, and the Signal Corps No. 1 (also known as the Wright Military Flyer) was produced, making it the world's first military airplane. (USCG.)

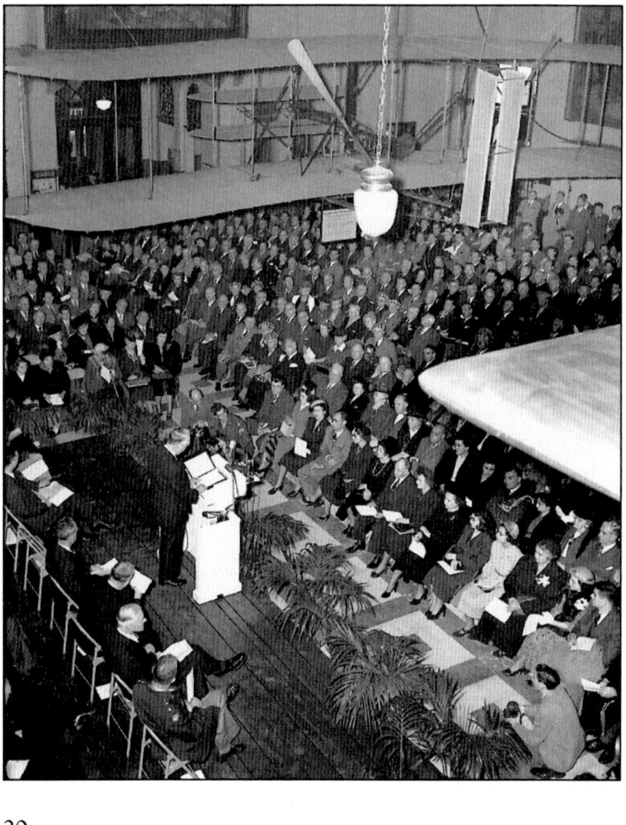

Remembering the Historic Flight. In ceremonies at the Smithsonian Institute in Washington, D.C., shown in this December 17, 1948, photograph, the original *Kitty Hawk* flyer was made a gift to the museum, where it remains today, on behalf of the estate of Orville Wright. The airplane had been at the Science Museum in London (England) since 1928. (USCG.)

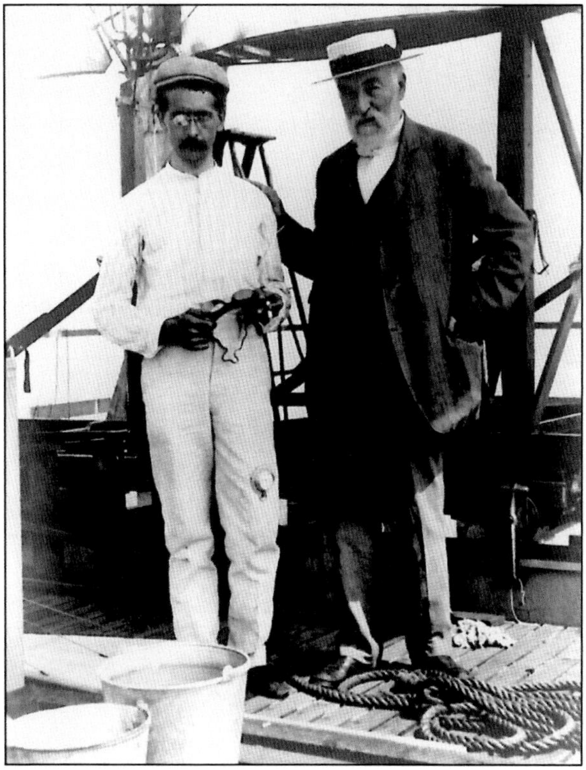

Samuel Pierpont Langley. The namesake of NASA Langley Research Center and Langley Air Force Base, Samuel Pierpont Langley lived from 1834 to 1906. His work in astronomy, physics, and aeronautics was pioneering, even if his design for a heavier-than-air flying machine was not. The director of the Smithsonian Institution in Washington, D.C., he successfully created unmanned, powered flight in 1896 when he built a steam-powered glider that flew for nearly a mile before it ran out of fuel. Flight attempts with a manned version in October and on December 8, 1903, failed. After the Wright brothers' success just days later, he gave up on the attempt. In the above photograph, he is shown with his assistant, Charles Manley, on the floating launching platform used for his glider, anchored on the Potomac River. (NASA.)

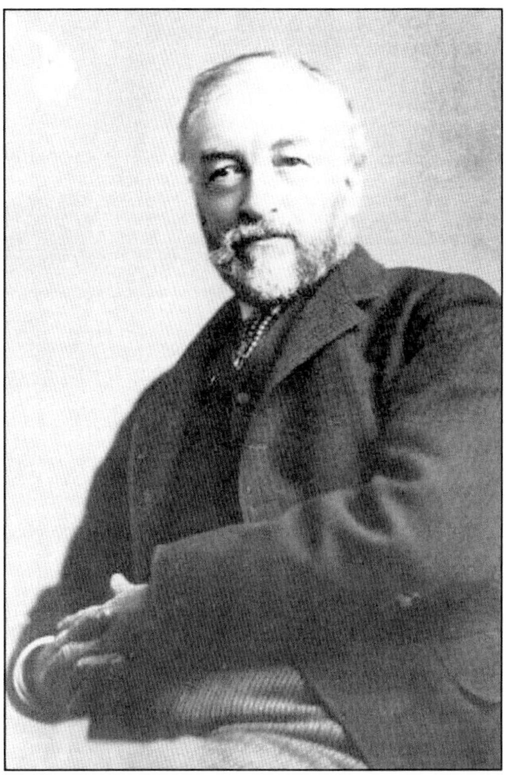

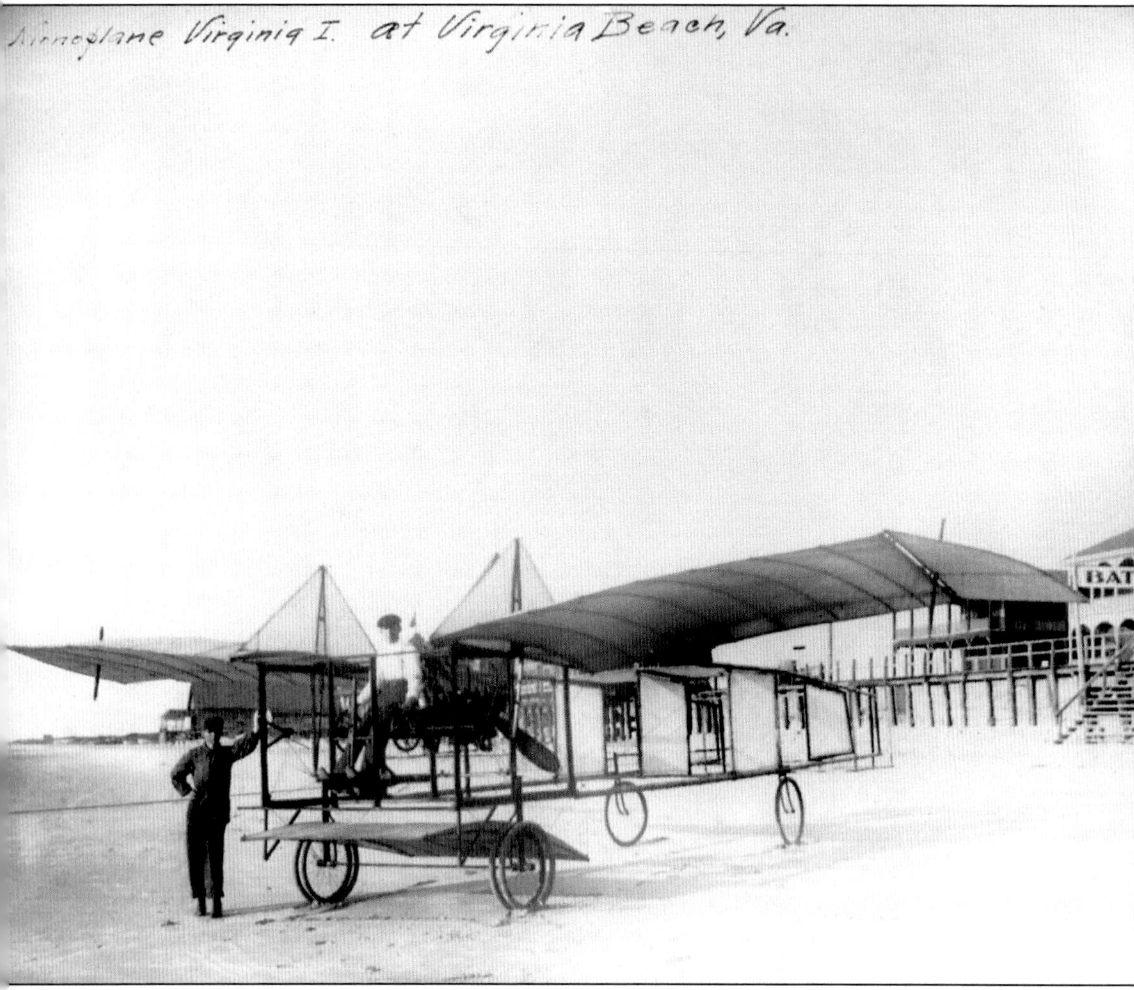

MONOPLANE *VIRGINIA I*. This August 1910 photograph shows the monoplane *Virginia I* at Virginia Beach. Fresh on the success of heavier-than-air flight just seven years earlier, many pioneers took up aviation as an interest. Advancements in flight came rapidly, allowing planes to navigate easier and stay aloft longer than the 12-second flight Orville Wright made in 1903. As with other areas of the country, Hampton Roads was passionate for flight, and many daredevils came and flew to the delight of thousands. Because there were few landing fields at the time, planes such as the one pictured here had to use anything flat and firm for a runway, like the beach or farmland. About the same time as this photograph was taken, Eugene B. Ely would be readying himself to take to the Hampton Roads skies, not as a thrill-seeker but as a visionary, flying off the deck of the USS *Birmingham* off the coast of Norfolk on November 14, 1910, and laying the groundwork for naval aviation and today's massive aircraft carriers. (National Archives.)

Two

Into the Wild Blue Yonder

As early as the Civil War, the military recognized the importance of aviation. But as the face of war changed, as it did in World War I, so did the face of military aviation.

Almost as soon as the Wright brothers made their famous flight in 1903, the application of their heavier-than-air flying machine was viewed with military uses in mind. Many of those applications started in Hampton Roads.

Pioneers in aviation came to the region; names like Ely, Curtiss, Mitchell, and Byrd left an indelible mark.

It was here that the mighty aircraft carriers had their start, along with the idea that airplanes could be successfully used to bomb targets. As the experiments with flight grew, so did the area military bases and their scope of operation.

This included the establishment of Langley Field, today Langley Air Force Base, one of the oldest continuously operating military aviation bases in the world. This also included the development of Naval Operating Base Norfolk, today the Norfolk Naval Air Station, the largest naval base in the world, and with Naval Air Station Oceana, today a Master Jet Base and the world's busiest naval air station.

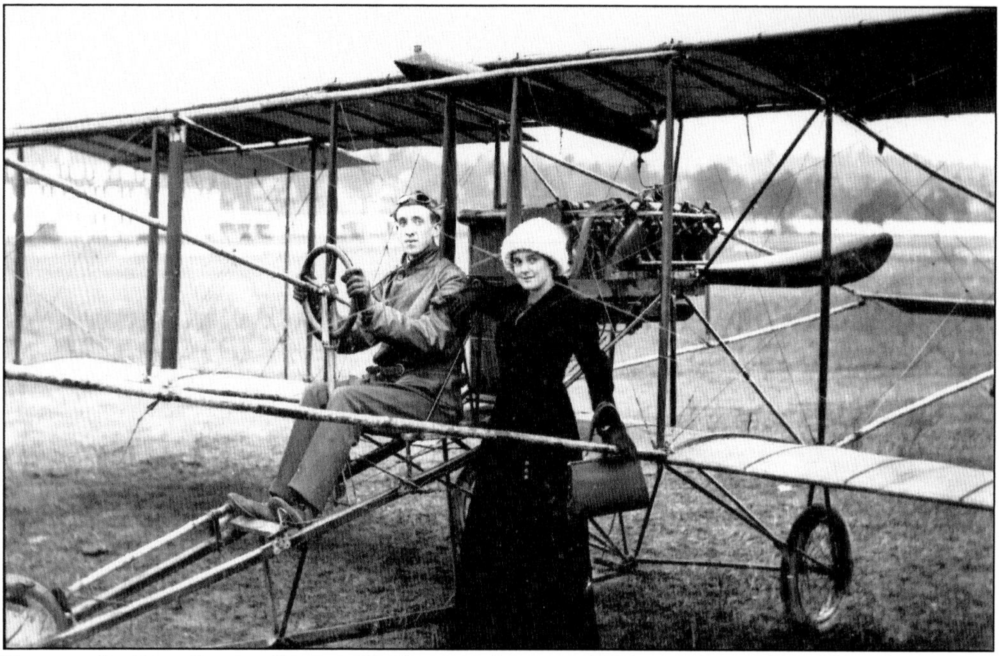

EUGENE B. ELY. Eugene Bruton Ely, born in Iowa in 1886, was an early, self-taught aviator. He pioneered military aviation by piloting a Curtiss biplane off the deck of a ship anchored in Hampton Roads and landing on shore. In this photograph, he is shown with his wife, Mabel. Ely died in 1911 in a plane crash in Georgia. (HRNM.)

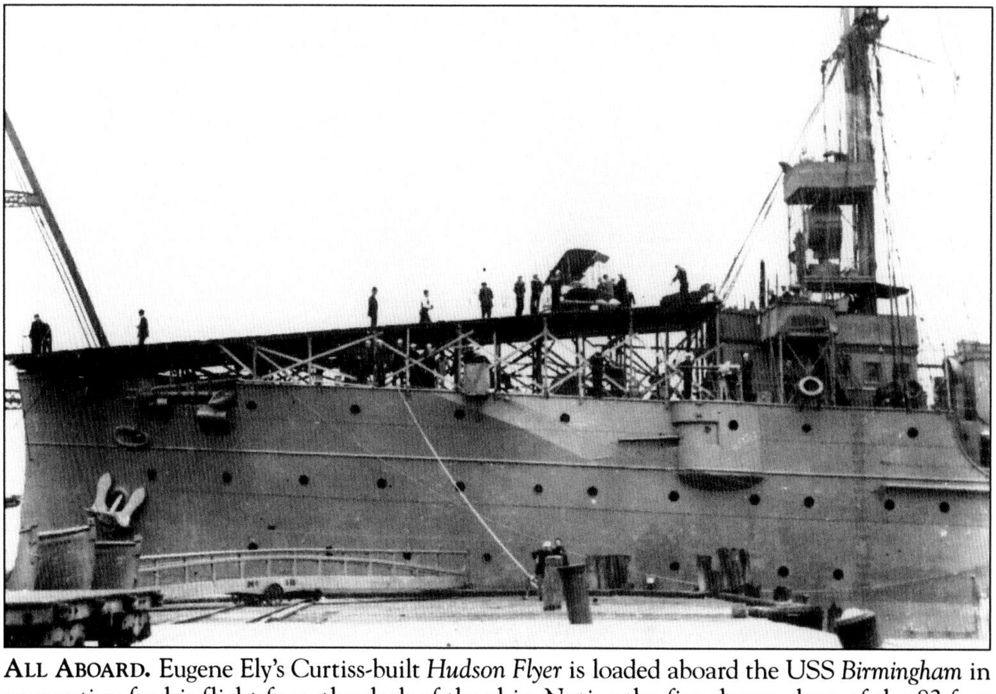

ALL ABOARD. Eugene Ely's Curtiss-built *Hudson Flyer* is loaded aboard the USS *Birmingham* in preparation for his flight from the deck of the ship. Notice the five-degree slope of the 83-foot ramp; the forward edge was 37 feet above water. Ely volunteered for the task (Wilbur Wright turned it down) out of patriotism and to settle a bet it could be done. (HRNM.)

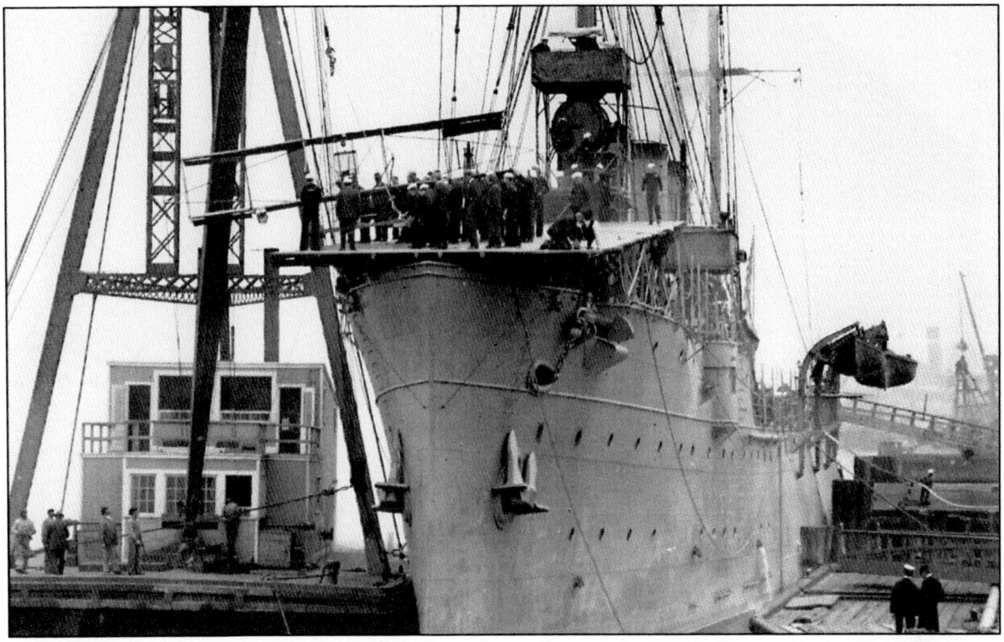

First Flight, Ship To Shore. With his plane aboard the USS *Birmingham,* Ely set out on November 14, 1910, to prove flight from a ship was possible. It was the birth of naval aviation when he took off from the cruiser, anchored off Fort Monroe, and landed at Willoughby Spit in Norfolk about three miles away. With money made from the flight, he bought his wife, Mabel, a diamond ring. (HRNM.)

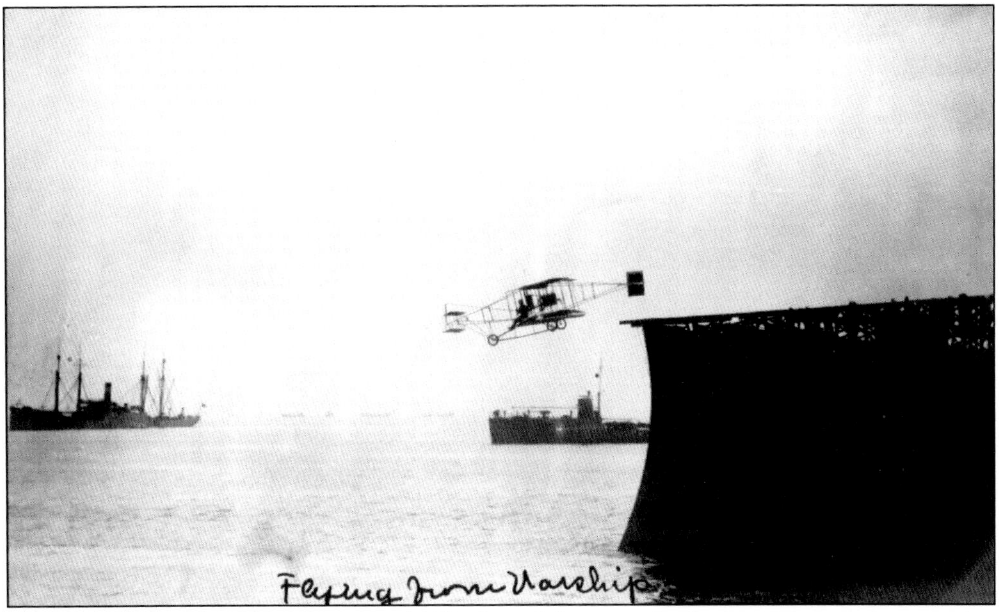

Leap of Faith. The take-off was rough; Ely dipped dangerously close to the sea, splintering his propeller and being splashed with saltwater. Still, he gained altitude, although he lost direction in an ensuing squall. When he landed in Norfolk, he did not know where he was and asked a resident who had rushed from her home, "Where am I?" Julia Smith replied, "Right between my house and the yacht club." (HRNM.)

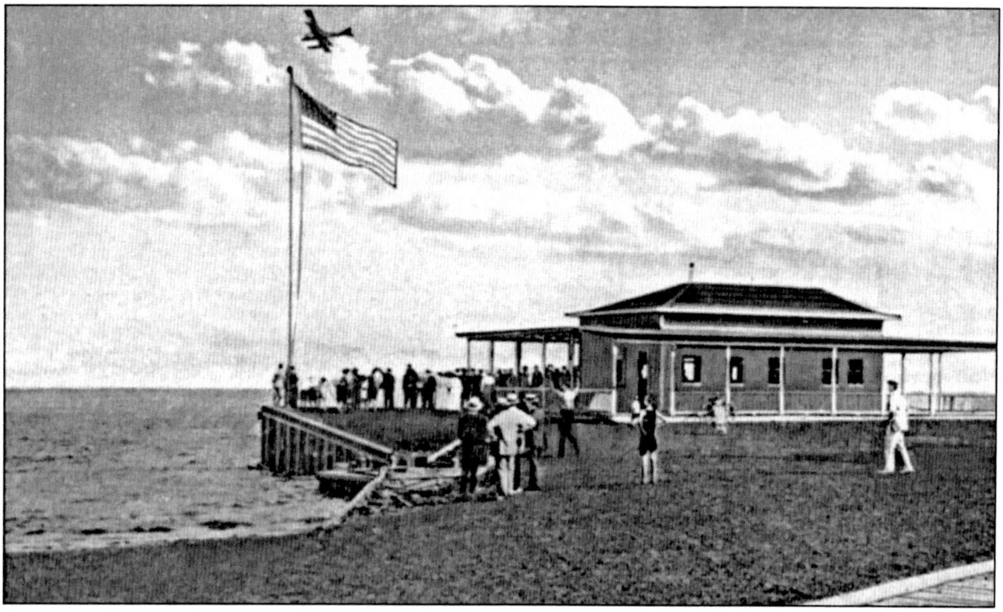

CURTISS FLYING SCHOOL. These vintage postcards show the Curtiss Flying School. Aviation pioneer Glenn H. Curtiss sponsored the Atlantic Coast Aeronautical Station on a 20-acre tract of land east of the Newport News Boat Harbor beginning in the fall of 1915, with Capt. Thomas Scott Baldwin as the school's head. Many civilian students later became famed World War I flyers: Victor Carlstrom, Vernon Castle, Eddie Stinson, and Gen. Billy Mitchell all trained here. The school also attracted a large number of Canadians who hoped to fly for the Royal Flying Corps. The facilities had a small land field and were on the harbor, ideal for flying boats (also known as hydroplanes), making this the first regularly used airport in Virginia. With the creation of additional military flying schools in the region, namely Langley Field in Hampton and the Norfolk Operating Base, and with limited land area to expand, the school was disbanded in 1922. (VASC; PEH.)

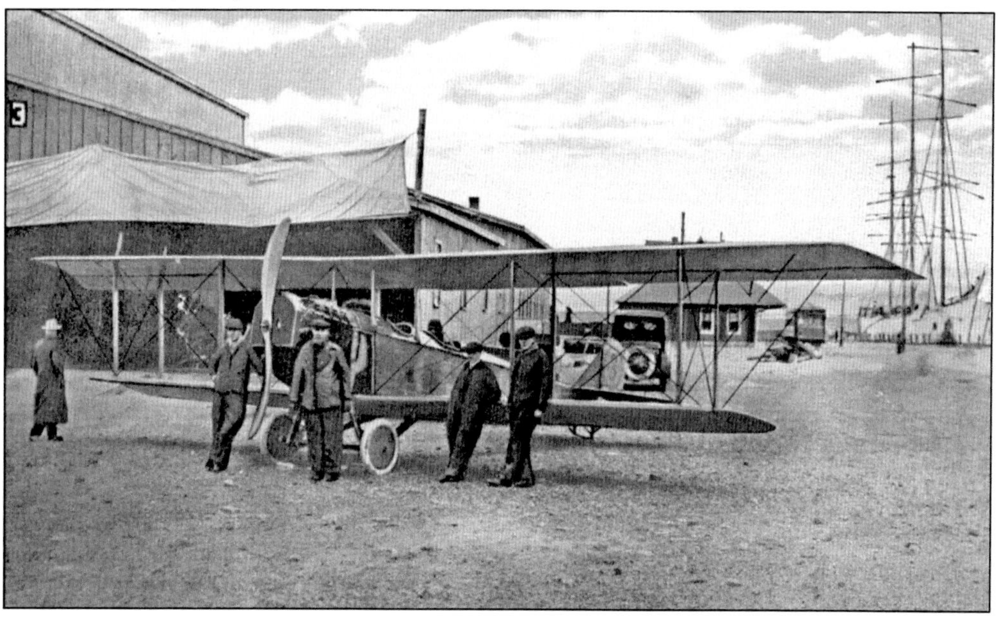

BILLY MITCHELL. Born William L. Mitchell in 1879, Mitchell journeyed each weekend from Washington, D.C., where he served in the Army Signal Corps to attend the Curtiss Flying School in Newport News. He led American aviation units in France during World War I and become one of the military's greatest supporters of air power; he is regarded as the father of the U.S. Air Force. He died in 1936. (U.S. Air Force.)

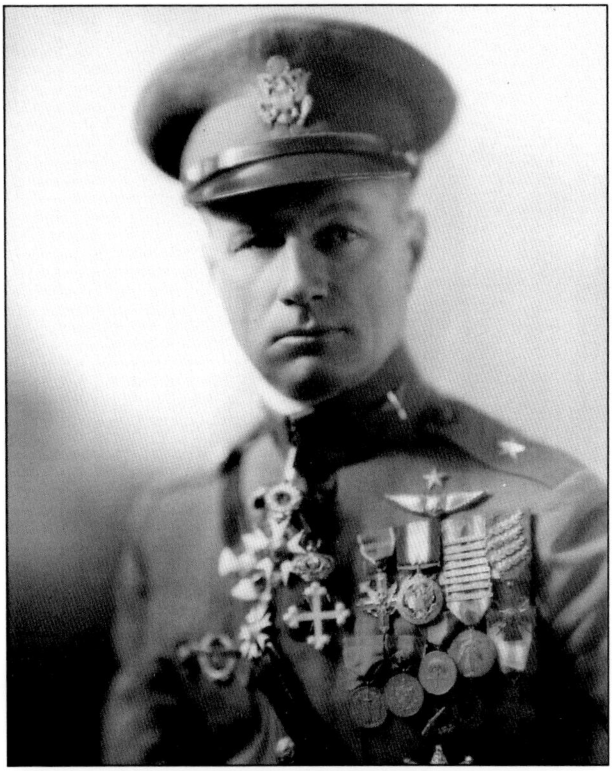

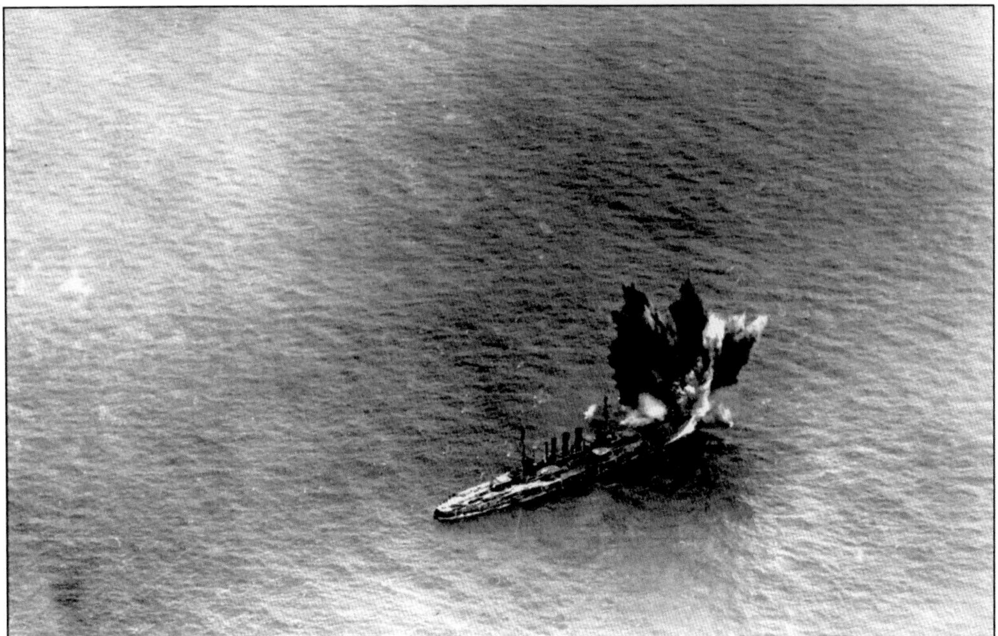

HISTORY IS MADE. To demonstrate air superiority, Billy Mitchell persuaded the army and navy to allow him to demonstrate the capabilities of the airplane by attempting to sink captured warships. In this photograph, he proves his point with the sinking of the German battleship *Ostfriesland* off Cape Henry on July 21, 1921. (U.S. Air Force.)

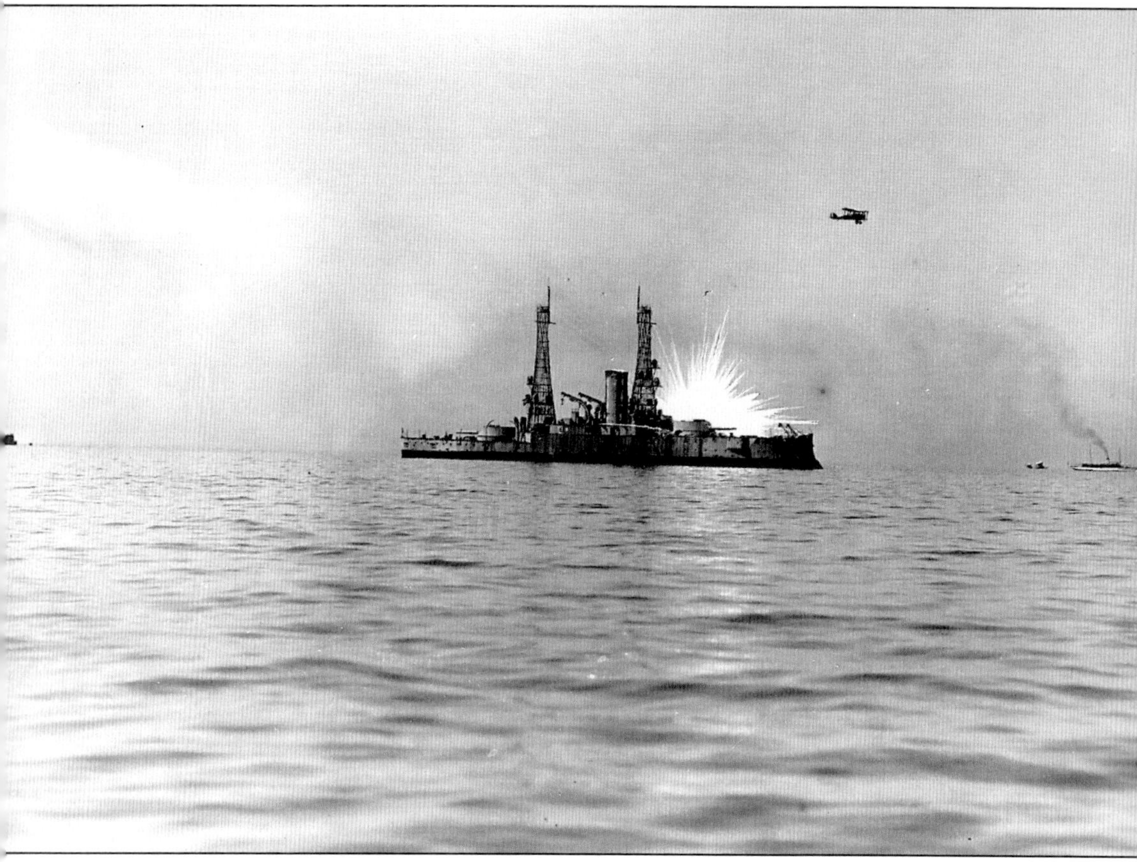

Bombs Away. Gen. Billy Mitchell said as early as 1906 that future conflicts would take place in the air, not on the ground. A strong proponent of military aviation, he spent his life trying to prove that point. Part of his belief was that surface forces were obsolete in the air age. "No surface vessels can exist wherever air forces action from land bases are able to attack them," he said. To prove his point, he successfully sank numerous ships using air power alone. Anchored off the coast of Cape Henry, the German carrier *Ostfriesland* became the first battleship sunk by bombs from an airplane on July 21, 1921. He demonstrated the concept of air superiority by dropping phosphorous bombs on the U.S. battleship *Alabama*, as shown in this photograph. Mitchell's career was controversial; in a scathing statement about the cause of the navy dirigible *Shenandoah*'s crash, he was court-martialed for insubordination in 1926—a ruling that was voided posthumously in 1955. (U.S. Air Force.)

RICHARD EVELYN BYRD. Born into a famous Virginia family in 1888, Byrd joined the navy and developed a passion for the airplane during World War I, later becoming a flying instructor for the military. He became a world-renowned explorer, most notably for his 1928–1930 Antarctic Expedition. It was the first of its kind to be mechanized, drawing on the use of airplanes, aerial cameras, snowmobiles, and massive communication resources. (National Archives.)

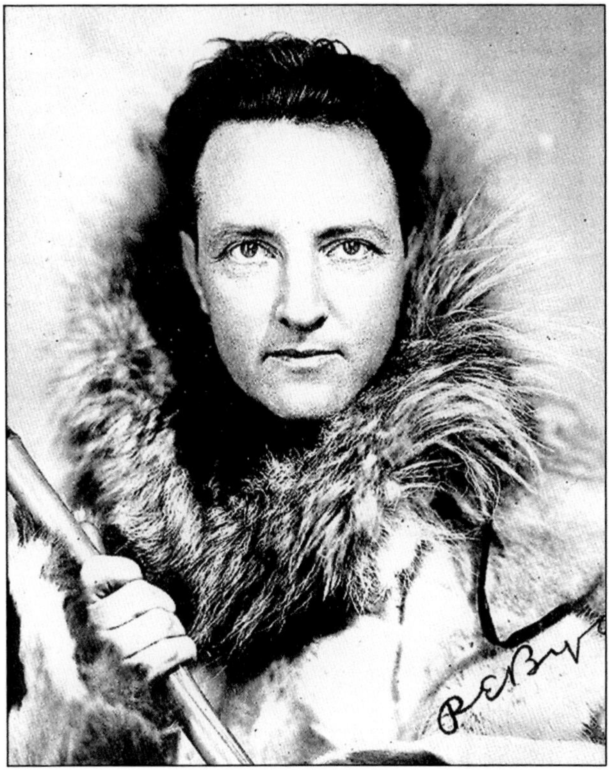

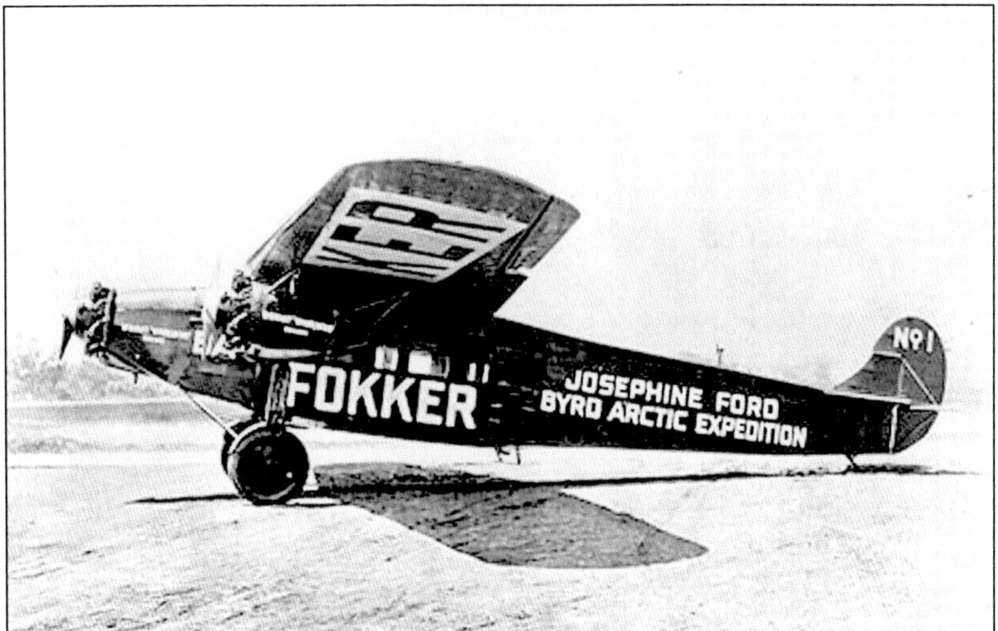

NEXT STOP, THE SOUTH POLE. Byrd utilized several aircraft in his first Antarctic Expedition, including the Fokker Trimotor seen here. Part of his expedition, including the *Eleanor Bolling*, loaded with 300 tons of supplies, left for the ice pack on September 25, 1928. Byrd would remain adventurous, continuing his worldwide expeditions until 1955. (National Archives.)

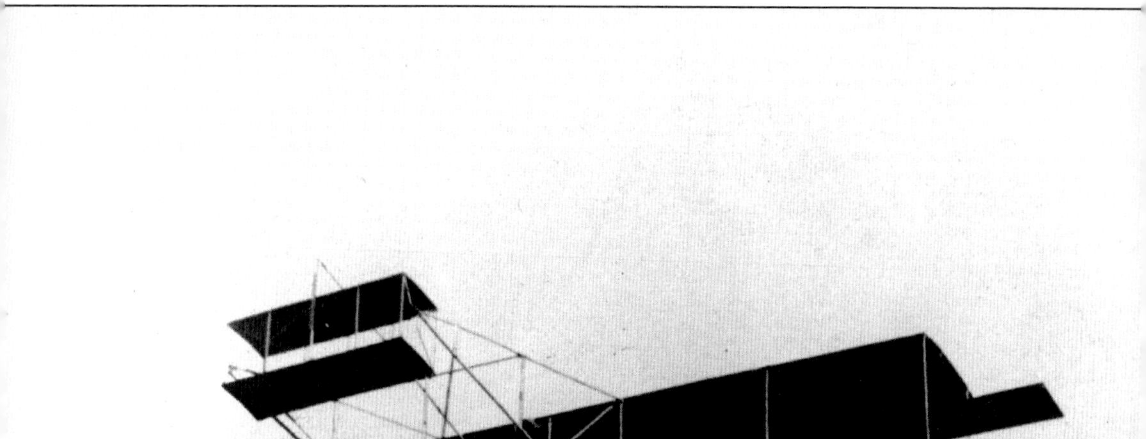

DAREDEVIL WANTED. The early days of aviation took a hearty breed to fill the cockpits, but many stepped up to the task with pioneers like Eugene Ely, Billy Mitchell, and Richard Byrd. Other fly-boys filled the seats differently—as daredevils. Because flying was so new, when an aviator came to town to put on a show, thousands turned out. That was the case with J. C. Mars, shown here in his Curtiss plane buzzing Hampton Roads on November 2, 1910. The show was part of an aviation meet sponsored by the *Ledger-Dispatch* newspaper. An account of the time said more than 10,000 folks turned out at the old 1907 Jamestown Exposition site to watch the spectacle. It was the first sustained aerial flight in Norfolk. The paper reported: "Mars reached an altitude of 100 feet on his first flight and 500 feet on his fifth. The cheering crowd could be heard for miles around when it realized the craft could really fly." (HRNM.)

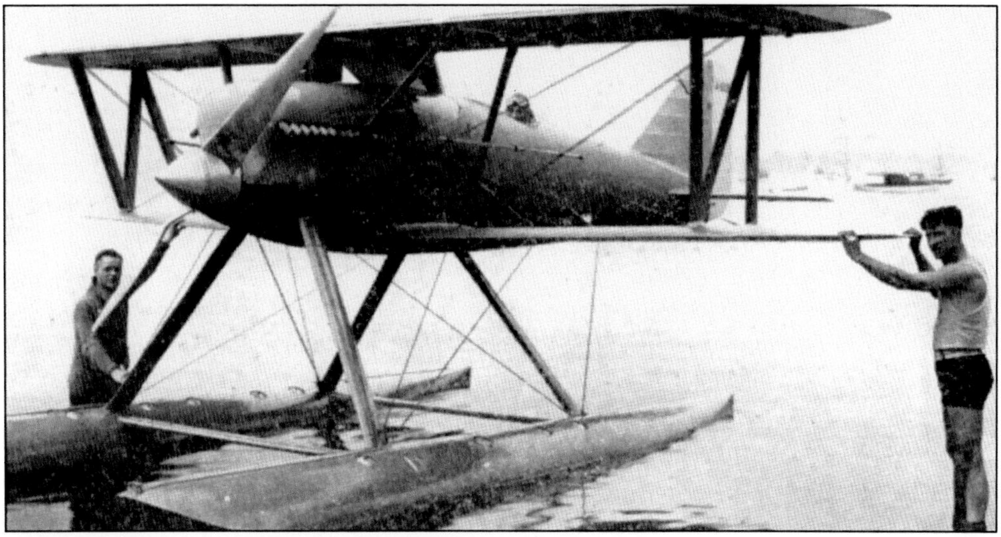

BY LAND, SEA, AND AIR. Hampton Roads was host in November 1926 to the International Seaplane Race for the Jacques Schneider Trophy at the Norfolk Naval Operating Base. Competing were teams from America and Italy. The annual event was called the "premier sporting event of the aeronautical world. The best designers of Europe and America exert every effort to produce seaplanes that will be faster than anything previously produced." The first competition was held at Monaco in 1913. In the above photograph, navy lieutenant David Rittenhouse stands with his Navy-Curtiss Racer, winner of the 1923 event in England at 177.4 miles per hour. The below photograph shows the course taken by the pilots during the competition. An Italian aviator won the race, flying at an average speed of more than 246 miles per hour. (NPL.)

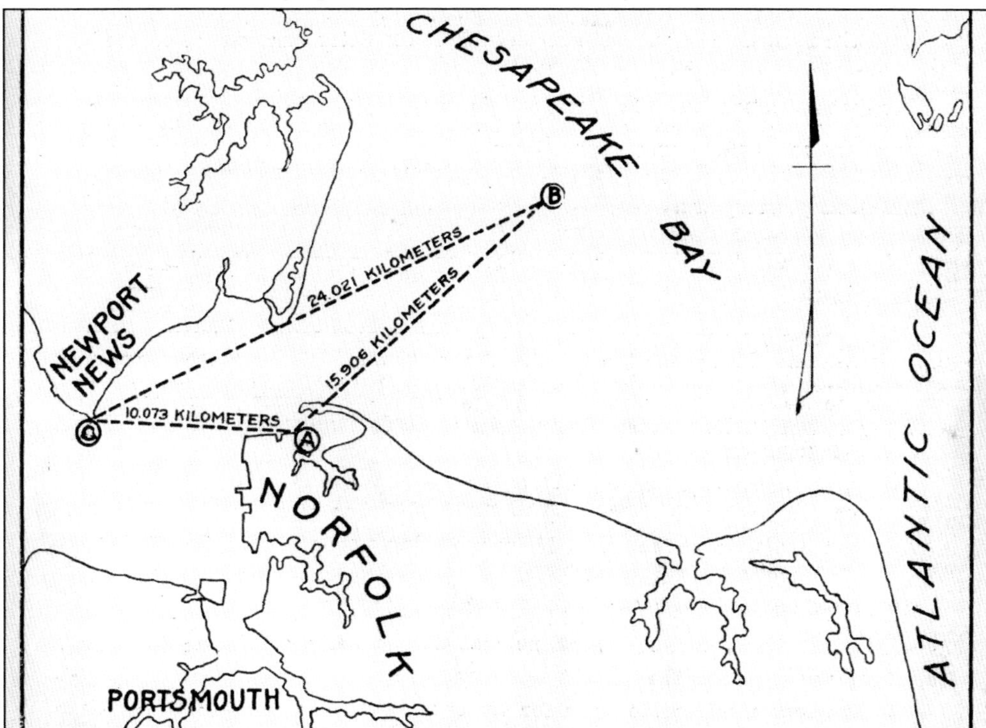

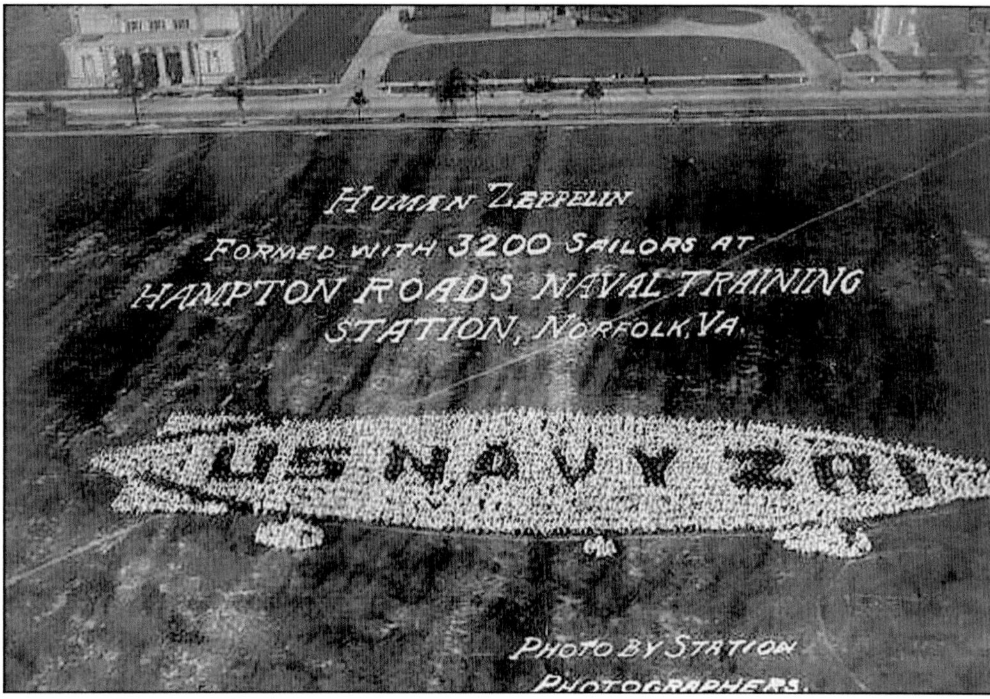

BUOYANT BUNDLES. In the above photograph, 3,200 sailors at the Hampton Roads Naval Training Station in Norfolk form a "human Zeppelin," spelling out "U.S. Navy ZR1." The ZR1, also known as the *Shenandoah*, was built in 1923 and was the first rigid, helium-filled airship constructed in the United States. Helium was used instead of hydrogen because of the horrific *Roma* accident in Norfolk the year before. Nonetheless, the *Shenandoah* crashed in 1925, and while it did not burn, the accident killed 14 of the 43 crewmen aboard. In the below photograph of about the same time, U.S. Army blimps, the T.C. 5 and T.C. 9 from Langley Field, Virginia, pass over the Washington Monument during a practice flight. (HRNM; Library of Congress.)

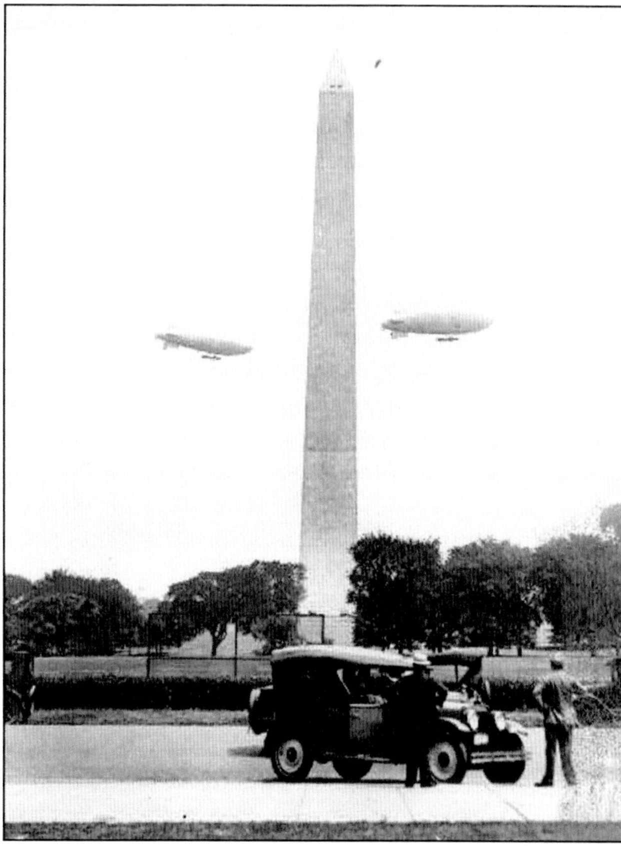

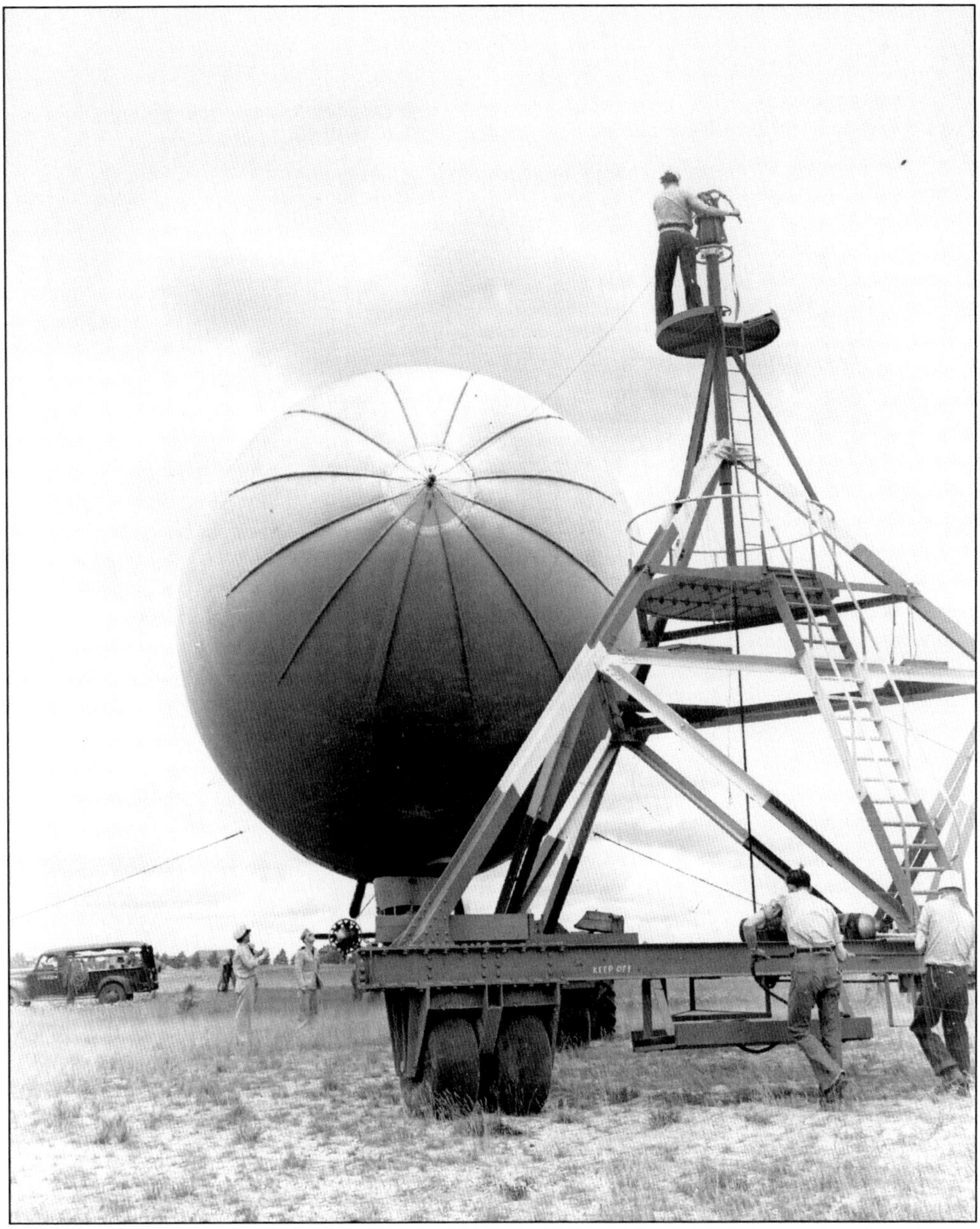

BLIMPIES. Hot-air balloons had been around since 1783, and by the 1890s, rigid airships began to emerge. While there was some use during World War I, the United States did not really get involved with dirigibles until the early 1920s. Airships grew into favor because they could fly further and carry more than an airplane, as well as land and take off where planes couldn't. The United States favored dirigibles and blimps until World War II, but their use has been limited since. This photograph shows a navy blimp used for anti-submarine patrol during World War II. (HRNM.)

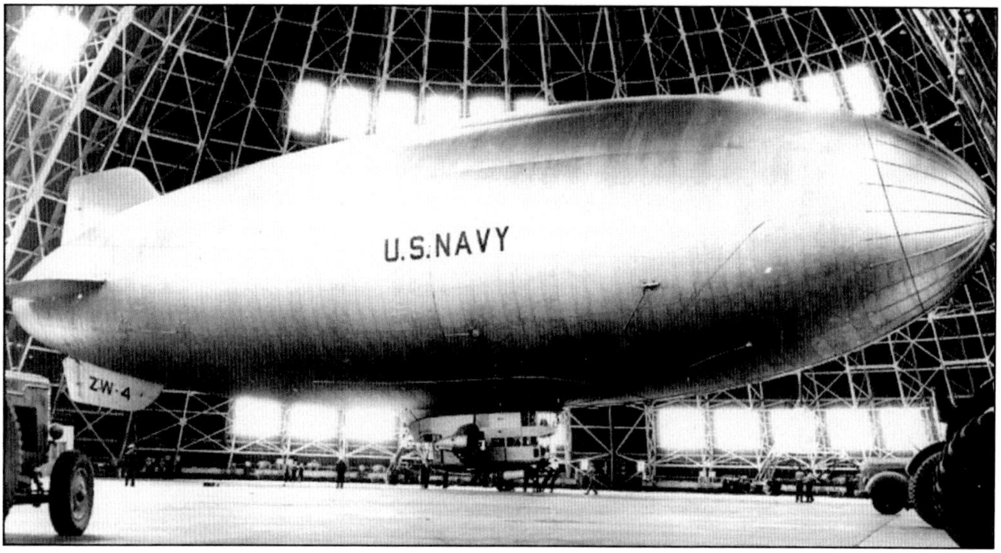

A Place To Call Home. During World War II, the U.S. Navy used blimps as a way to patrol for enemy submarines off the coast. In an era before helicopters and satellites, blimps proved to be an effective way to keep an eye on things. This blimp is housed inside an enormous hanger at the Weeksville Naval Air Station in northeastern North Carolina, about an hour south of Norfolk. The station was established in 1942 to coordinate blimp patrols. (HRNM.)

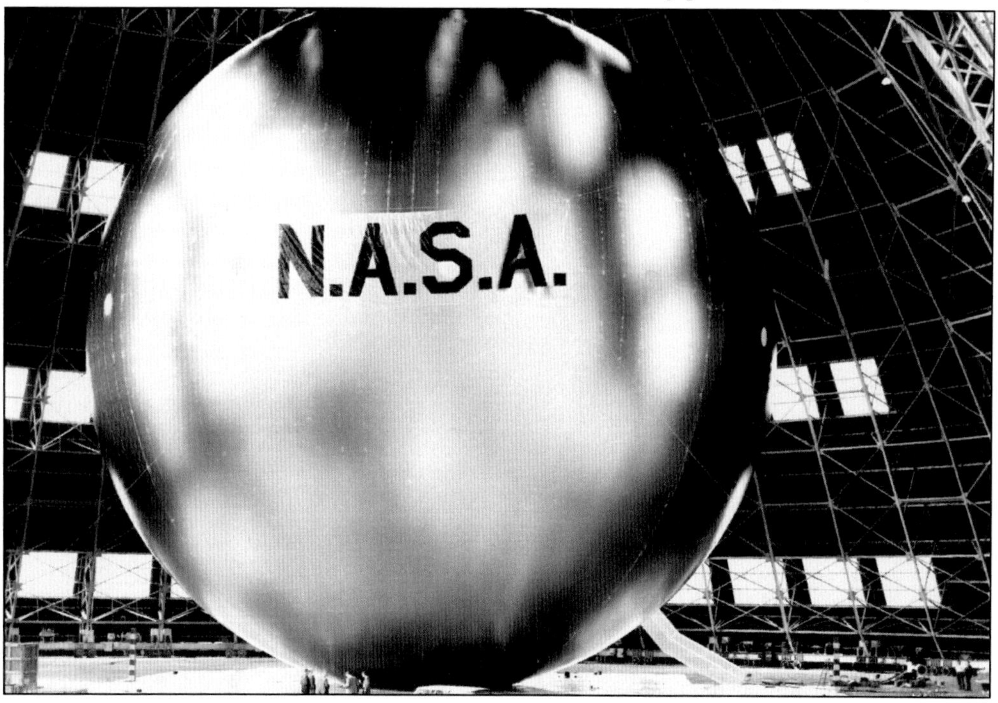

Did You Hear an Echo? This odd blimp was an Echo satellite, NASA's first communications satellite experiment. Each craft was a large metallic balloon designed to act as a passive reflector of microwave signals; communication signals were bounced off of it from one point on earth to another. The project lasted from 1960 to 1969. Here is one of the "satelloons" in the former navy blimp hanger at Weeksville, North Carolina. (NASA.)

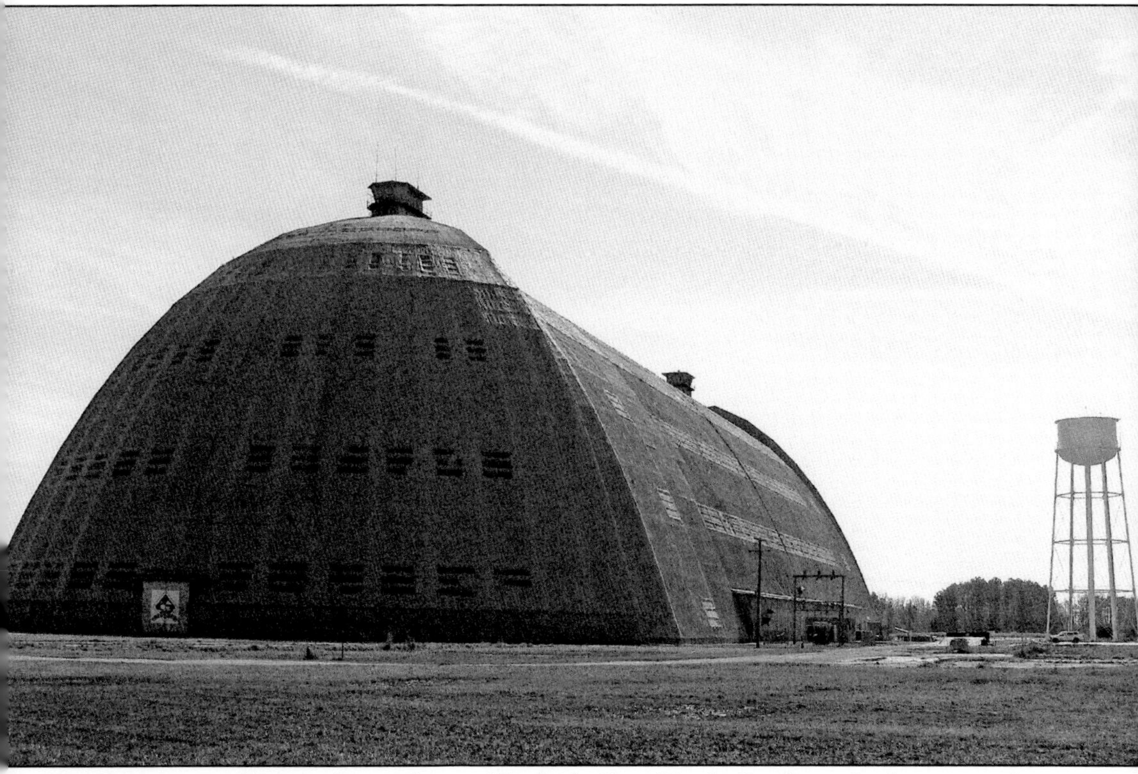

THE SKINNY ON BLIMPS. Located near Elizabeth City, North Carolina, the hanger at the former Weeksville Naval Air Station is huge. Built in 1941, the structure is 960 feet long; its two clamshell doors alone weigh 420 tons each. It stands 190 feet tall and is 328 feet wide. There are 7.3 acres of space inside. The hanger was built to be a Mid-Atlantic base during World War II for the navy's blimp operations; it had enough space for 12 navy K airships. In 1943, an even larger companion hanger was built and designated the world's largest wooden building, but it was destroyed in a fire in 1995. After World War II, the blimps left, but in 1947, a navy blimp squadron was reassigned to Weeksville. By the mid-1950s, at least 10 blimps and 12 helicopters were stationed there. However, that squadron was decommissioned in 1957, and the blimps left for a final time. Today, the hanger is in use by TCOM, L.P., a company that maintains and repairs blimps. (PEH.)

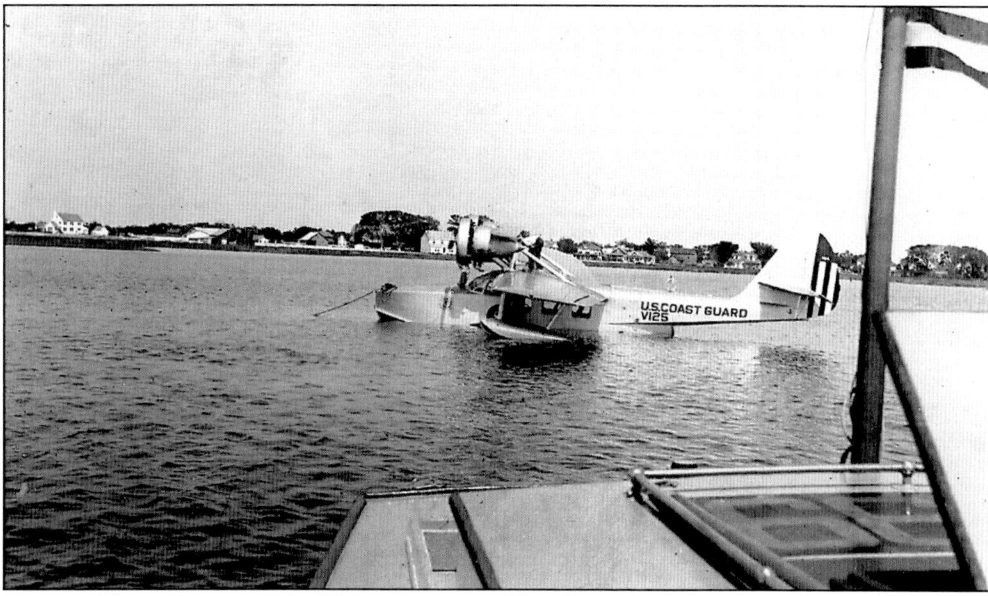

AERIAL COAST PATROL. The U.S. Coast Guard has been involved in aviation in one way or another since the Wright brothers' first flight in 1903; it was members of the U.S. Life Saving Service, a forerunner of today's Coast Guard, that assisted the Wrights in a number of ways, including providing weather reports. In 1916, Pres. Woodrow Wilson created the Aerial Coast Patrol, which today is part of the operations that guard the nation's coastline and provide search-and-rescue missions. Hampton Roads is home to the Coast Guard's Fifth District, and helicopters and airplanes fan out across the Mid-Atlantic from the region. The above photograph shows a vintage Coast Guard seaplane at a North Carolina base. The below vintage photograph shows a Coast Guard rescue at sea. (OCGS.)

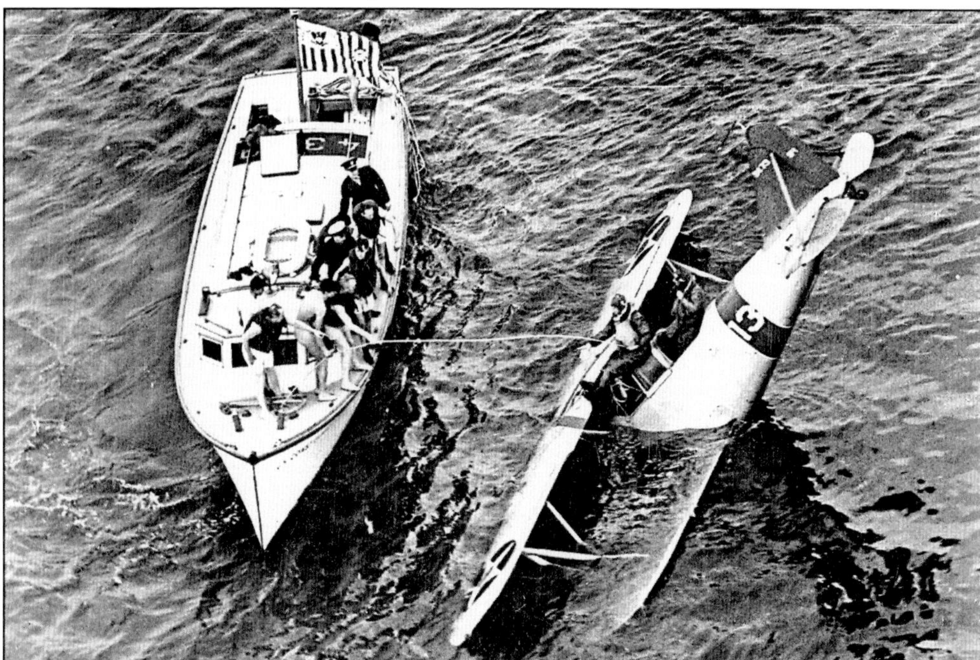

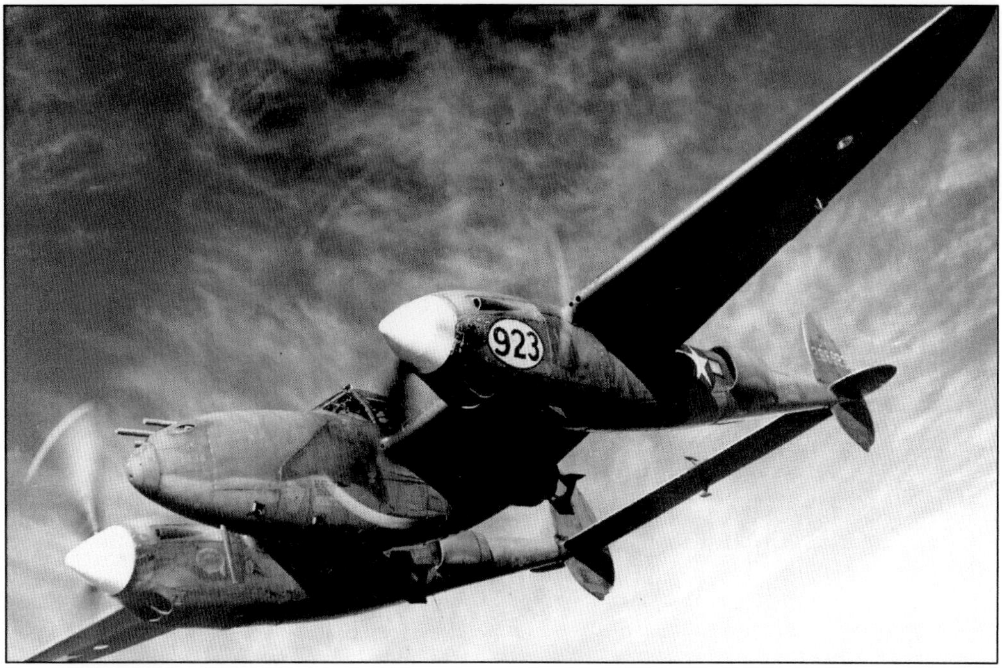

Langley Field. Established in 1917 as Langley Field, today Langley Air Force Base is one of the oldest continuously active air bases in the United States. Hangers built in 1918 housed the JN-4 Curtiss Jenny and deHavilland DH-4 bomber. For a while, the base would be home to lighter-than-air craft, such as the *Roma*. In the 1920s, Langley played a part in crafting the concept of air power, when Gen. Billy Mitchell flew his experimental bombing runs from there. The grassy field grew in the 1930s and became a major airfield of the Army Air Corps. By World War II, planes such as those shown in these photographs flew from paved runways. Today Langley is home to the First Fighter Wing and headquarters of the Air Combat Command. (Library of Congress.)

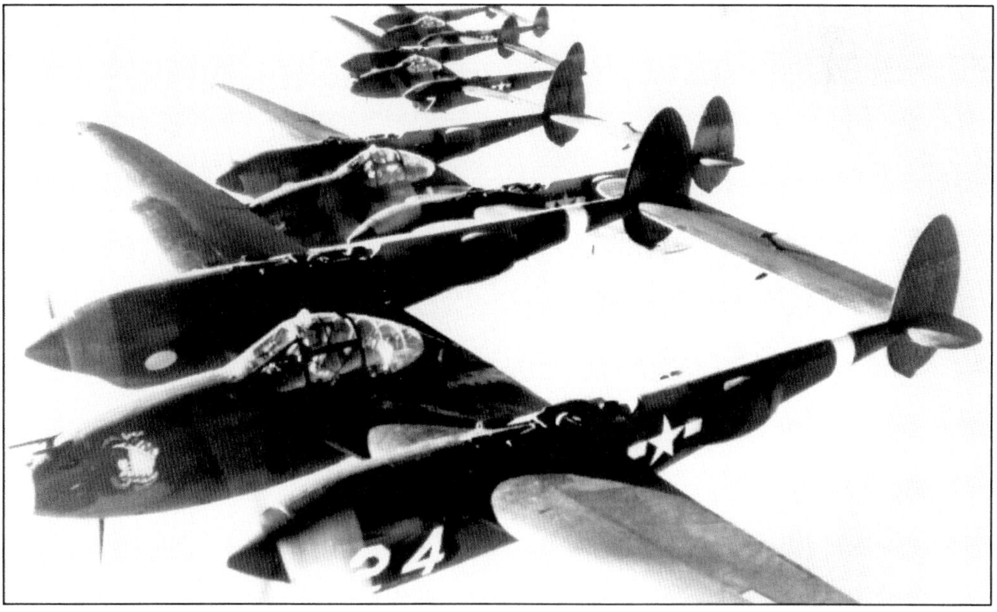

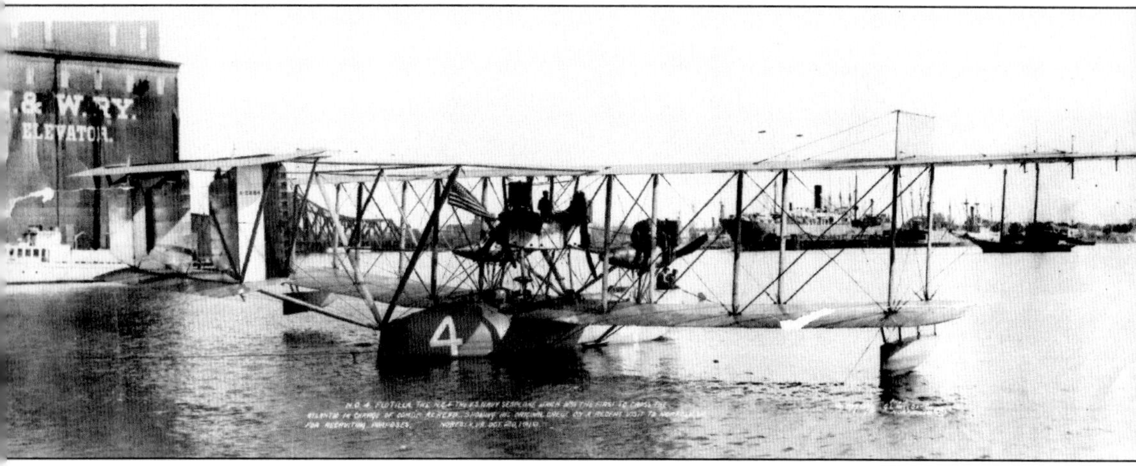

Off We Go. Aviation was little more than a decade old when plans for Naval Station Norfolk were developed. The base has its roots with the Naval Air Detachment, Curtiss Field (the Atlantic Coast Aeronautical Station) in May 1917. Later that year, with a staff of five officers, three aviators, ten enlisted sailors, and seven aircraft, the group moved to the Norfolk side of the water and was renamed Naval Air Detachment, Naval Operating Base, Hampton Roads. The aircraft, all seaplanes, were flown across the harbor and moored to stakes in the water until canvas hangers were constructed. The move gave the detachment a better place for operations, accessibility to supplies from Naval Station Norfolk, and room for expansion. Shown in this October 1919 photograph at the base is Comdr. A. C. Read and his crew in their NC-4 Flotilla seaplane, the first to cross the Atlantic, from Rockaway Beach, New York, to Plymouth, England. (HRNM.)

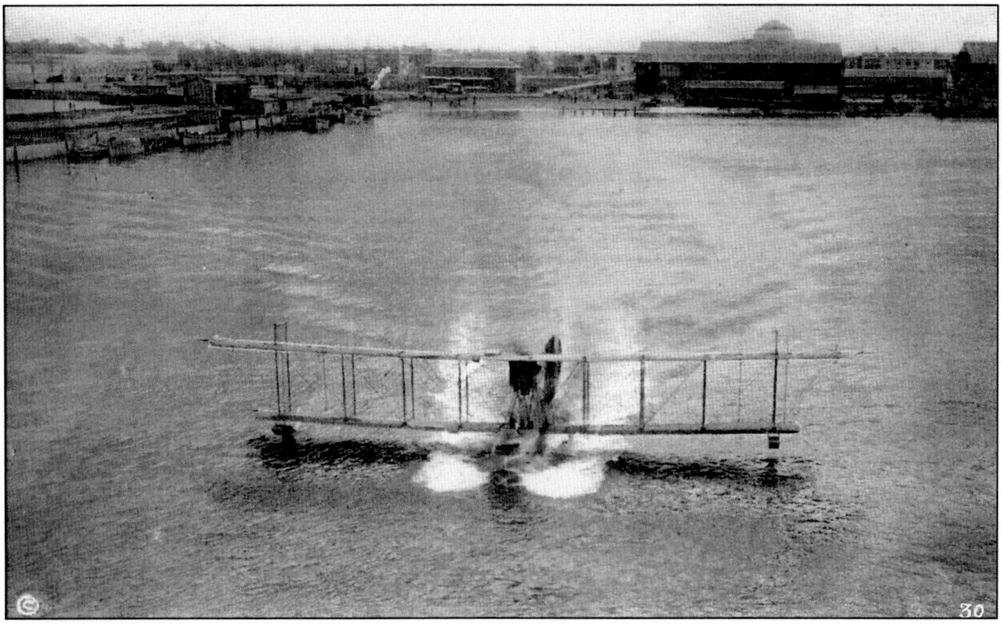

EARLY SCENES OF NAVAL OPERATING BASE NORFOLK. These two postcards come from a series postmarked 1922 and give a glimpse at the early aviation scene at Naval Operating Base Norfolk. At this time, land plane use was limited. The base operated largely as a harbor for seaplanes, as indicated in the top photograph, which has the title "Starting Out." The base also operated lighter-than-air craft, like the blimp seen in the below photograph, titled "Starting up for Observation." Built on the site of the former 1907 Jamestown Exposition, some of the former festival buildings can be seen in each picture. (PEH.)

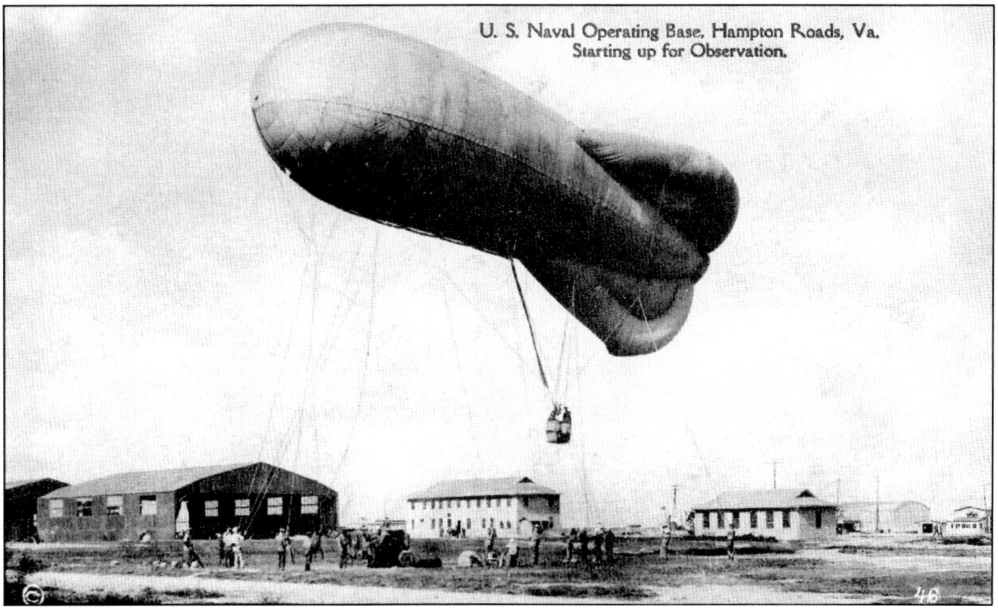

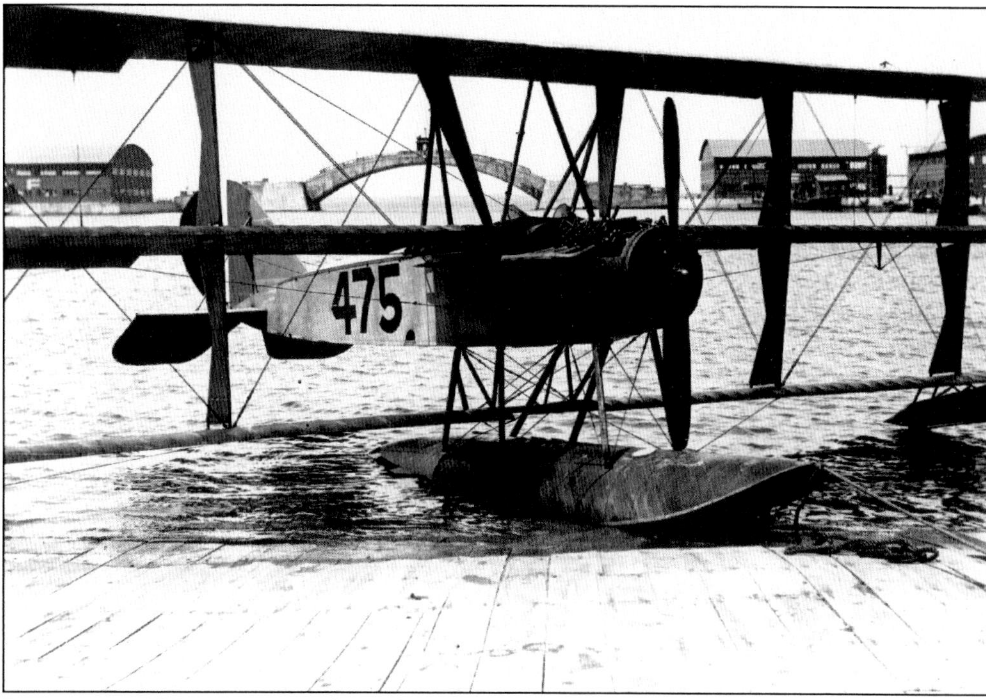

PLANES AT NOB NORFOLK. These photographs show some of the types of aircraft that were operating in the early days of NOB Norfolk. Note that both are seaplanes, taking advantage of the large adjacent harbor. In the above July 1918 photograph is an experimental triplane, the Curtiss L-type. In the bottom May 1919 photograph is a Curtiss HA Dunkirk fighter. (HRNM.)

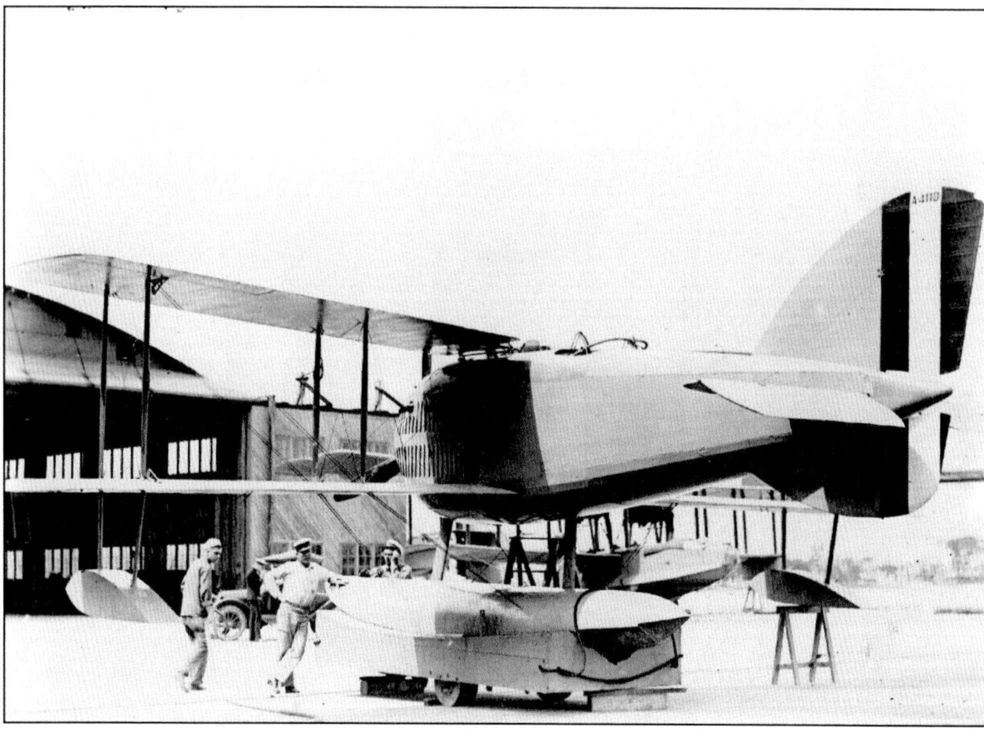

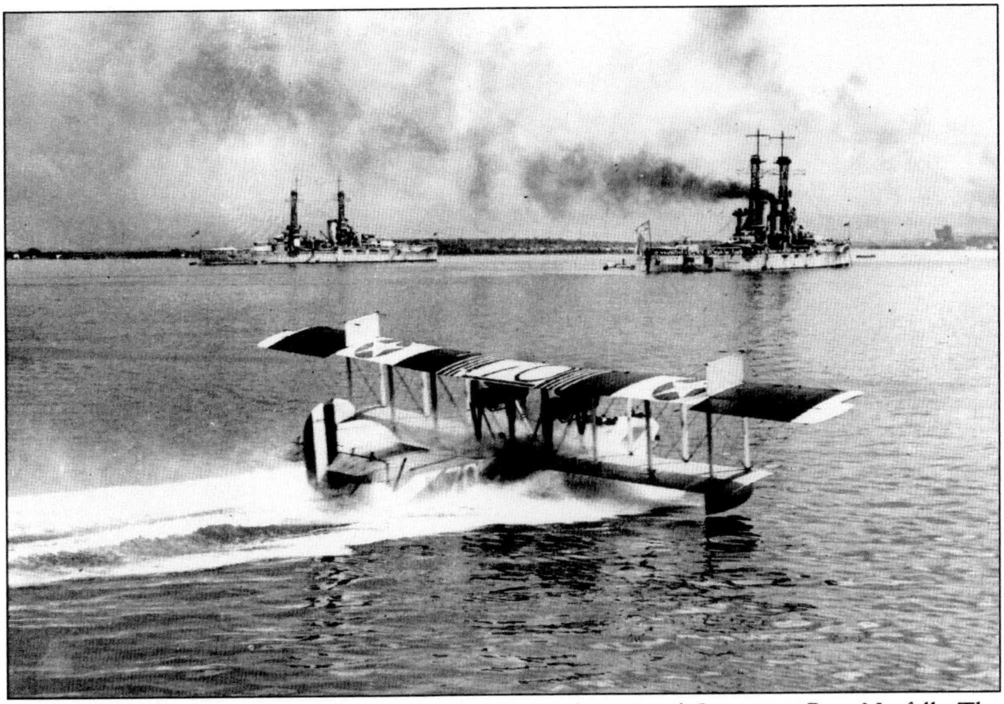

NAME THAT PLANE. These photographs show aircraft at Naval Operating Base Norfolk. The top photograph is a Curtiss F-5L seaplane, *c.* 1920, of the Atlantic Fleet Air Detachment. In the bottom photograph, neither the type of aircraft nor the crew is noted; however, the men are in navy uniforms. A myriad of aircraft could be seen at NOB Norfolk, many of them Curtiss-built. Curtiss had strong ties to the area: he started an aviation school in Newport News in 1915, which would give rise to the flight detachment at NOB Norfolk. (HRNM.)

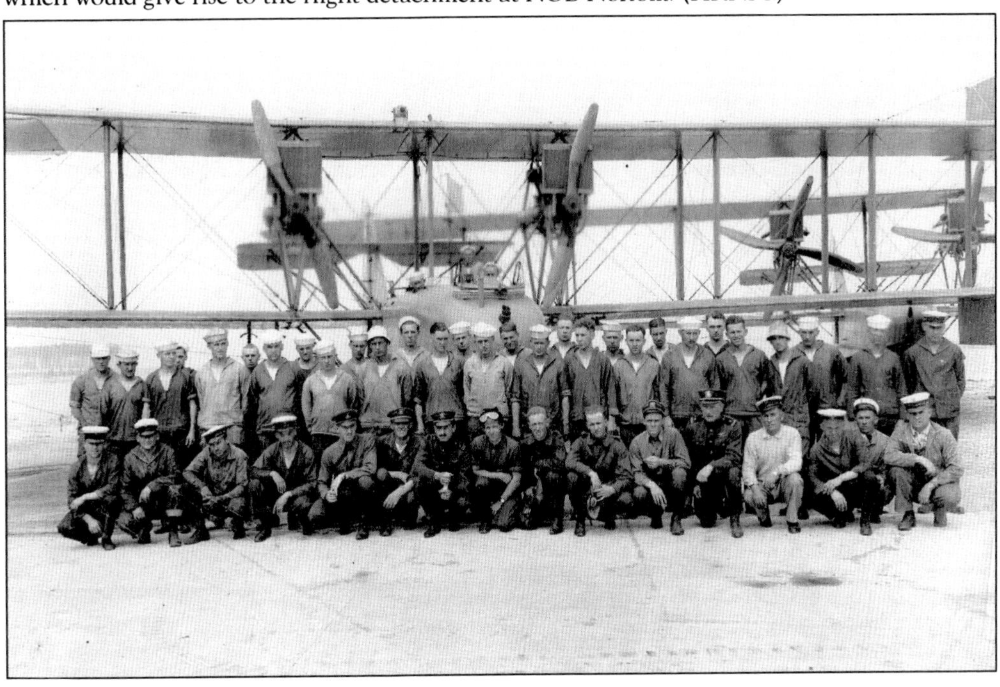

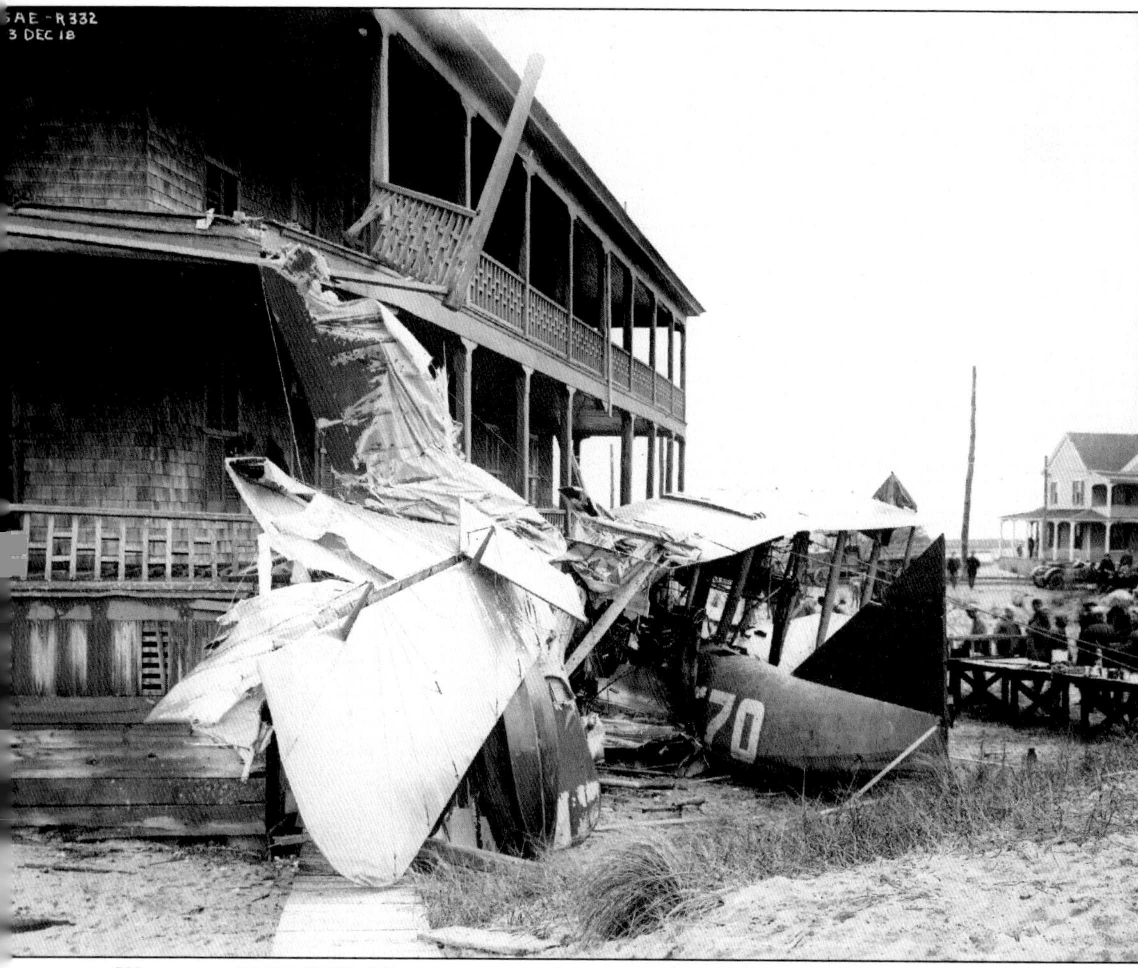

WRECK OF H-12 #770. The experimental aircraft H-12 #770 crashed into a neighborhood in Norfolk on Friday, December 13, 1918, killing two men aboard; it became Norfolk's first crash involving a home in a residential area. The seaplane was returning to the Norfolk Naval Base from a Maryland base when it crashed into the old Willoughby Club at Willoughby Spit. The plane had landed on the water in Little Bay and was attempting a take-off when it plummeted into a corner of the double-decker porch of the club. Fortunately, the club had been shuttered for the winter. Aboard the plane, Thomas Vincent (Delco) Jones and Llewellyn W. Alexander died; Robert Palmedo (the pilot), D. Thomas, and W. V. Avery were injured. The accident could have proven worse: just on the other side of the club were occupied cottages. (HRNM.)

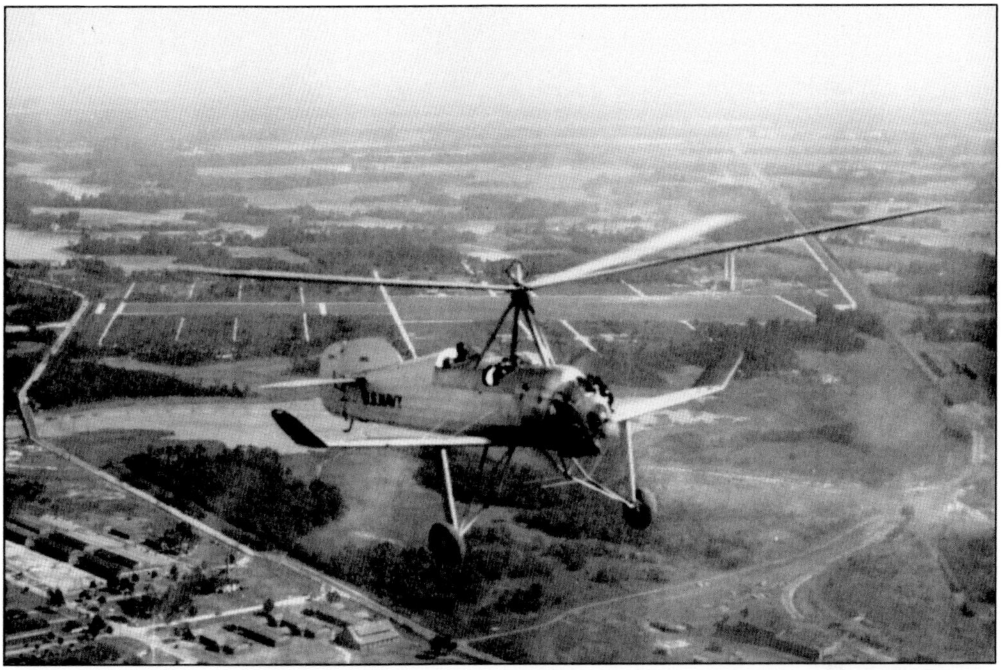

MORE AIRCRAFT AT NOB NORFOLK. Over the years, aviation operations at NOB Norfolk expanded. While a large seaplane base was maintained, aircraft of other types were also entering the scene, such as the Auto Gyro, seen in the above photograph, taken sometime in the early 1930s. Of note in this picture is the old East Camp in the center of the photograph. This area would be acquired in 1940 to grow the base. In the bottom *c.* 1932 photograph is a Great Lakes BG-1 airplane, made by the Great Lakes Aircraft Corporation. Note the reference to Quantico on the side of the aircraft. (HRNM.)

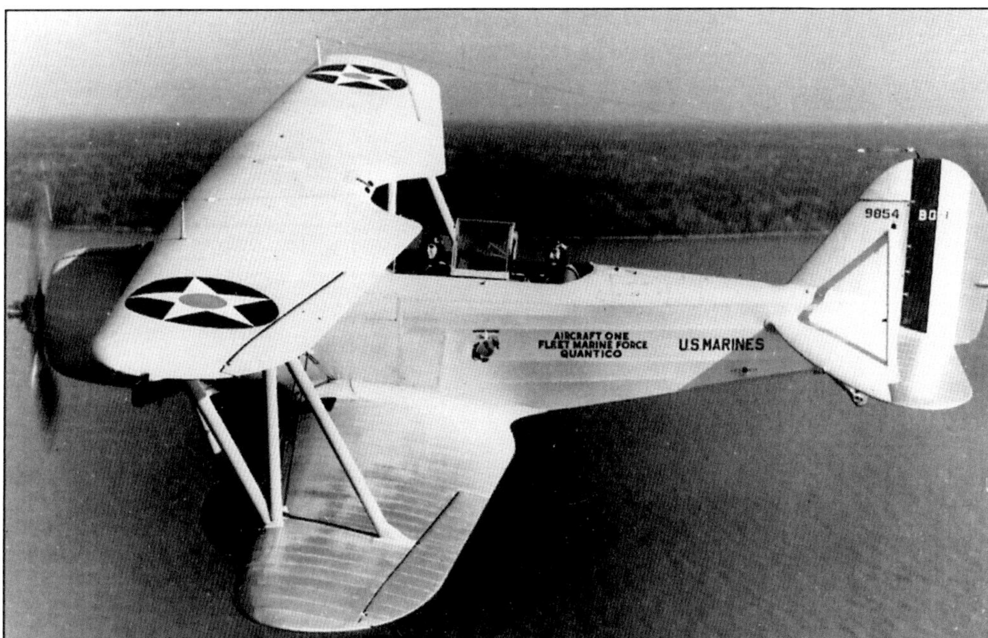

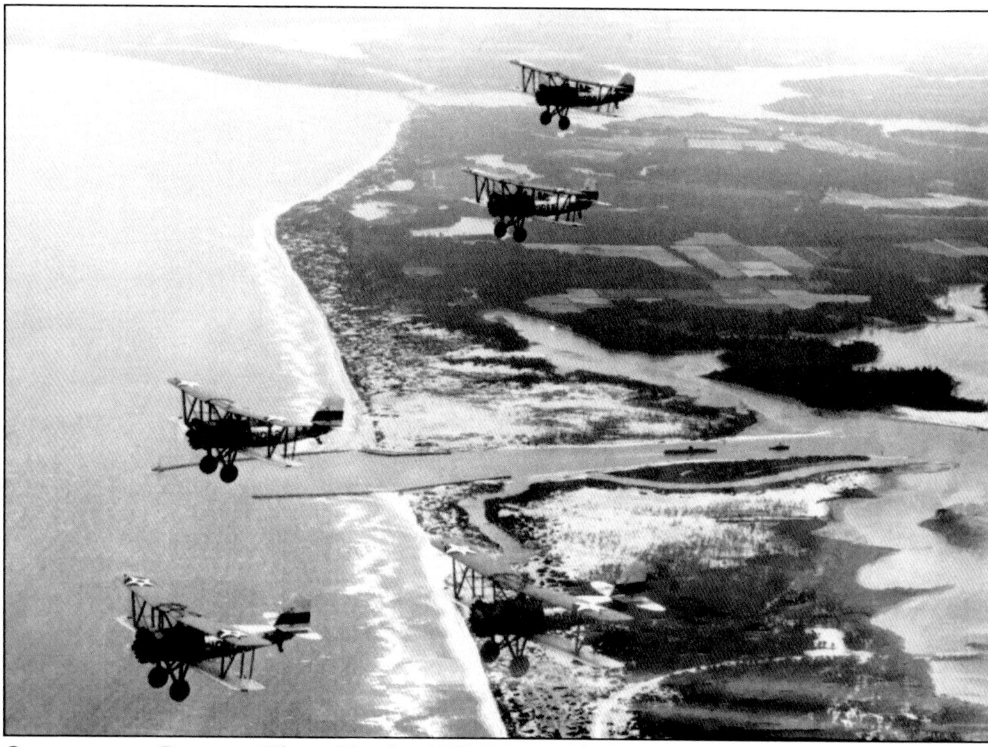

Observation Planes. These Vought 02U Corsair observation planes were carried aboard cruisers and launched by catapult. They are seen here over Little Creek around 1930. Visible in the photograph is Cape Henry in the extreme top left and the Virginia Beach shoreline in the top right. Note the railroad barge being towed by tug; this was a Pennsylvania Railroad operation from Norfolk to Cape Charles. (HRNM.)

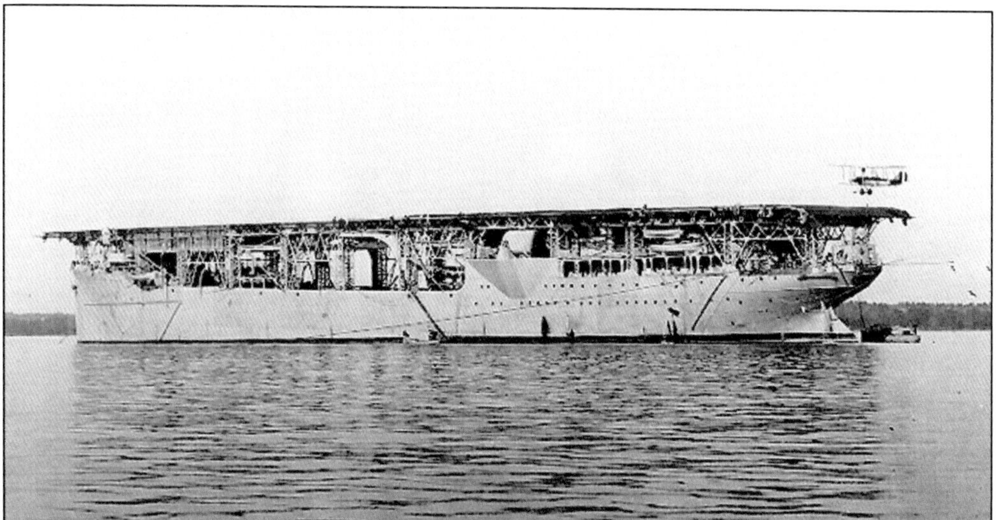

Flattop. In 1910, Eugene Ely was the first to fly from the deck of a ship, becoming a pioneer in naval aviation. Here the USS *Langley* is pictured *c.* 1923. Built as the *Jupiter*, it was converted into the first United States aircraft carrier at the Norfolk Naval Shipyard. It led the way to advancements, as seen in the Vought aircraft in the top photograph. (HRNM.)

FURTHER AIR CARRIER ADVANCES. From Eugene Ely's first flight came advances in aircraft carriers, like the USS *Enterprise*, which carried these Douglas TBD Devastators. The planes in this World War II–era photograph are attached to the Torpedo Squadron. The advantages in launching planes from ships were great, and aircraft carriers have been instrumental in every American conflict from World War II to today. (HRNM.)

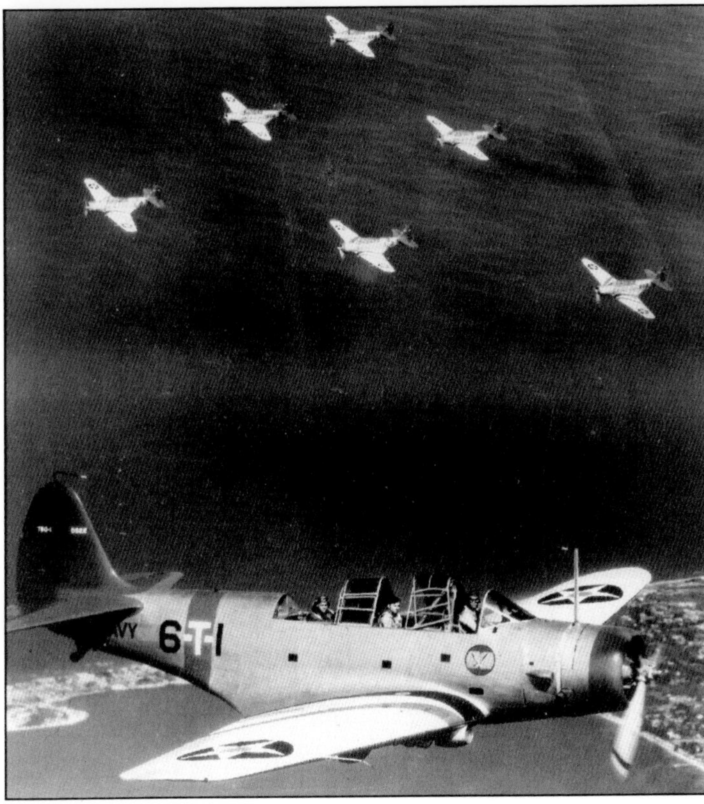

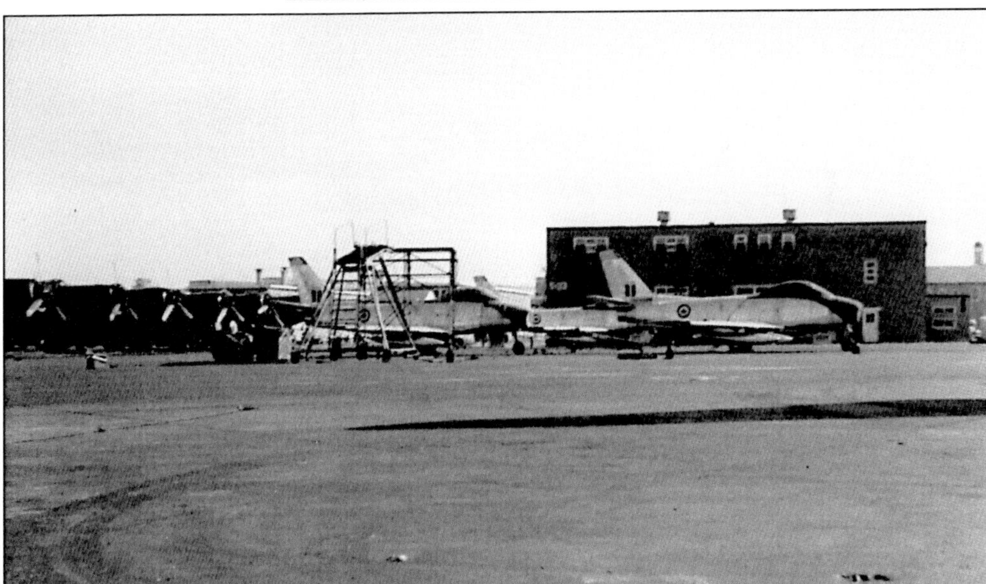

AN INTERNATIONAL FLAIR. This October 1951 photograph shows Canadian F-86 Sabre jets used by NATO at Naval Air Station Norfolk. When the United States entered NATO (North Atlantic Treaty Organization) in 1949, aircraft and crew from partner countries were seen at the field. Today, it is not uncommon to see jets from the military of other nations at Naval Station Norfolk for training and the like. (HRNM.)

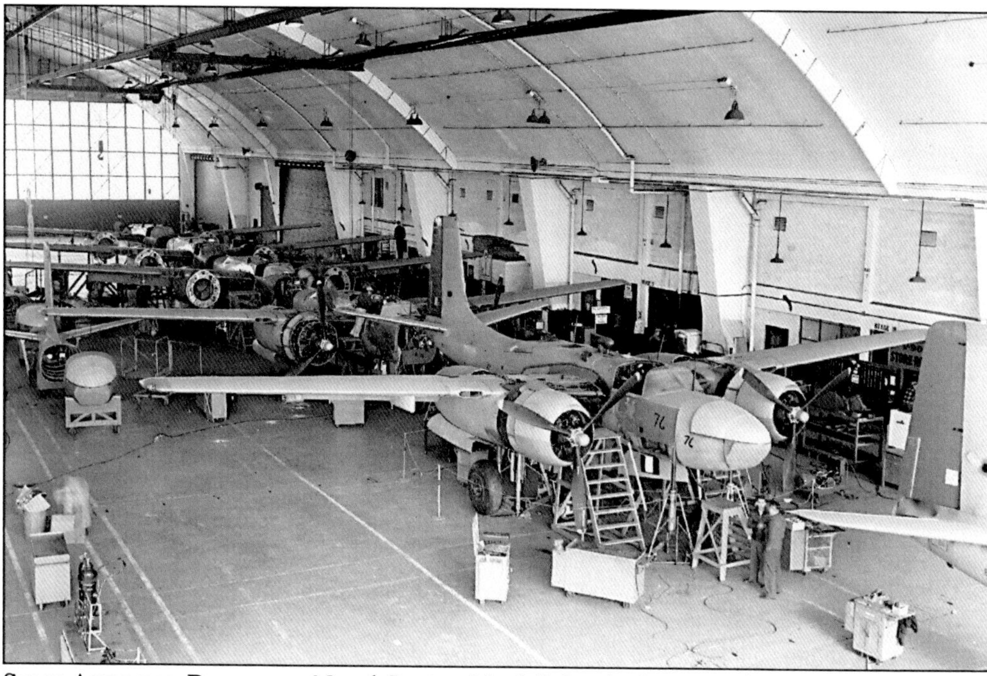

Some Assembly Required. Naval Station Norfolk has had many roles over time, including being a homeport for ships, a landing field for planes, a training facility, and an assembly plant. In the above March 1950 photograph, planes get their final touch at the Aircraft Final Assembly on the base. In the bottom photograph from May 1942, aircraft maintenance is learned at the Advance Base A Training Unit in Hanger 2. This is not only a working facility but sleeping quarters, too, for 1,100 men; note the beds in the upper right corner of the photograph. (HRNM.)

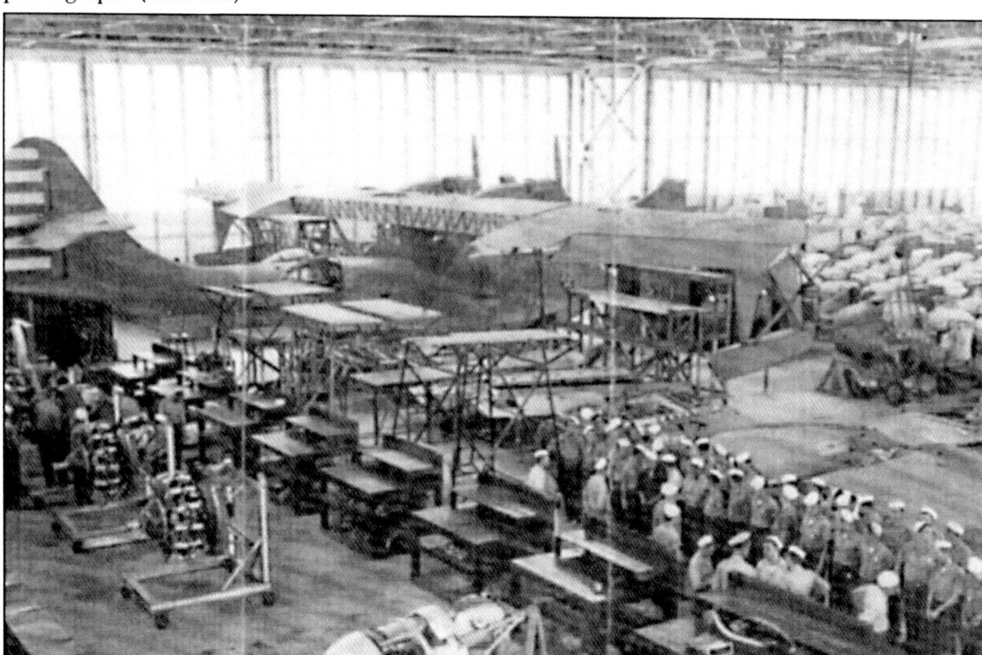

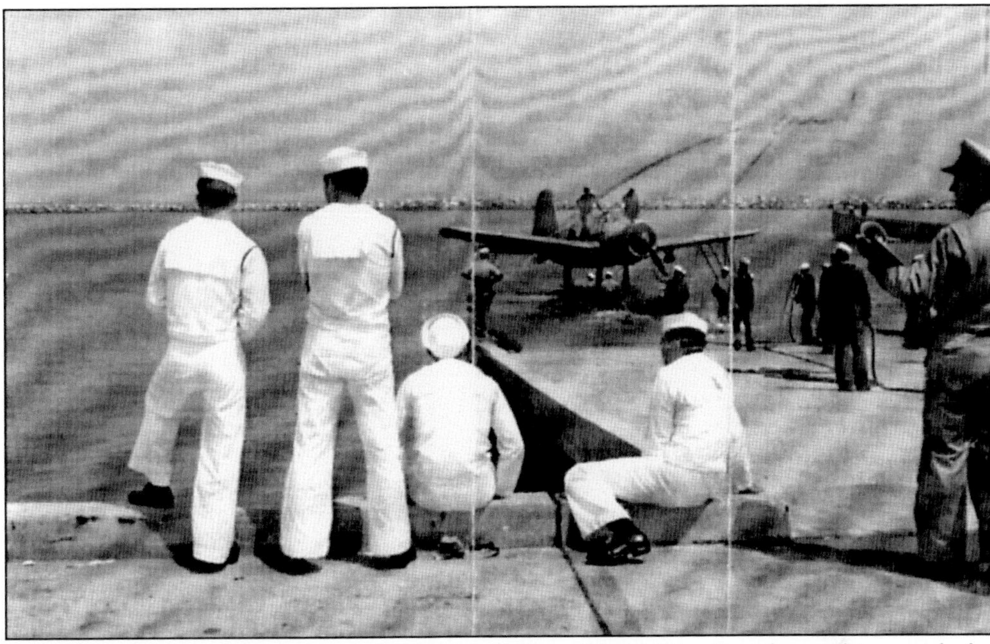

The War Effort. The impact of NOB Norfolk in World War II is far-reaching; with few exceptions, navy air squadrons that fought in the war trained in Norfolk. The air station also trained numerous British fighter squadrons and French and Russian patrol squadrons. From 1943 to the end of the war, a total of 326 U.S. units were commissioned and trained under the control of AIRLANT (Commander Air Force, Atlantic Fleet; now Naval Air Force Atlantic Fleet). The base was also involved in West Coast operations; in 1944, the year of peak production, 16 carriers, 20 carrier air groups, 57 carrier-based squadrons, 21 patrol squadrons, and 18 aviation units were deployed to the Pacific. The above seaplane ramp is shown in July 1942. The below photograph shows a PBM3 in the water at the seaplane base in November 1942. (HRNM.)

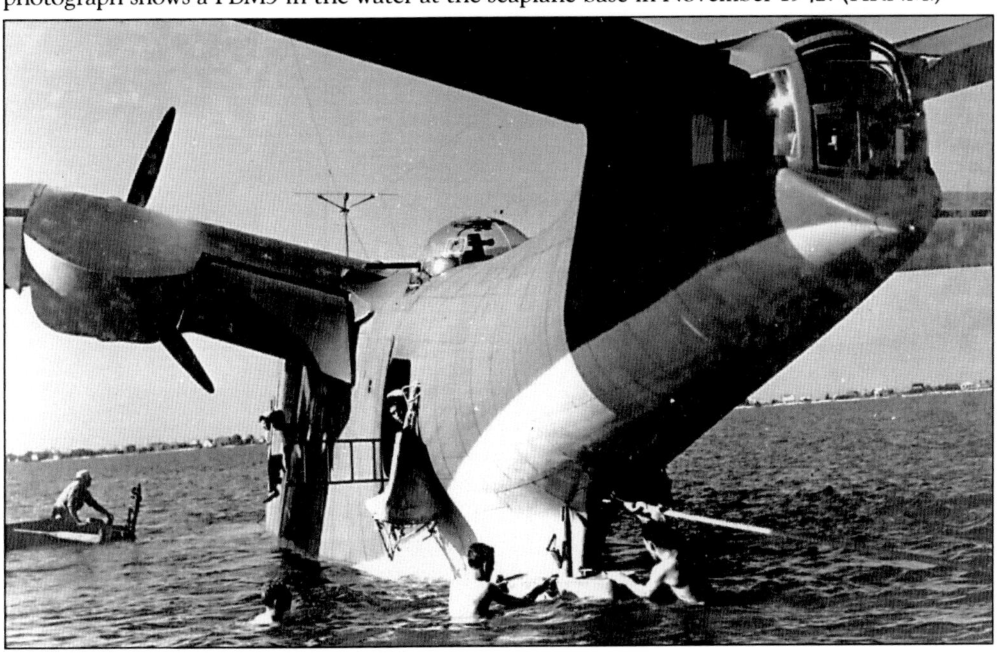

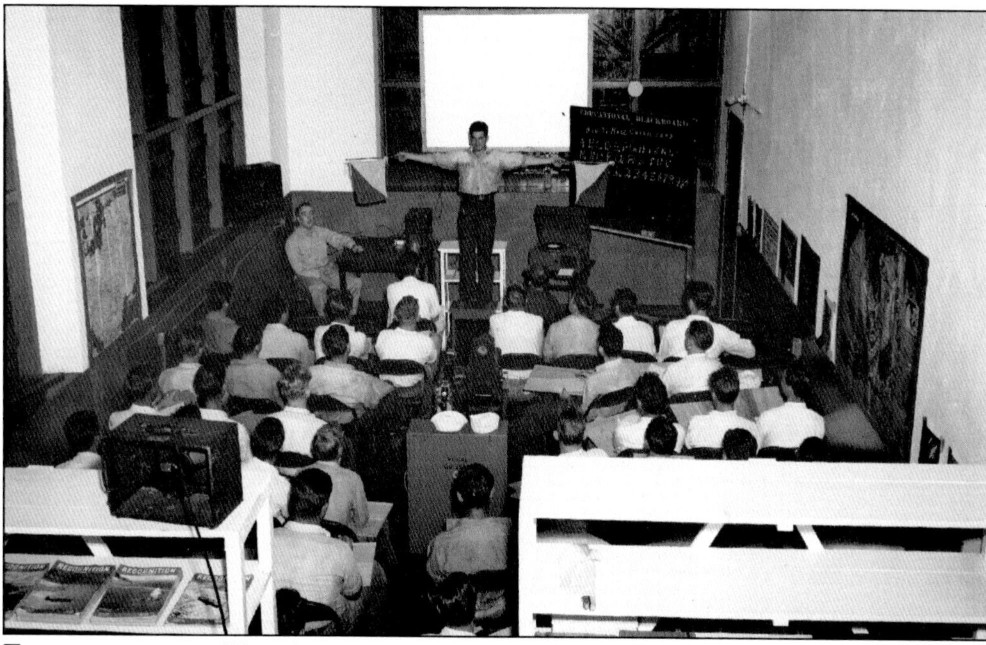

TRAINING FOR THE WAR. It was constant training during World War II, as shown in these photographs: the top picture is an aviation training unit, the bottom picture is a radio class. During World War II, NOB Norfolk grew exponentially. In manpower, the station leaped from an average of 2,076 officers and enlisted in December 1940 to 16,656 active-duty in December 1943. For the first six months of 1943, there was an average of 700 flights per day, which represents a take-off or landing every two minutes around the clock (the average today is one every six minutes). Flight operations grew, and by 1943, there were outlying fields at Chincoteague, Whitehurst, Reservoir, Oceana, Pungo, Fentress, Monogram, and Creeds, Virginia, as well as Elizabeth City, Edenton, Manteo, and Harvey Point, North Carolina. (HRNM.)

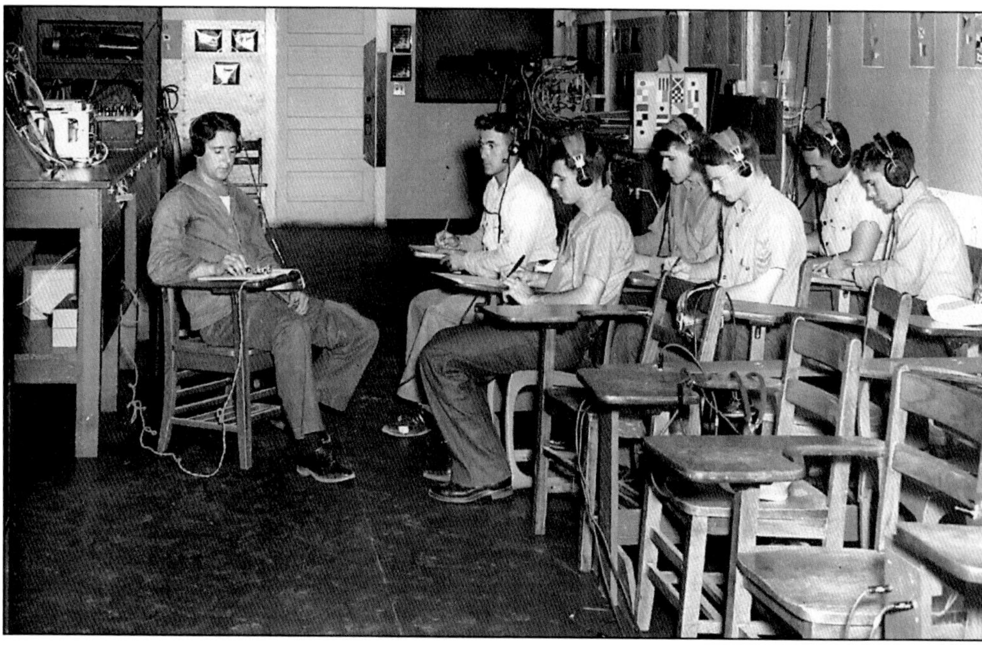

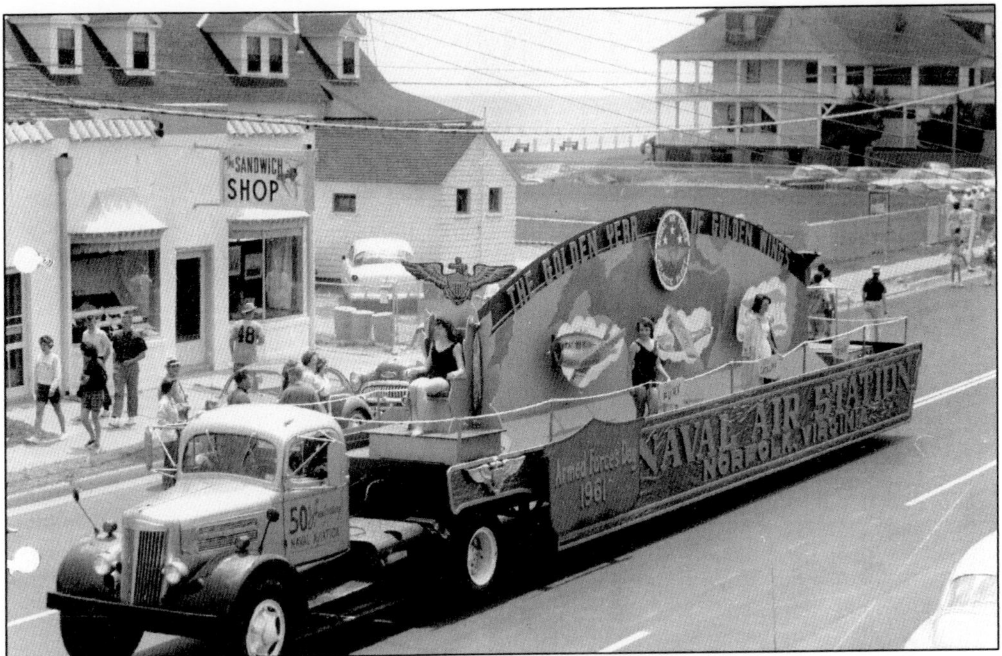

ARMED FORCES DAY. This *c.* 1961 photograph shows girls from Virginia Beach High School participating in Armed Forces Day. Even after World War II and the Korean War, things kept hopping around the military bases, largely due to buildup associated with the cold war. To show troop support, folks turned out for events like this and Memorial Day. (HRNM.)

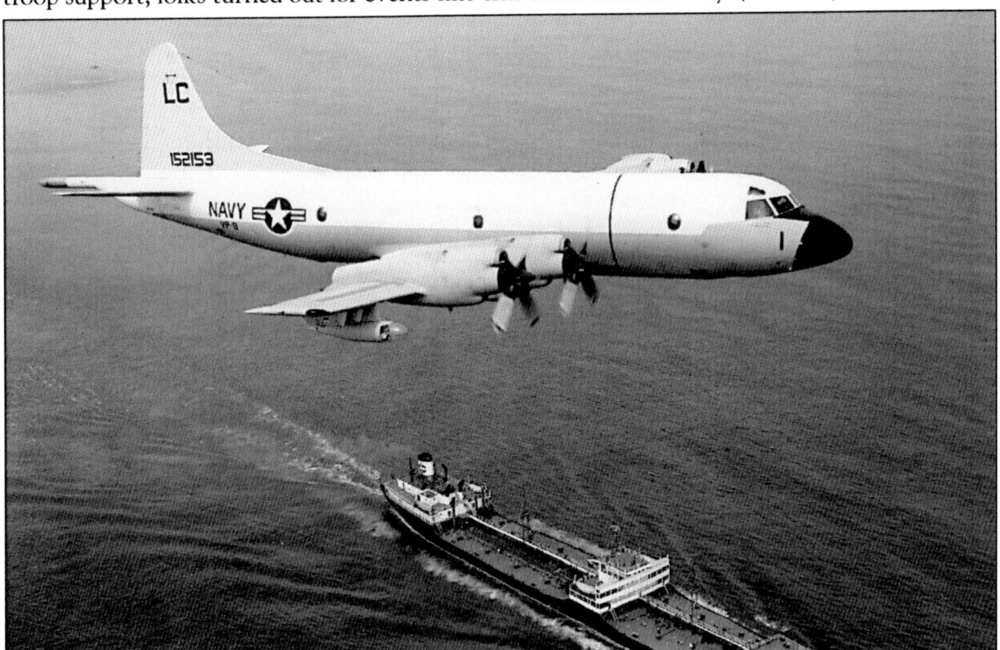

P-3C ORION IN FLIGHT. This 1965 photograph shows a navy Orion in flight over Norfolk. The four-engine, long-range turboprop patrol aircraft was used for submarine detection and other maritime surveillance. During the cold war, it was a frequent sight around Hampton Roads and is still being used today in the Iraqi conflict. (HRNM.)

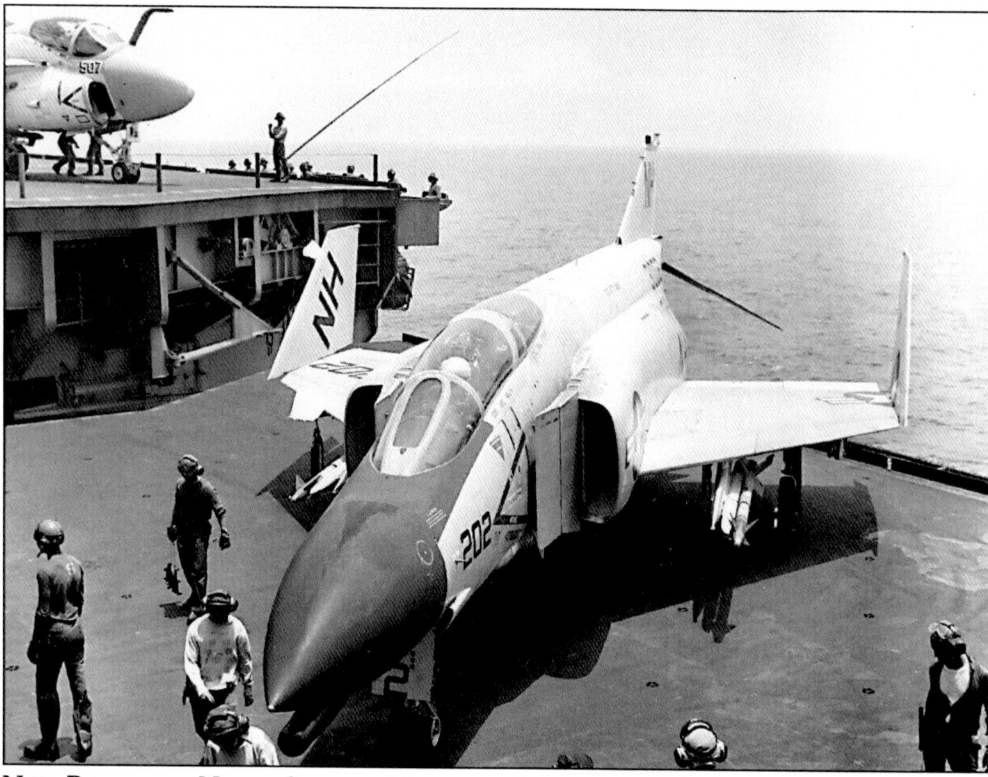

NEW ROLES FOR NAVAL STATION NORFOLK. Beginning in the late 1960s, Naval Station Norfolk (as well as Langley Air Force Base) began to see action related to the Vietnam War. In the above photograph, a McDonnell Douglas F-4 Phantom II is lowered into the hanger deck of an aircraft carrier after a strike on Haiphong Pol Storage in April 1967. The Grumman A-6A Intruder, seen in the bottom photograph, flies over Cape Henry. It saw action during conflicts in the 1980s and during the first Gulf War. (HRNM.)

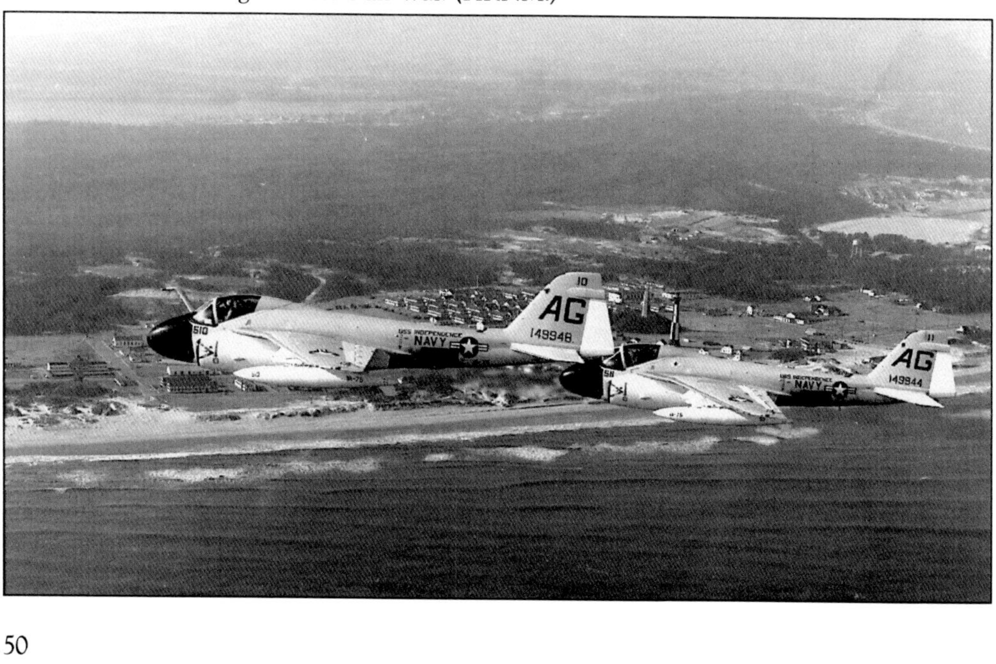

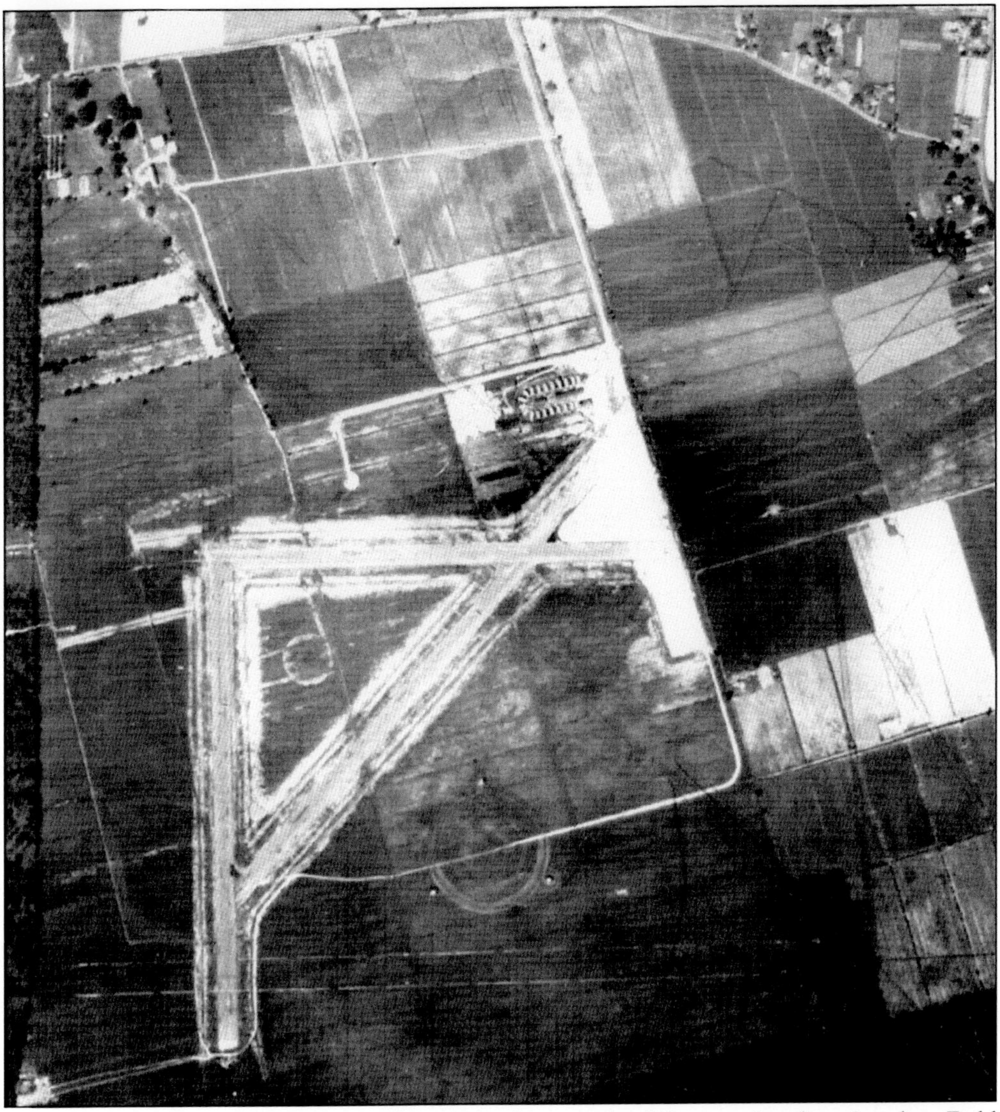

BUILD IT AND THEY WILL COME. This 1940s photograph of Oceana Auxiliary Landing Field has no resemblance to today's Naval Air Station Oceana, designated a Master Jet Base. Carved from a farm in present-day Virginia Beach, Oceana has grown to become one of the largest and most advanced air stations in the world, comprising some 6,820 acres (including its Dam Neck Annex). There are four runways—three measuring 8,000 feet long and one measuring 12,000 feet long. All combine to fulfill the base's mission to train and deploy the navy's fighter/attack squadron of F-14 Tomcats and F/A-18 Hornets. Oceana is a busy base: pilots stationed here fly approximately 219,000 operations annually. Operations are supplemented with the use of Naval Auxiliary Landing Field Fentress in Chesapeake, Virginia, Naval Station Norfolk Chambers Field in Norfolk, Virginia, and the Navy Dare County Range in North Carolina, all under the base's command. (NASO.)

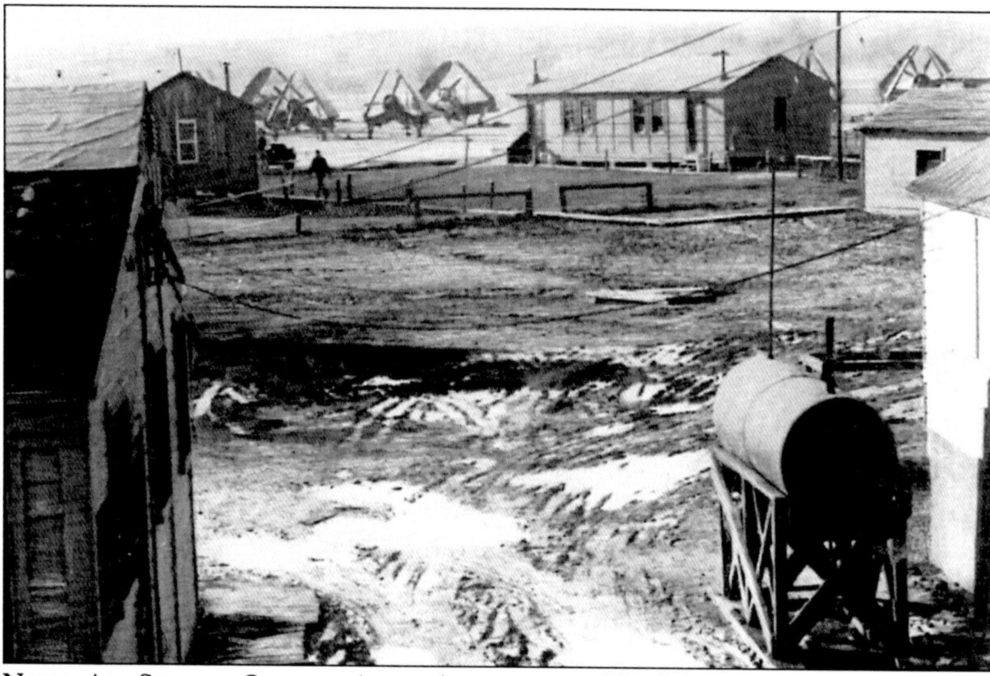

NAVAL AIR STATION OCEANA. As naval operations at Naval Operating Base Norfolk (now Norfolk Naval Air Station) expanded with the approach of World War II, 328 acres from Potter's Farm, near the tiny community of Oceana in present-day Virginia Beach, were eyed for an auxiliary landing field (ALF) in 1940 to supplant pilot training. From the muddy field, as shown in the top picture, c. 1944, a simple triangular airfield was laid out, along with a handful of Quonset huts and a 312,000-gallon fuel storage tank. By 1942, ALF Oceana upgraded to Naval Air Auxiliary Station (NAAS). By war's end, the number of men and aircraft tripled, and in 1952, it became NAS Oceana. In the bottom photograph, Bombing Squadron Three (VB-3) is shown with their Curtiss SB2C-5 Helldivers. The planes are shown at the old North Station in 1945 (the North Station closed and operations moved to the south side of the field in the mid-1950s). (NASO.)

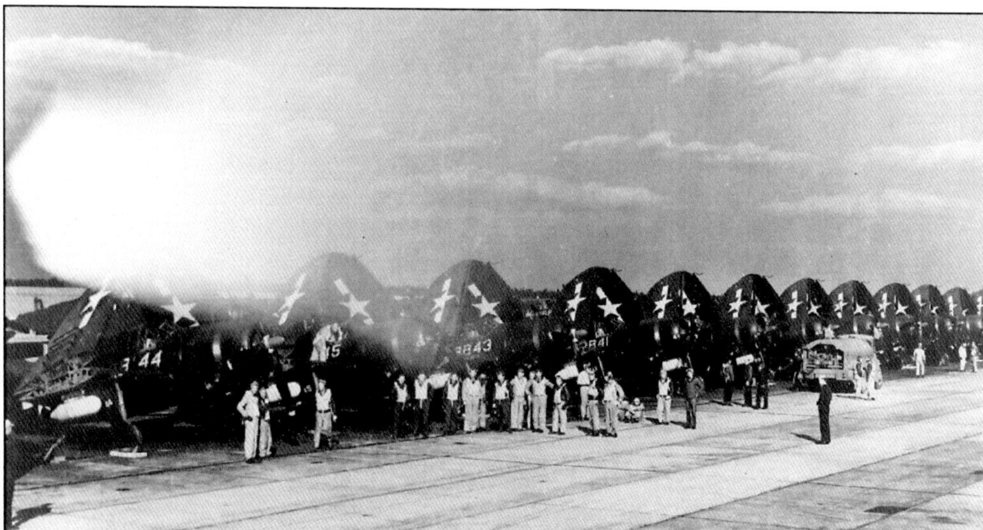

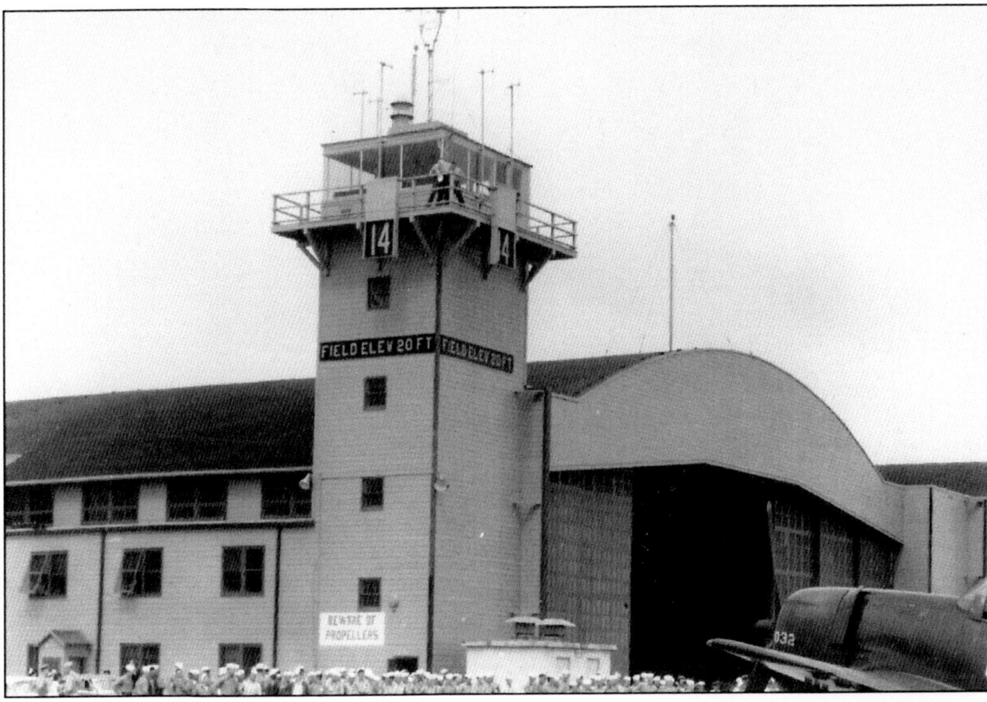

GROWTH AND EXPANSION. As war efforts grew, so did ALF Oceana. Calls for expansion came just months after the field initially opened, and the military started eyeing adjacent farmland. Today, NAS Oceana is more than 16 times its original size. In 1942, a new designation of Naval Air Auxiliary Station (NAAS) Oceana came. The above photograph was taken at the old North Station; the photograph at the left of five Grumman F6F-5 Hellcats was taken over southern Virginia Beach fields. Today, the base is in danger of closing or having portions of its operation moved by the BRAC, or Base Realignment And Closure Committee, because of encroachment of residential and commercial interests in Virginia Beach; Oceana is literally surrounded on all sides by homes and businesses. For years, many residents have been lobbying for efforts to quiet some of the jet noise from the base. In the meantime, Oceana remains a vital part of naval operations and of the Virginia Beach community. (NASO.)

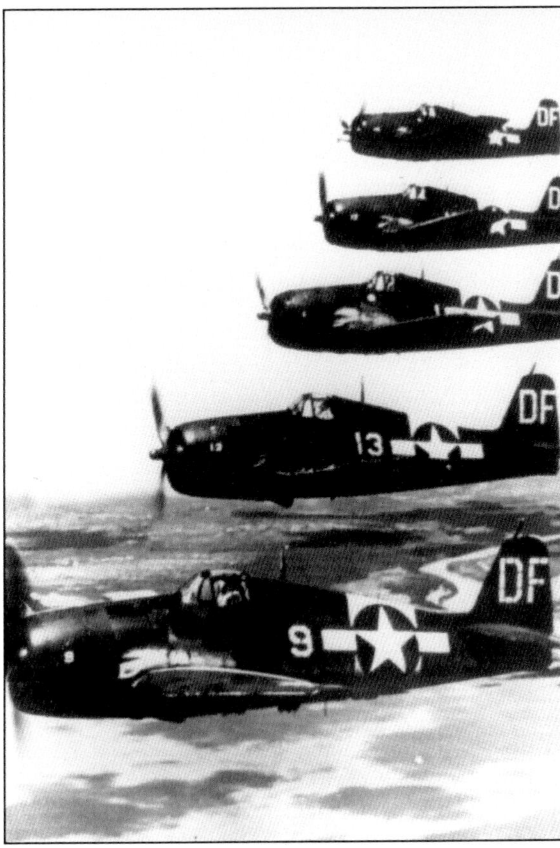

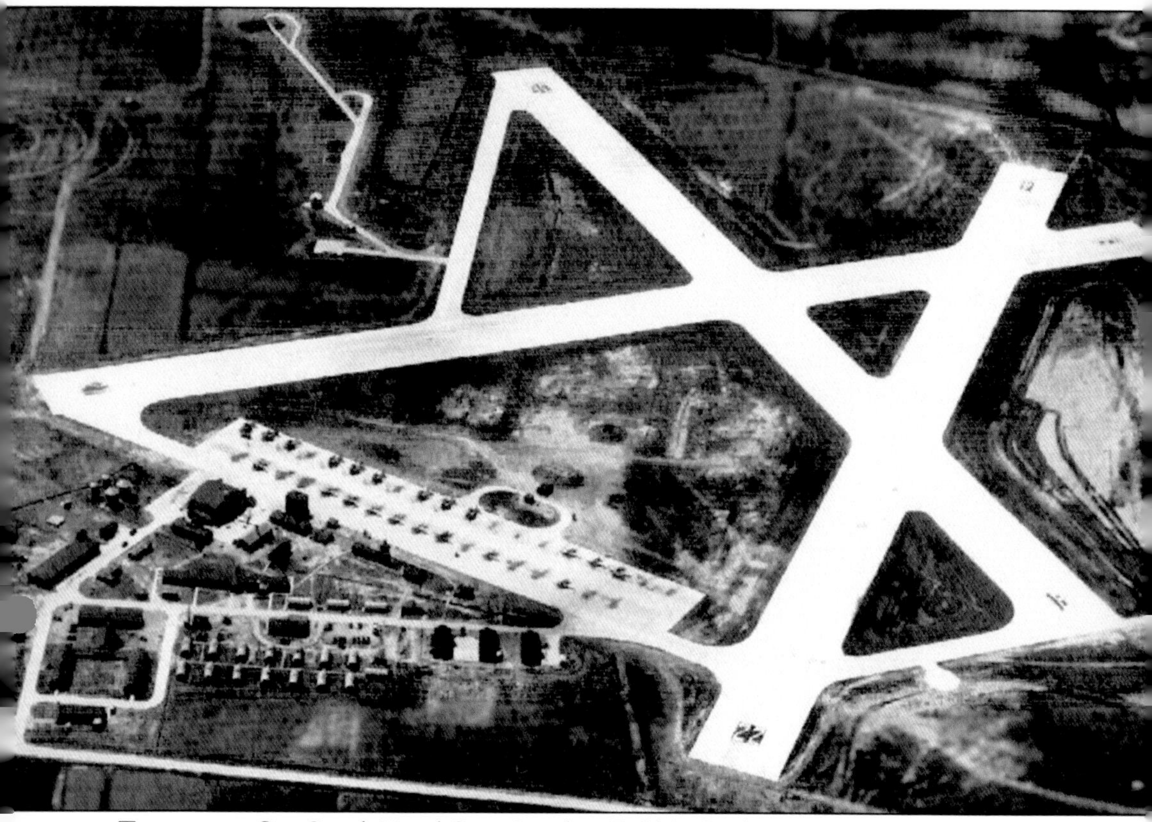

Touch and Go. Creeds Naval Outer Landing Field (NOLF) in rural Virginia Beach, as shown here, was one of many fields build in Hampton Roads to support training operations during World War II. Planes, particularly from Norfolk Naval Air Station, would use this field and others; most would be abandoned shortly after the war. Other fields included Pungo NOLF, Whitehurst NOLF, Monogram Naval Auxiliary Air Station/Driver, Chincoteague Naval Auxiliary Air Station/Wallops Island (still open), and Auxiliary Landing Field (ALF) Fentress (still open and assigned to Naval Air Station Oceana). Curiously, some of these fields, although unused for years, still exist and serve other purposes: in Virginia Beach, the Creeds NOLF (decommissioned by the navy in October 1945) is today used by the Virginia Beach Police Department for a variety of training exercises. (PEH.)

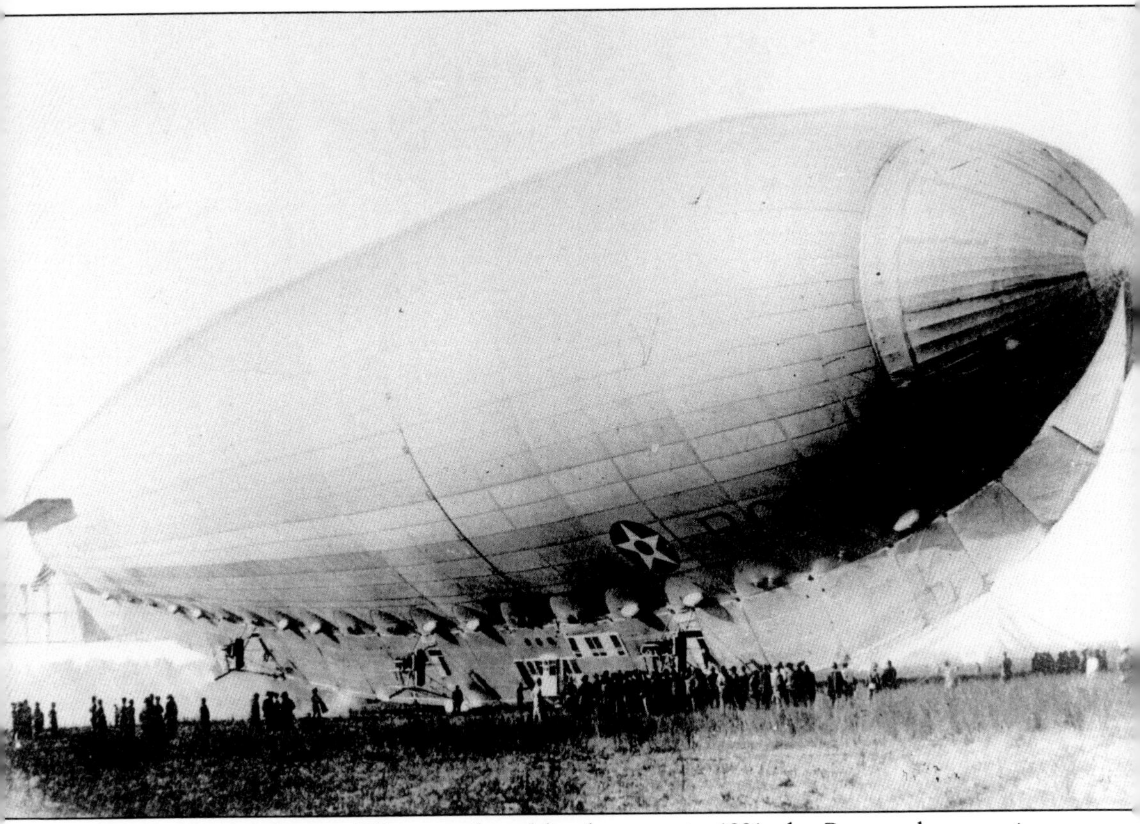

The Army Airship Roma. When purchased by the army in 1921, the *Roma*, a large semi-ridged airship made in Italy, became the biggest dirigible in U.S. military service. The ship was big: 410 feet long, 92 feet tall, and capable of carrying passengers and cargo at a quick clip. Built in 1919, it had drawn attention across Europe for its size, speed, and range; now it belonged to America. It was packed and sent to Langley Field in Hampton and prepared to be put into service. The giant silver ship became a frequent site over Hampton Roads as the Langley crew trained at the controls of the finicky craft. Then, on February 21, 1922, the *Roma*, cruising over Naval Operating Base Norfolk, tilted forward and began a descent earthward. As it lumbered along, crew members threw out what they could to lighten the load in hopes of saving the ship, but it was not enough: the nose of the hydrogen-filled craft hit the ground and brushed into a high-voltage electric line. It exploded into a giant fireball. (NPL.)

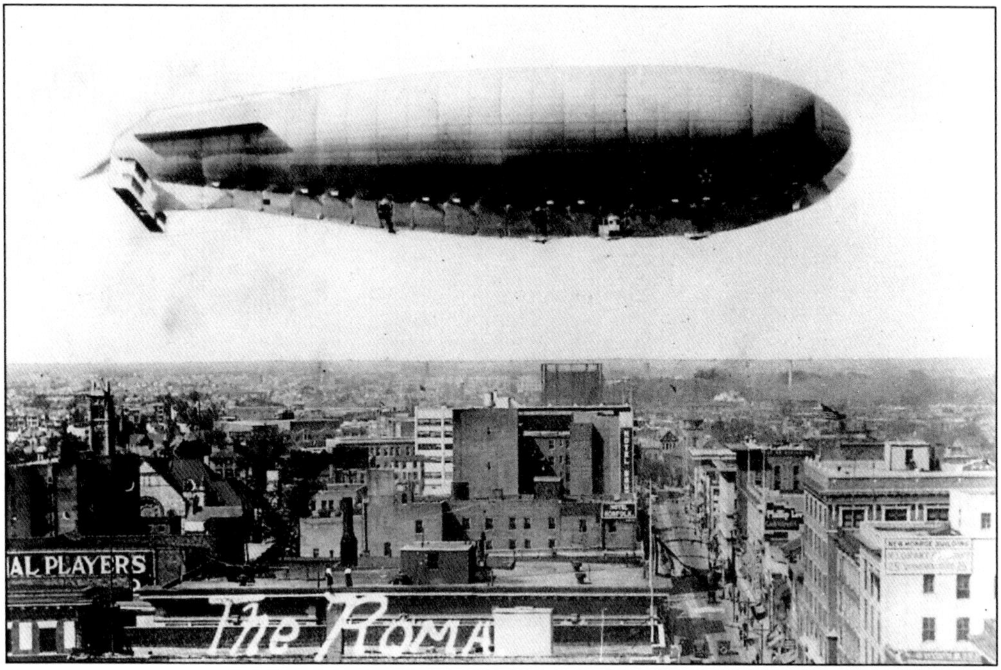

SILVER SHIP OF THE SKY. The *Roma*, seen in the above photograph sailing over Norfolk, was a beautiful ship by all accounts. Being semi-rigid, it was a cross between a blimp and a dirigible. The keel housed a control room, navigation space, passenger cabin, the outriggers that held the engines, and a rudder and elevator. Inside, gas cells held more than a million cubic feet of hydrogen. Based at Langley Field, the Italian-made craft was seen often over Hampton Roads in late 1921 and early 1922. Capt. Dale Mabry was the skipper when it exploded after hitting electric lines near the army's Quartermaster Depot, site of today's Norfolk International Terminal. Of the 45 aboard, 34 died. Today there is a small concrete monument that simply reads "U.S. Army Dirigible Roma Crashed Here, Feb. 21, 1922" to mark the spot. (NPL.)

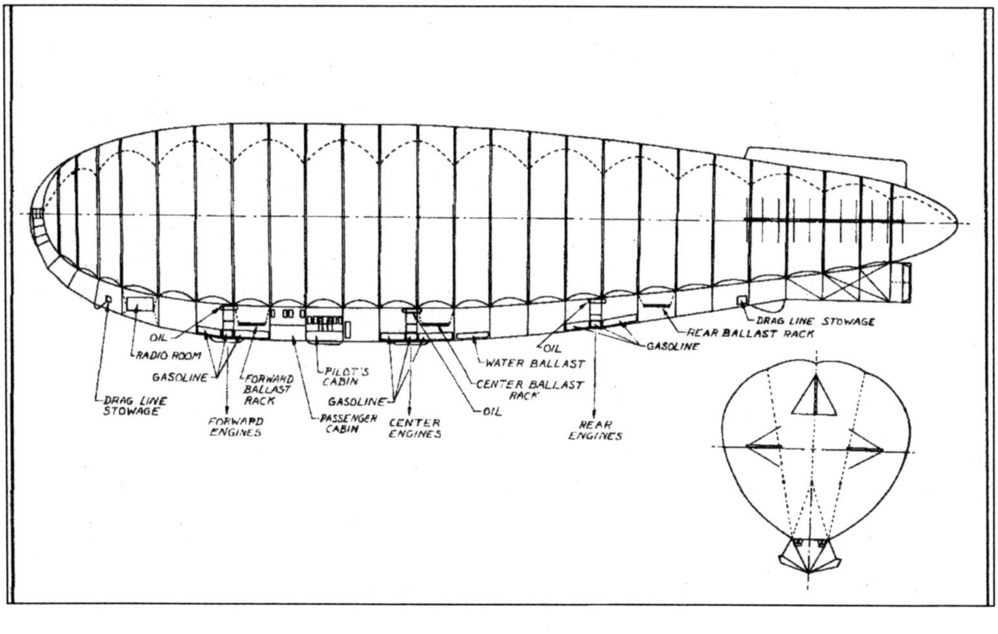

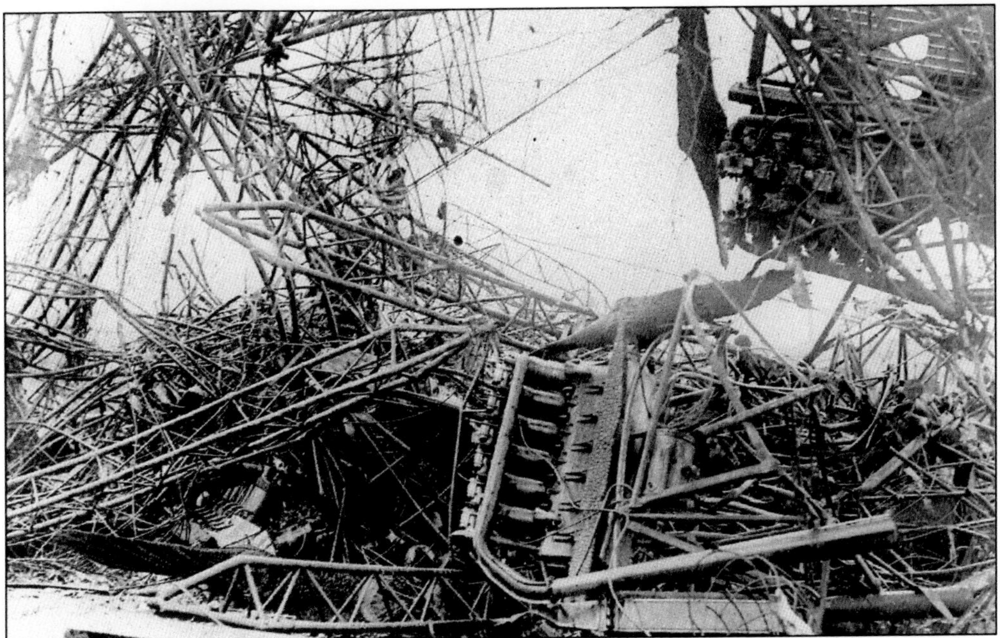

"My God, Boys." Those were the last words spoken by *Roma* captain Dale Mabry when he realized his giant hydrogen-filled airship was going to crash. During a flight over Norfolk on February 21, 1922, the crew noticed the ship become difficult to control. The keel started to buckle, and the tail began to come loose. The nose dropped, and the ship tilted towards the ground. Just south of Naval Operating Base Norfolk, it hit the ground and slammed into electrical wires; the hydrogen exploded immediately, killing 34 of the 45 aboard. These vintage photographs show the result. The bottom photograph is of the crash scene near the army's Quartermaster Depot. The electrical wires that the airship hit are near the center of the photograph near the curve of the road. (NPL.)

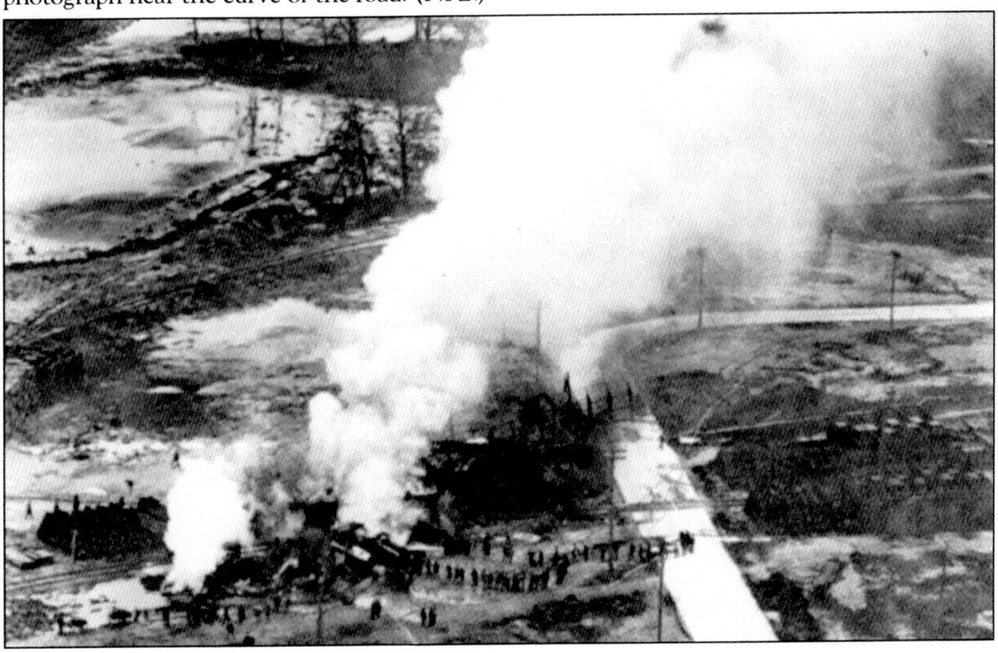

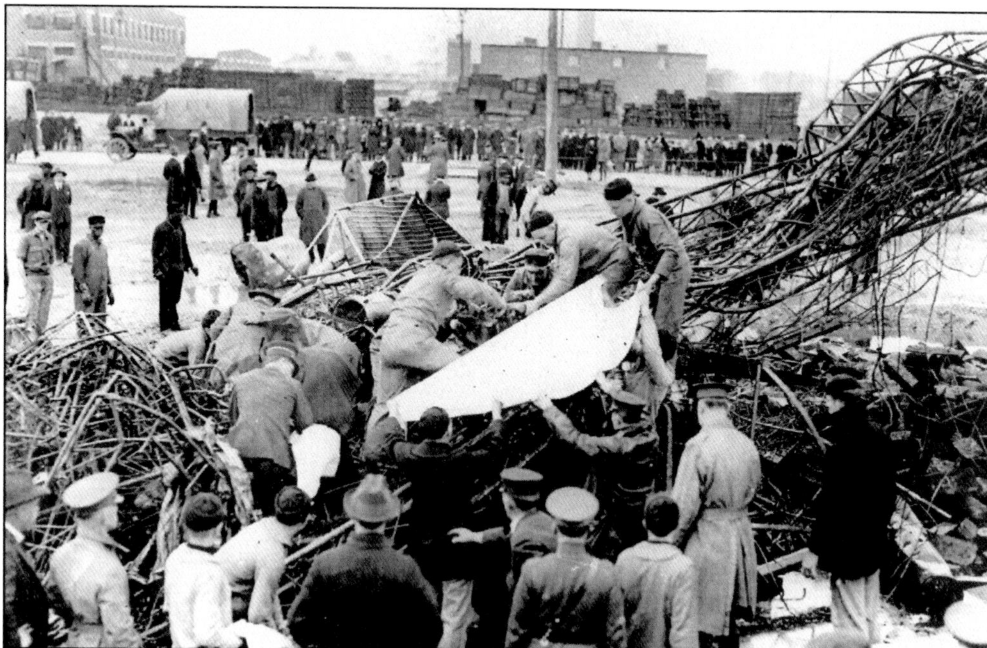

THIRTY-FOUR PERISH IN GIANT BLIMP *ROMA*. That headline greeted readers of the *Virginian-Pilot* on February 22, 1922, the day after the Langley Field–based airship crashed to the ground, hit electrical lines, and exploded. These vintage photographs show the crash site; the above photograph shows bodies being removed from the wreckage. The fireball burned the victims to "a cracklin' " said one rescuer. Another said one skull "shrunk in the heat and burned away to the size of a fist." Although the disaster rivaled the 1937 crash of the *Hindenburg*, there were no movie reels to capture the horror, and the incident has faded from many people's memories. (NPL.)

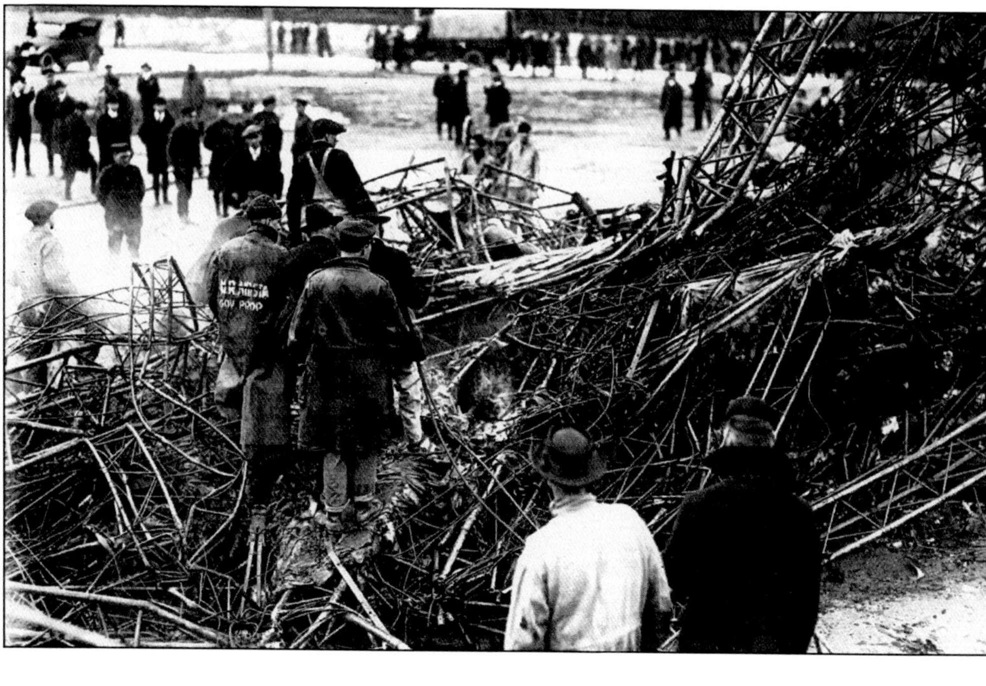

Three

THE RACE FOR SPACE

When Pres. John F. Kennedy proclaimed that America would put a man on the moon by the end of the 1960s, NASA Langley Research Center scientists at the Hampton, Virginia, facility got right on the job.

In fact, the entire Lunar Orbiter project was coordinated and managed right here in Hampton Roads; all of the space heroes of the 1960s lived and trained here—Alan Shepard, Neil Armstrong, John Glenn, Buzz Aldrin, and many more.

In many ways, the race for space was like the race for heavier-than-air flight just a half-century before—except, with the cold war against the former Soviet Union raging, much more seemed at stake. The region was right behind all the developments.

The role Hampton Roads played in early space exploration cannot be underscored. As a testament, a major museum, the Virginia Air and Space Center (http://www.vasc.org) is a legacy to the early days of space flight as well as current developments in exploration.

Today NASA Langley Research Center (and NASA Wallops Island Flight Center, just up the Eastern Shore) are still instrumental in developing procedures used in space exploration, with research and the occasional launches into space from the Wallops Island facility.

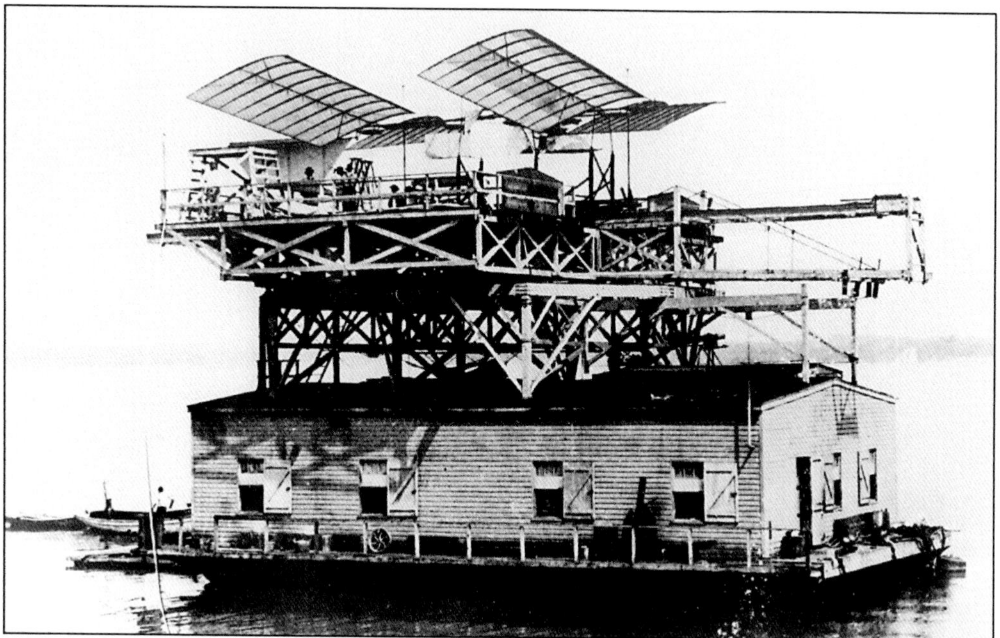

The Langley Aerodrome. The Langley Aerodrome was the brainchild of a group led by Samuel Langley. Shortly after this photograph was taken, the December 8, 1903, manned tests of the Aerodrome ended in failure, as it fell into the Potomac River. Langley had other successes, however, and they are memorialized in the naming of NASA Langley Research Center and Langley Air Force Base. (NASA.)

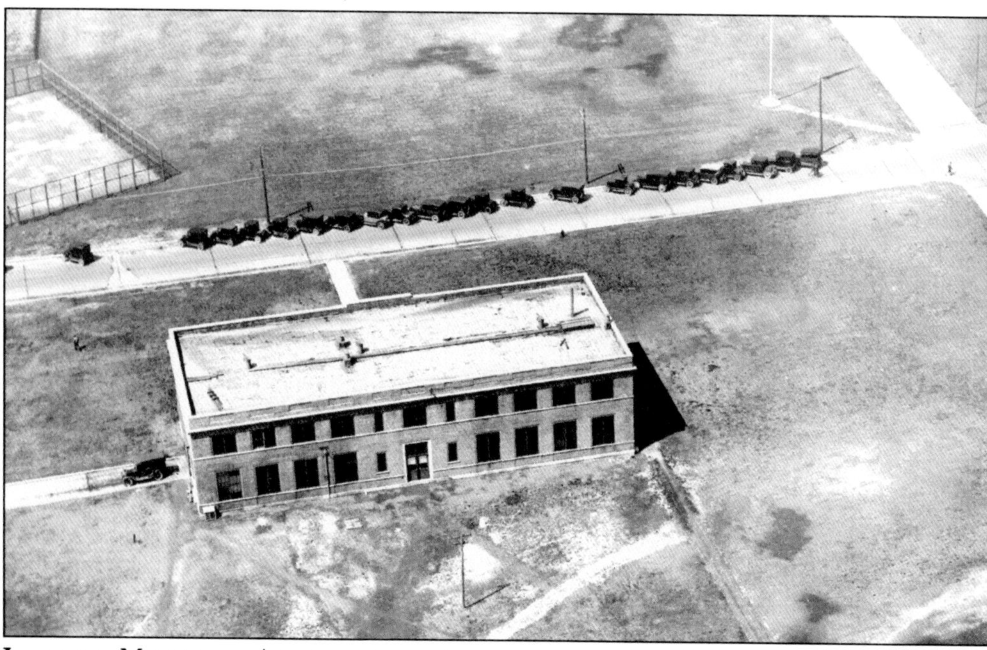

Langley Memorial Aeronautical Laboratory. This 1918 photograph shows the laboratory shortly after its completion. Today the facility is NASA Langley Research Center. Langley continues to forge new frontiers in aviation and space research, as it has since 1917, when it was established as the nation's first civilian aeronautics laboratory. (NASA.)

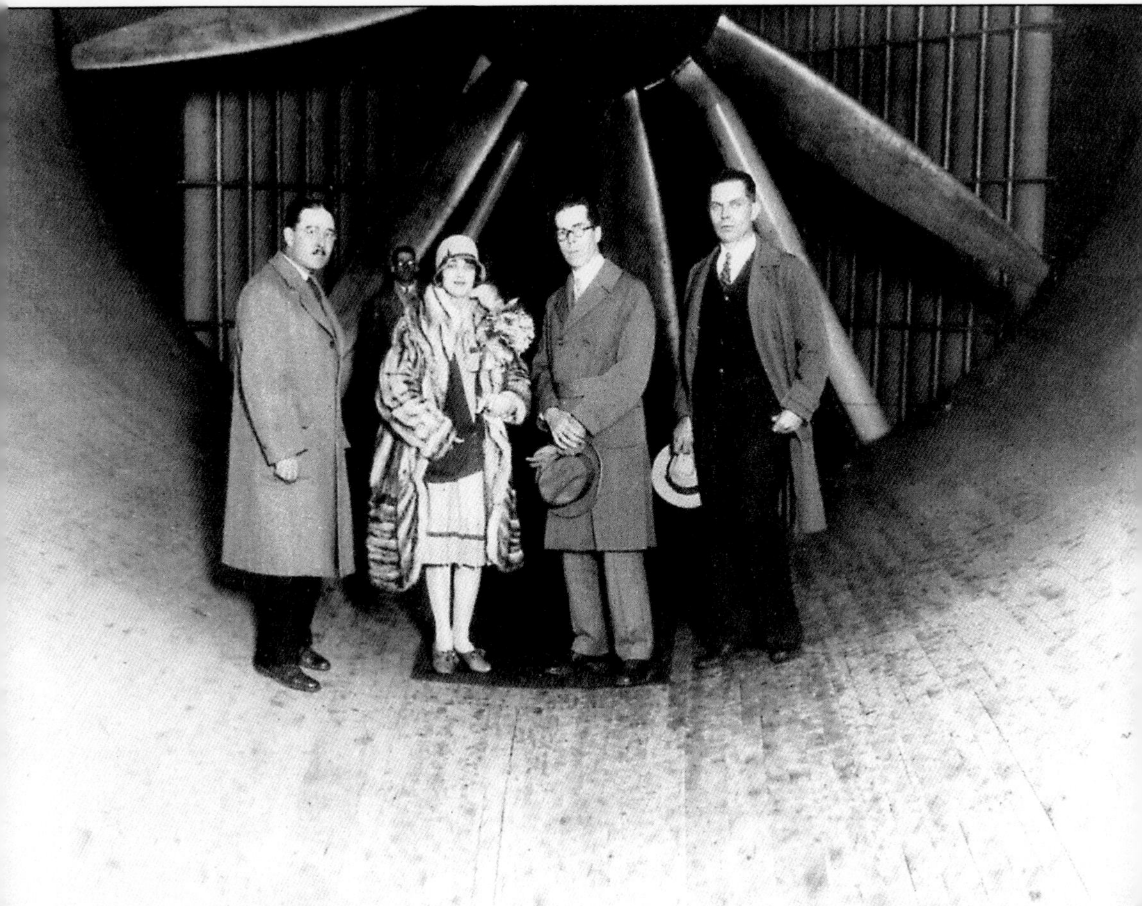

Windy City. Standing in front of this wind tunnel in this May 17, 1928, photograph are, from left to right, Tom Carroll, National Advisory Committee for Aeronautics (NACA) test pilot; Ruth Elder; Dr. H. J. E. Reid, NACA Langley director; and Dr. Ed Sharp. Chartered in 1915, NACA was operational from 1917 until 1958. The National Aeronautics and Space Act of 1958 created NASA from NACA. Even though the Wright brothers had been the first to fly a heavier-than-air craft, by the beginning of World War I in 1914, the United States lagged behind Europe in airplane technology. NACA was created as an independent government agency for research purposes to close that gap and to put the nation in the lead in aeronautics. By the end of the second decade of the 20th century, and into the 1920s, NACA conducted many types of test flights that involved both models and full-scale aircraft. Many of these tests took place in a series of wind tunnels NACA developed. (NASA.)

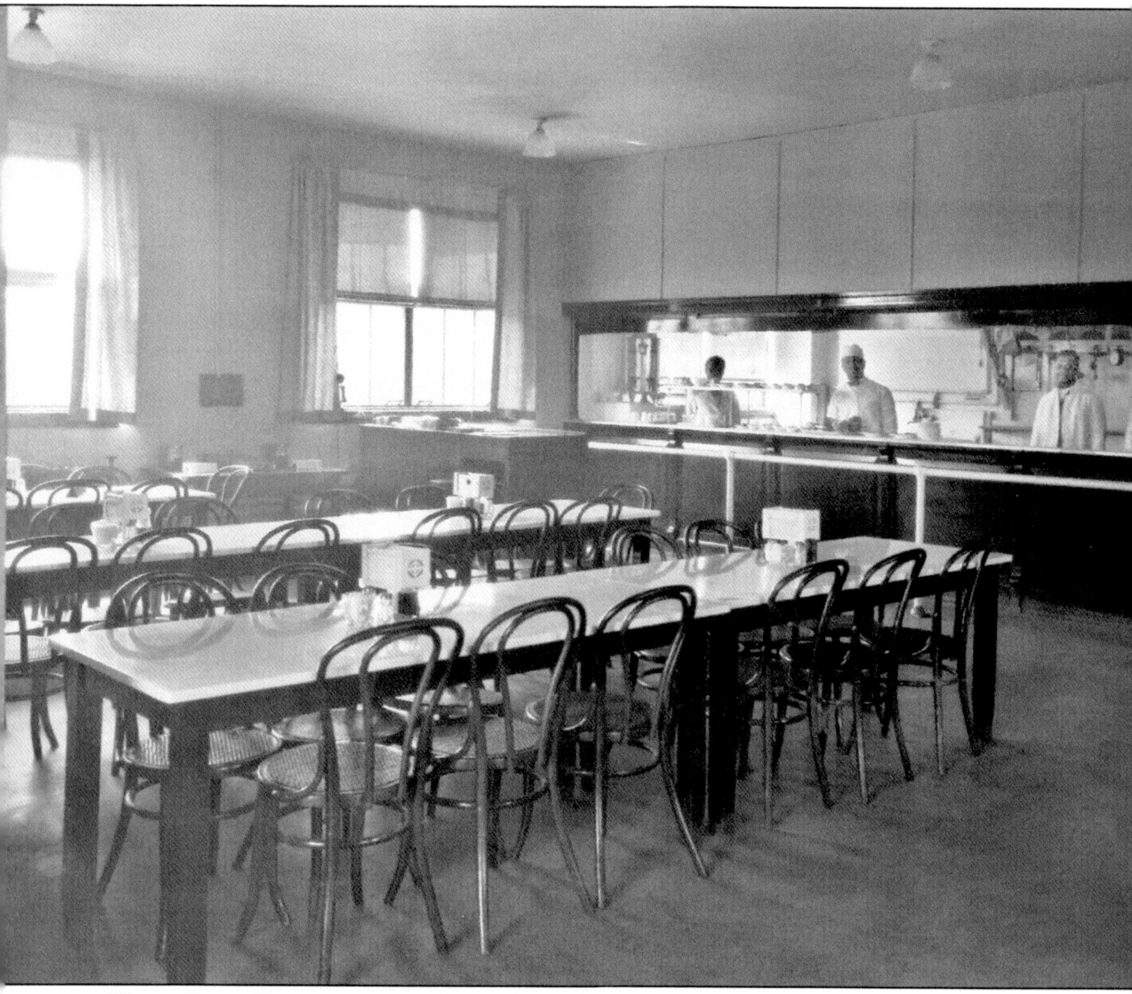

HAVE YOUR EQUATIONS AND EAT THEM, TOO. This vintage photograph shows the white marble tabletops of the Langley lunchroom. The slick tables were a boon to researchers, who often sketched tabletop equations while they ate. Afterwards, their marks could easily be wiped clean with a hand or a napkin. Some of those equations may have been of ways to improve the aerodynamics of aircraft, which the agency did in a number of ways. There were many advances, such as the NACA Cowling, for which the agency won the Collier Trophy in 1929. The cowling not only reduced drag by covering the engine but also improved the cooling of the engine. NACA expanded their influence in the field of aviation by recruiting top-notch engineers and scientists to work in even larger and more advanced technological facilities. (NASA)

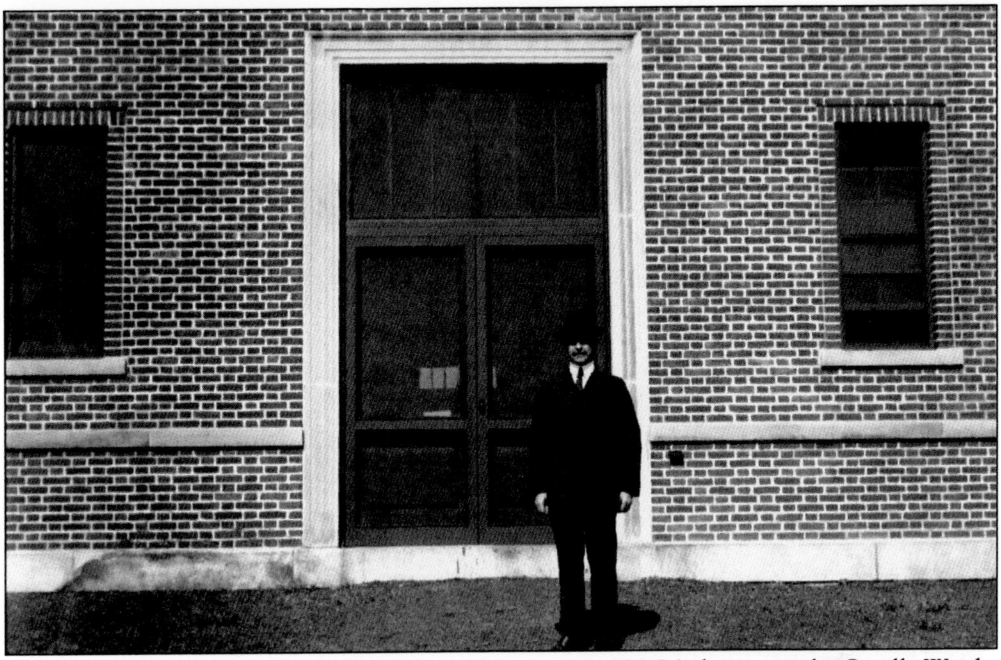

A Very Important Visitor. VIPs were nothing new to NACA, but a visit by Orville Wright in July 1922 was a treat to many NACA engineers, who looked at him as a hero. Engineer David L. Bacon and physicist Frederick H. Norton escorted Wright around the laboratory during his stay. (NASA.)

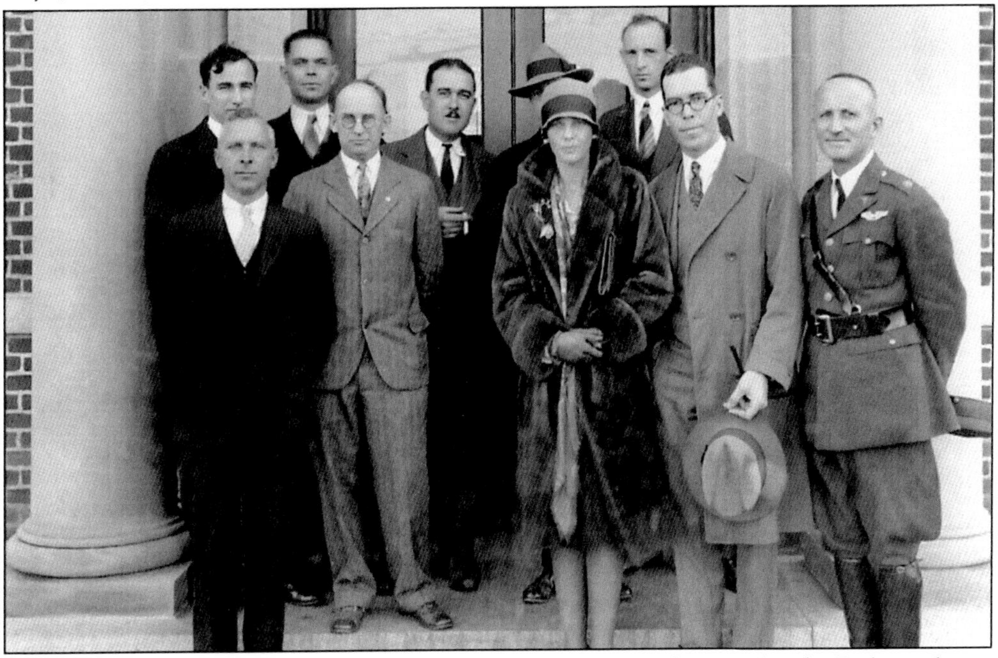

The First Lady of Aviation. Another special visitor to Langley was Amelia Earhart, shown in this November 1928 photograph. Shown from left to right are (first row) E. A. Meyers, Elton Miller, Amelia Earhart, Henry Reid, and Lt. Col. Jacob W. S. Wuest; (second row) Carlton Kemper, Raymond Sharp, Thomas Carroll, unidentified, and Fred Weick. (NASA.)

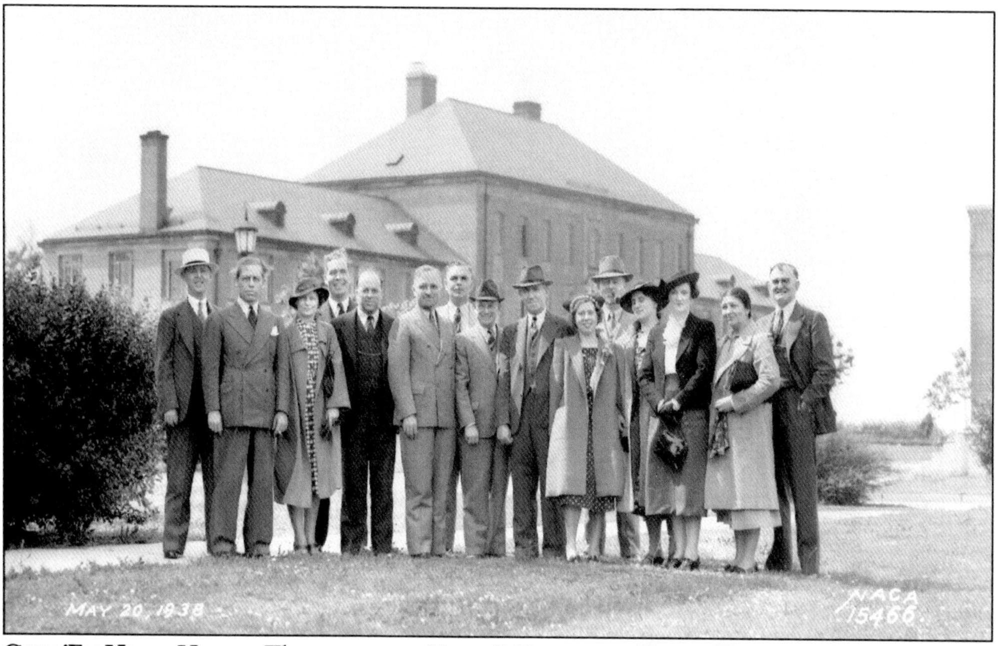

GIVE 'EM HECK, HARRY. Then a senator, Harry S. Truman and his staff tour Langley Field on May 20, 1938. Later, when he became president, Truman was responsible for creating the Department of the Air Force when he signed the National Security Act of 1947; it became effective the next year and ended the 40-year association the Air Force had had with the U.S. Army. (NASA.)

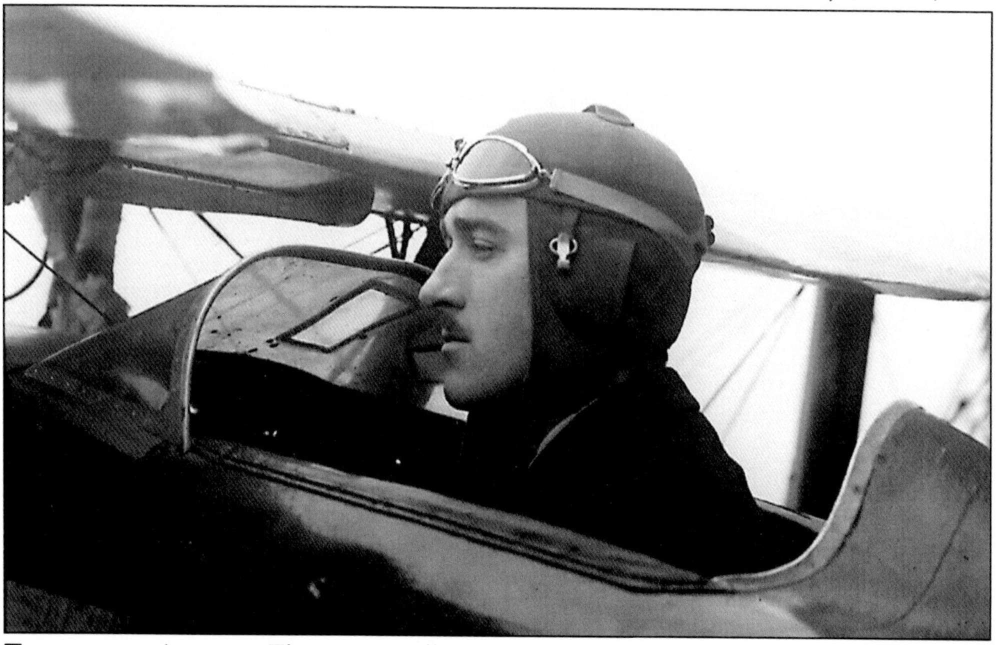

TESTING THE AIRWAYS. Thomas Carroll, seen in this c. 1930 photograph, was NACA's and Langley Field's first civilian test pilot—a very dangerous job indeed. He may have taken to heart a word of advice in the first handbook issued with the Curtis-Wright flyer, "Do not spin this aircraft. If the aircraft does spin it will return to earth without further attention on the part of the aeronaut." (NASA.)

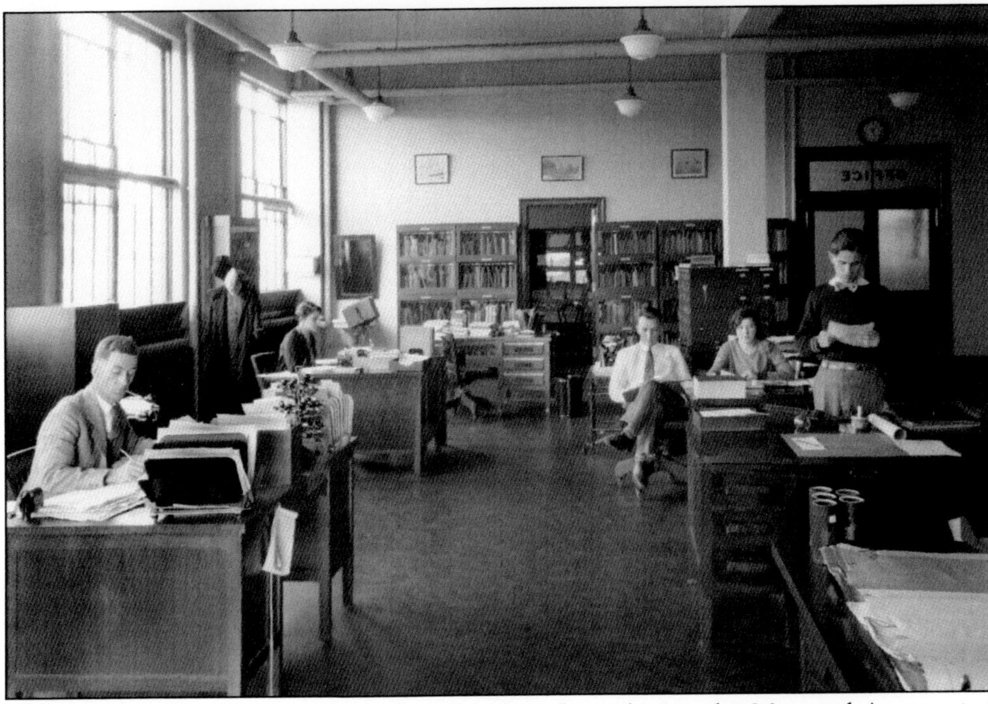

HARD WORKERS. There was a lot of hard work to do at the Langley Memorial Aeronautical Laboratory; engineers were tasked with finding ways to improve the aerodynamics of aircraft. The above photograph shows Langley administrative offices in 1927. Note the blueprints on the table at the lower right corner and the rubber stamp tree on the man's deck in the left foreground. The bottom photograph shows Langley's human computers at work in 1947. The women in the picture performed mathematical computations for male staff. (NASA.)

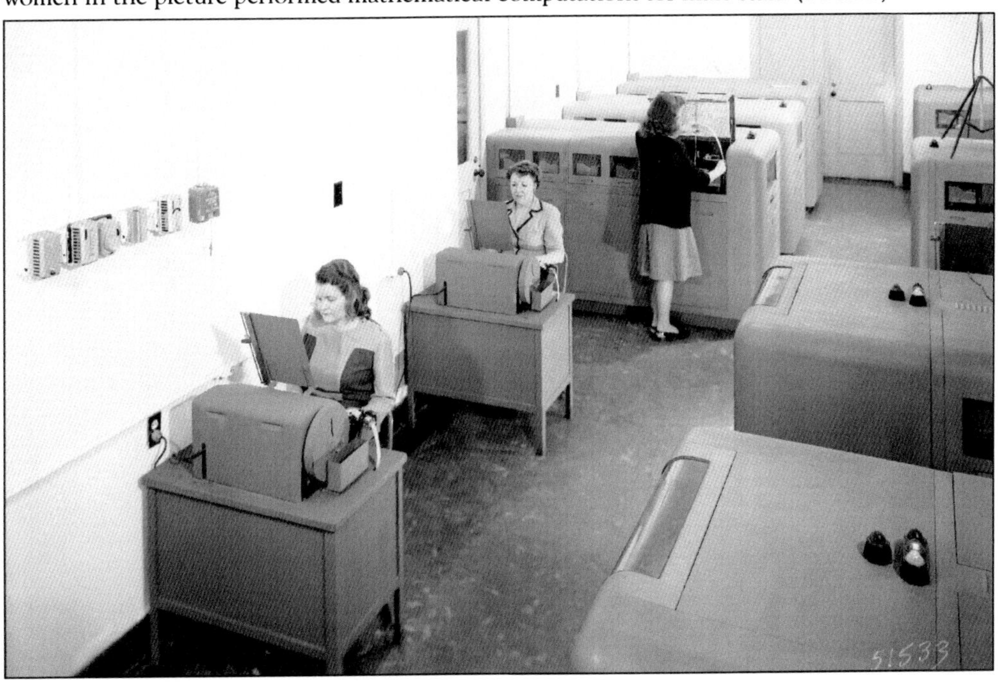

OFF WE GO. The Langley Memorial Aeronautical Laboratory (LMAL) was created in 1917, making it the nation's first civilian aeronautics laboratory. As part of LMAL, the National Advisory Committee for Aeronautics (NACA) was created as an independent government agency for research purposes to close the gap that had grown with Europe, as the latter became more advanced in aeronautics, and to put the nation in the lead in the field. Land along the Back River in Hampton, shown in the below 1952 photograph, was used for this purpose. Today the site is home to NASA Langley Research Center and Langley Air Force Base. (NASA.)

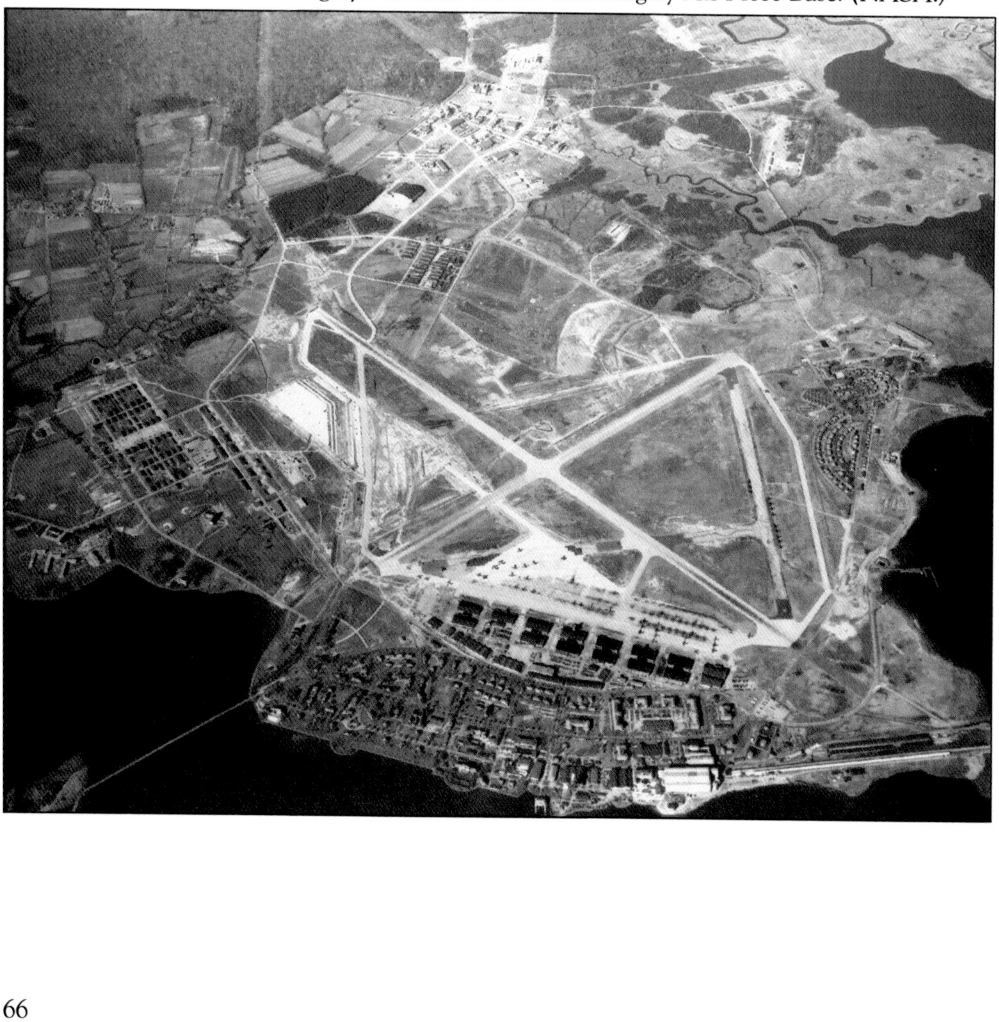

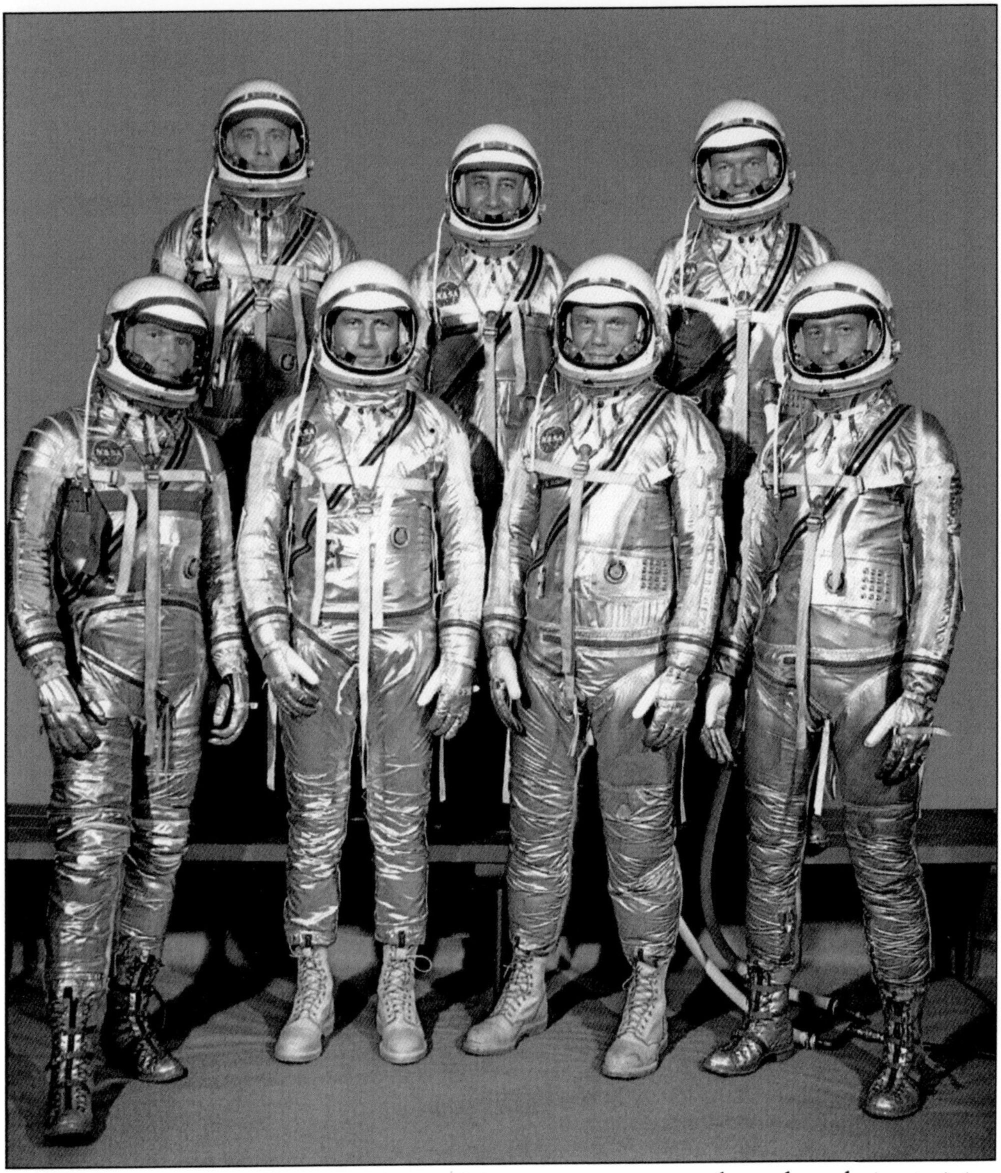

THE MERCURY SEVEN. The original seven Mercury astronauts are shown here during training at NASA Langley Research Center in the early 1960s. From left to right are (first row) Walter Schirra, Donald "Deke" Slayton, John Glenn, and Scott Carpenter; (second row) Alan Shepard, Virgil "Gus" Grissom, and L. Gordon Cooper. The suits were the ones used by the astronauts during their Mercury space flights. While familiarizing the astronauts with the Mercury set-up, Langley employees helped them to specialize in the technical areas crucial to the overall success of Project Mercury. Langley staff also guided and monitored the astronauts' activities through the many spaceflight simulators and other training devices built at the center expressly for the manned space program. In less than three years, Project Mercury proved that men could be sent into space and returned safely to Earth, setting the stage for the longer-duration Gemini flights and the Apollo lunar landings. (NASA.)

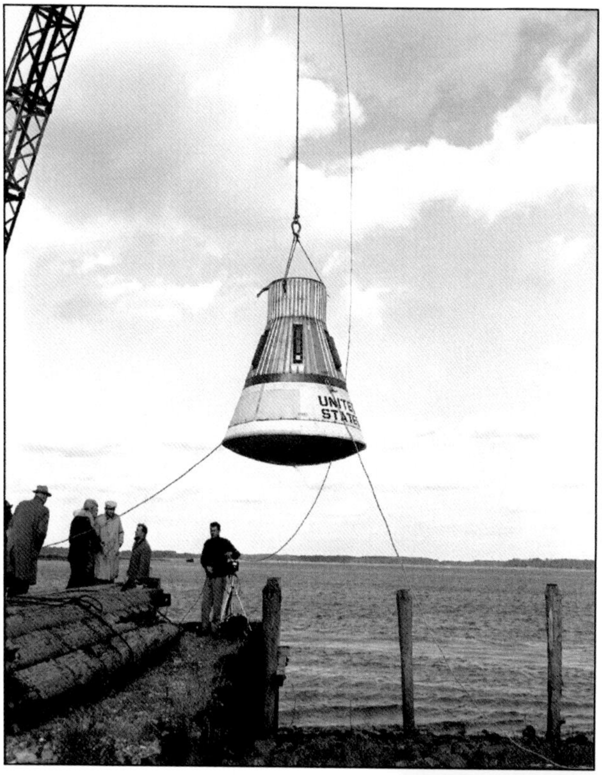

PRACTICE MAKES PERFECT. Plenty of research and testing goes into every project at the NASA Langley Research Center. In the 1959 photograph at left, the "Little Joe" capsule is test dropped at Langley's Back River and recovered from shore by crane. In the below photograph, Sam, the rhesus monkey, gets checked out after his ride in the Little Joe spacecraft in 1959. Sam experienced three minutes of weightlessness during flight. Animals were often used during test flights for Project Mercury to help determine the effects of space flight on humans. Seven Little Joes were launched from Wallops Island between 1959 and 1961. (NASA.)

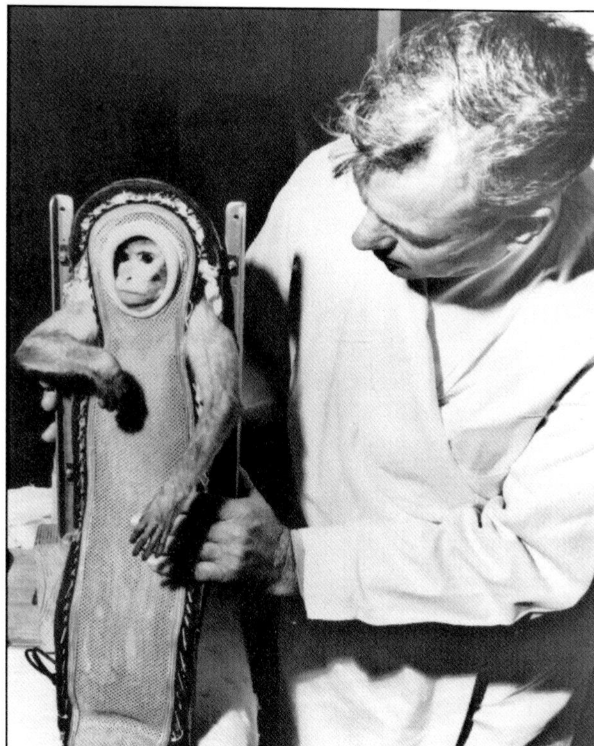

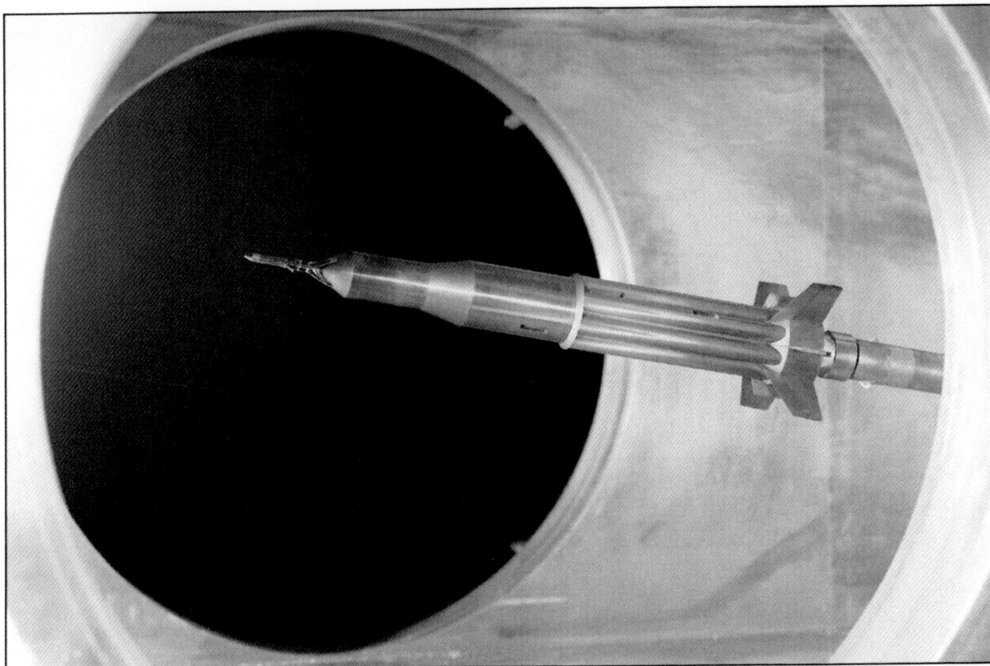

TO INFINITY AND BEYOND. NASA Langley Research Center has been involved in early space flight effort through research, training, and support. Those efforts continue today. The above March 1962 photograph shows wind tunnel tests of a Saturn rocket model. It was the Saturn rocket that propelled the Apollo astronauts into space. In the below December 1961 photograph, a test on a 50-foot parawing is made to see how safely it will bring down a model of a manned space capsule. The test was done from a few thousand feet above Palm Tree Island, an old army bombing range near Langley Field. (NASA.)

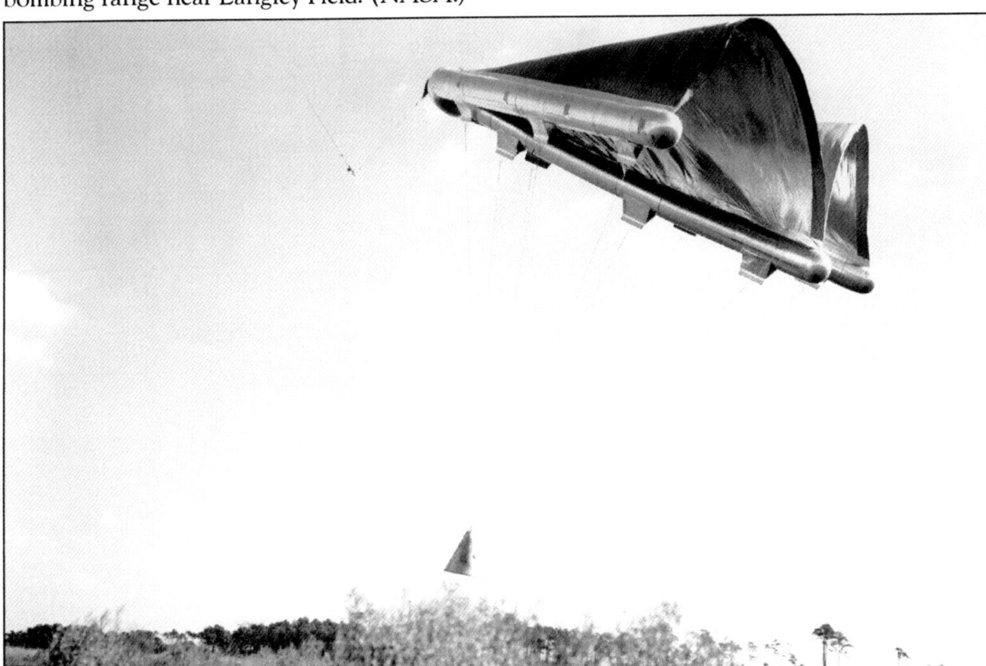

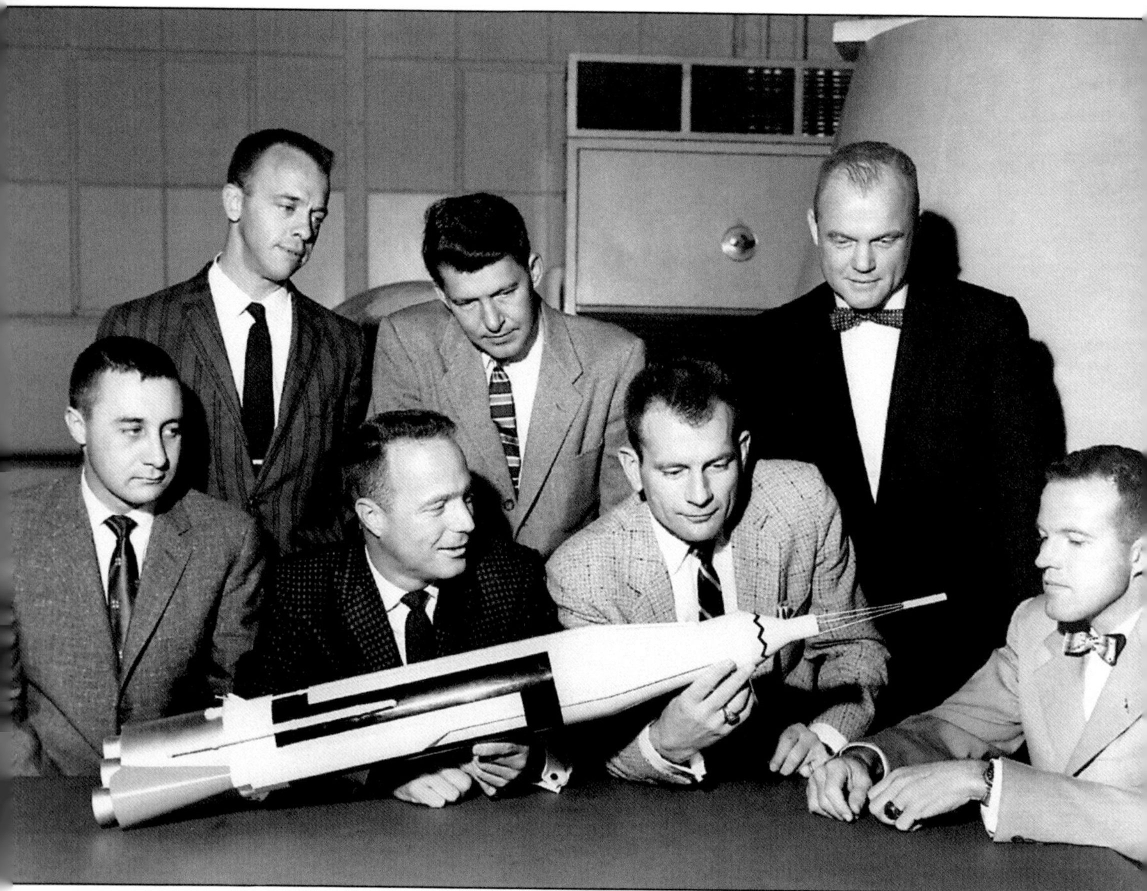

ORIGINAL SEVEN ASTRONAUTS INSPECT MERCURY MODEL. The original seven Mercury astronauts were, from left to right, (first row) Virgil "Gus" Grissom, Scott Carpenter, Donald "Deke" Slayton, and Gordon Cooper; (second row) Alan Shepard, Walter Schirra, and John Glenn. The Mercury 7 astronauts were introduced to the American public in April 1959. The criteria for selection were as follows: less than 40 years old; less than 5-foot-11-inches tall: excellent physical condition; bachelor's degree in engineering or equivalent; test-pilot school graduate; minimum of 1,500 hours flying time; and qualified jet pilot. Even so, the process of choosing the first astronauts was elaborate and rigorous. Once selected, the astronauts began their training program at Langley. This included a wide-range of training, from a graduate-level course in introductory space science to simulator training and scuba-diving. Training continued until the Langley Space Task Group was transferred to Houston, Texas. (NASA.)

EDWIN "BUZZ" ALDRIN. Aldrin is shown here in June 1969 at the NASA Langley Research Center's Lunar Excursion Module (LEM) Simulator. Aldrin became one of the first humans to walk on the moon after practicing in this simulator. The LEM allowed Apollo astronauts to study and overcome problems that could have occurred during the final 150-foot descent to the surface of the moon. (NASA.)

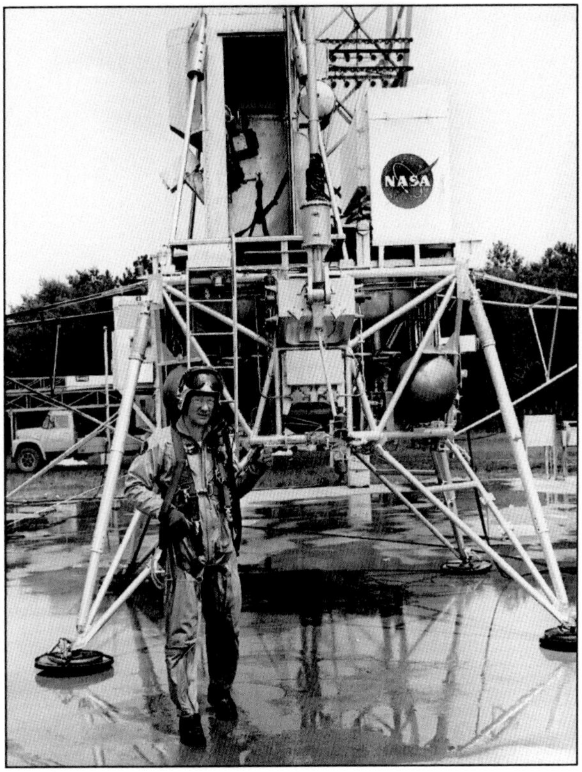

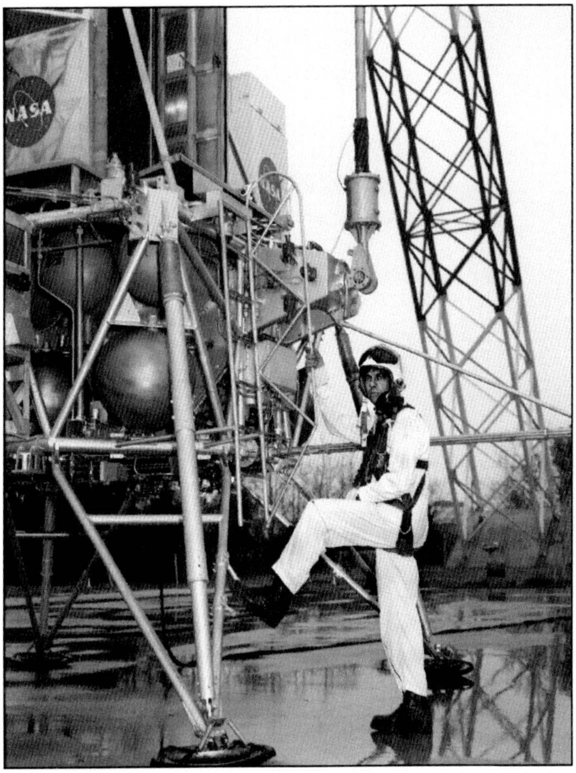

ALAN SHEPARD. Shepard was one of approximately 20 astronauts who used the Lunar Landing Research Facility and its associated Lunar Excursion Module Simulator, pictured here, to practice piloting during the final descent to the moon's surface. Shepard was the only Mercury astronaut to go on and make a lunar landing. This facility was designated a National Historic Landmark in 1985. (NASA.)

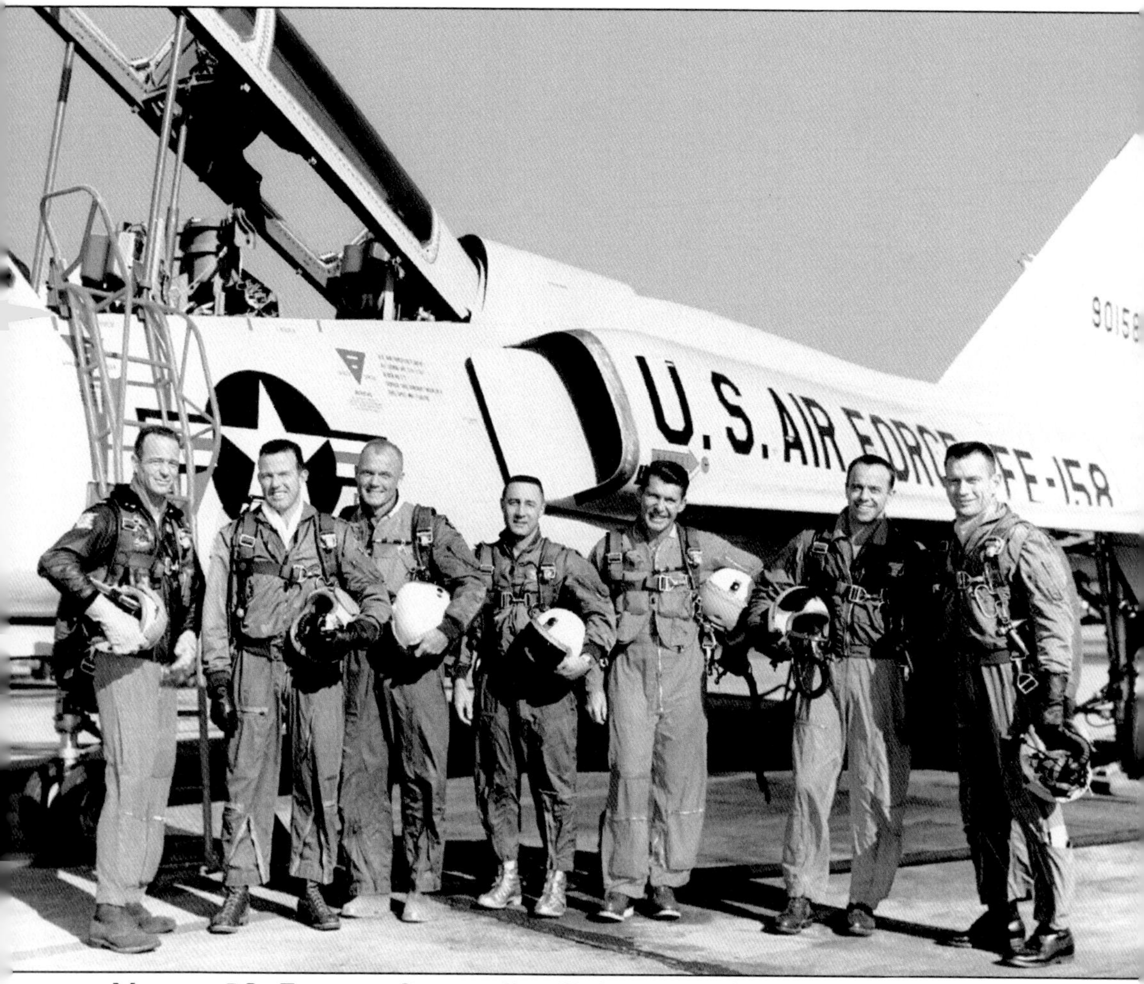

MERCURY 7 IN FRONT OF CONVAIR F-106B AIRCRAFT. This January 1961 photograph shows the Mercury 7 astronauts in front of a U.S. Air Force Convair F-106B aircraft during training at NASA Langley Research Center. Chosen from hundreds of applicants, the seven men were all test pilots. Standing in front of the aircraft, from left to right, are Lt. M. Scott Carpenter, Capt. Gordon Cooper, Col. John H. Glenn Jr., Capt. Virgil "Gus" Grissom, Lt. Comdr. Walter Schirra, Lt. Comdr. Alan B. Shepard Jr., and Capt. Donald K. "Deke" Slayton. Langley staff helped the astronauts train in specialized areas crucial to the overall success of Project Mercury. Langley staff also guided and monitored the astronauts' activities through the many spaceflight simulators and other training devices built at the center. In less than three years, Project Mercury proved that men could be sent into space and returned safely to Earth, setting the stage for the longer-duration Gemini flights and the Apollo lunar landings. (NASA.)

CHECK OUT MY NEW SUIT. NASA Langley researcher Kenneth R. Yenni tries out a proposal for an Apollo space suit, as shown in this March 1967 photograph. Project Apollo was conducted from 1961 to 1972 and included the Apollo 11 mission in July 1969 that sent man to the moon. (NASA.)

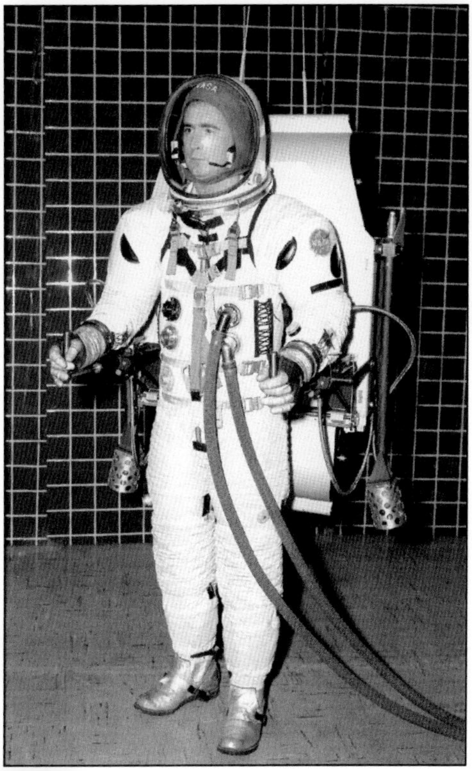

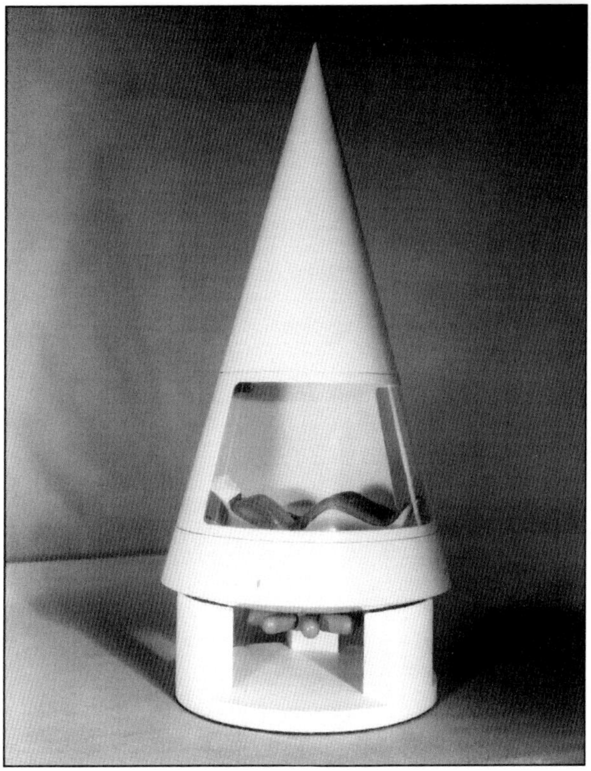

YOU'VE GOT A POINT. This August 1958 photograph shows a scale model of a proposed Mercury capsule shape, known as A. Project Mercury ran from 1959 through 1963 with the goal of putting a man in orbit around the earth, which was accomplished by John Glenn on February 20, 1962, in *Friendship 7*. Early planning and research was done by NACA; the program officially was carried out by the newly created NASA. (NASA.)

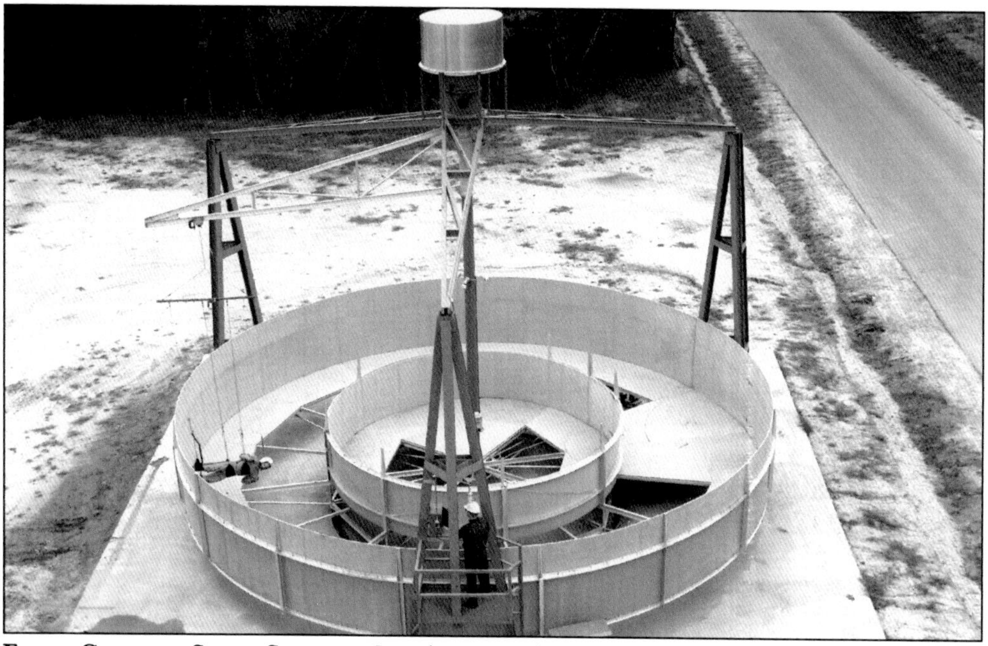

Early Concept Space Station. Langley researchers are always looking ahead at a variety of concepts as they relate to aeronautics and space travel. In this 1964 photograph, a Langley engineer takes a walk in simulated zero-gravity around a mock-up of a full-scale, 24-foot-diameter space station. (NASA.)

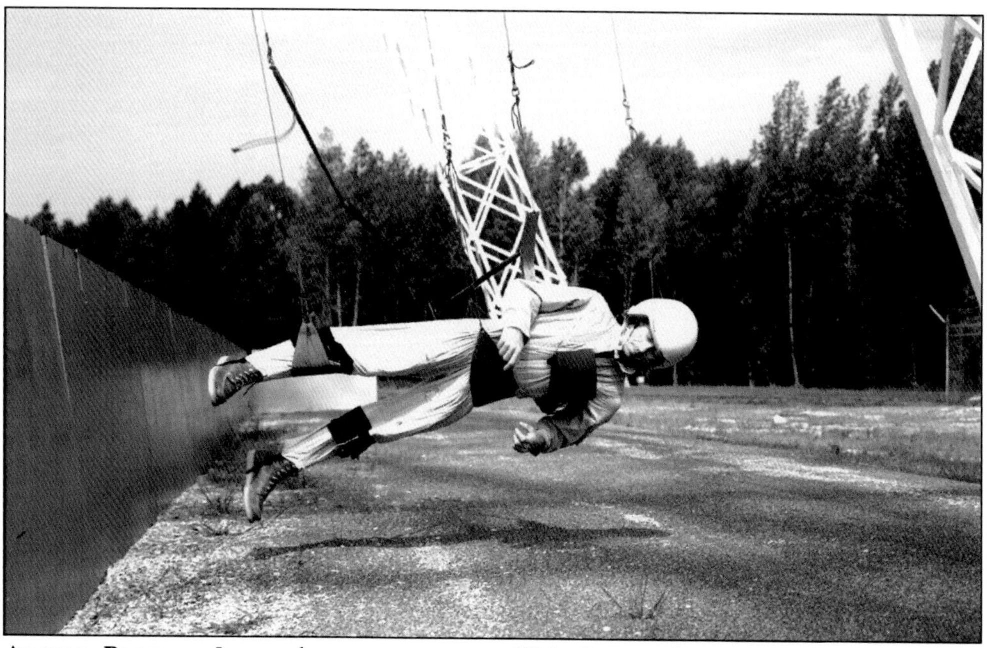

Apollo Project. In another test, astronaut Walt Cunningham examines the Reduced Gravity Walking Simulator located at the Lunar Landing Facility, as shown in this 1965 photograph. Researchers noted the effects of zero or reduced gravity while the subject walked, jumped, or ran to test a variety of factors, including fatigue, energy expenditure, and speed of locomotion. (NASA.)

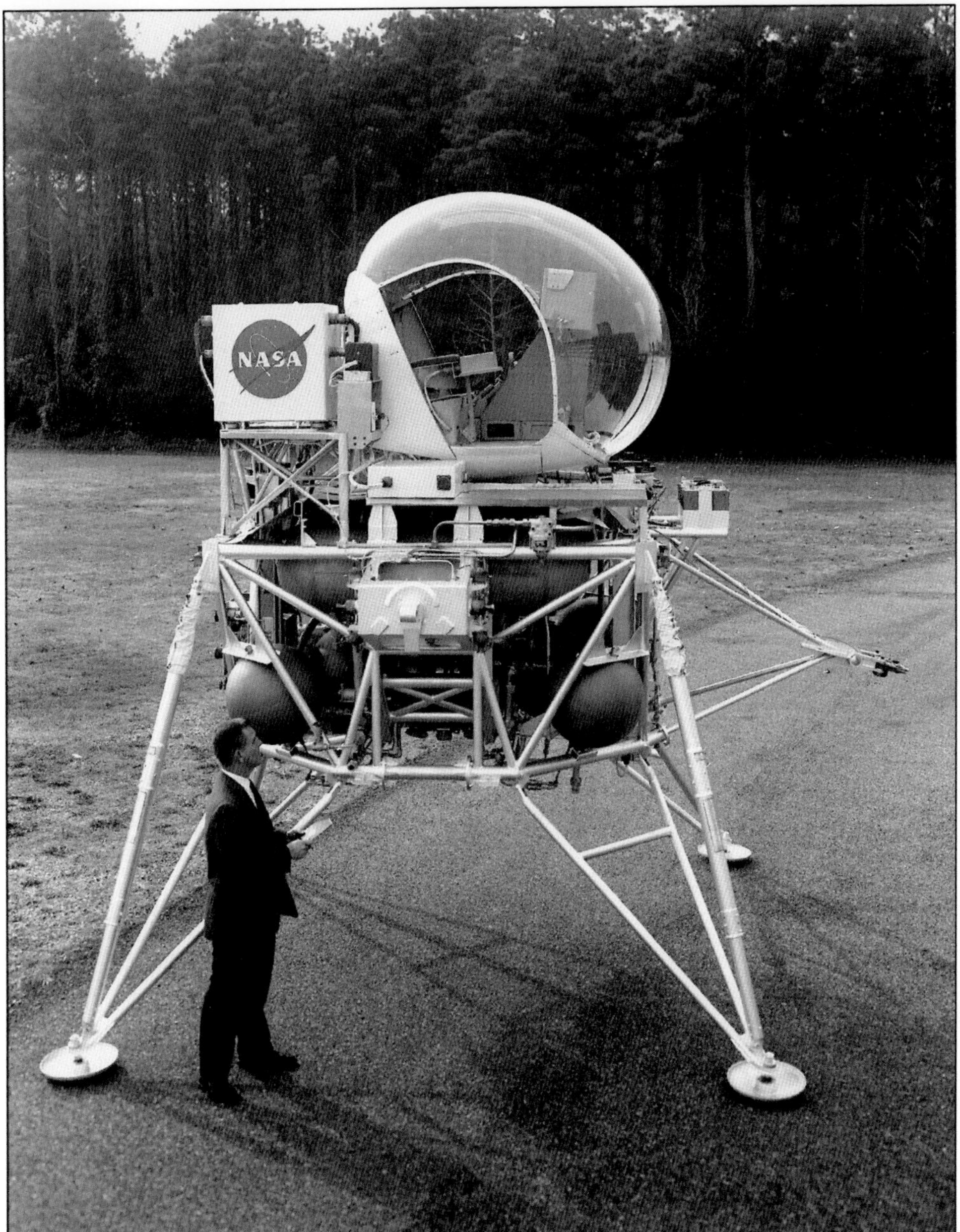

NEED A LIFT? A vehicle for the Lunar Landing Research Facility at NASA Langley Research Center is shown in this 1963 photograph. At this point, Project Mercury had come to a successful end; the program, with a goal of putting a man in orbit around the Earth, ran from 1959 through 1963. That goal was accomplished when John Glenn circled the globe in *Friendship 7* on February 20, 1962. Now NASA was gearing up for Project Apollo, which started in 1961 and ran until 1972. Researchers on Project Apollo devoted their time and talents to landing a man on the moon and returning him safely to Earth; it did so with the Apollo 11 mission in July 1969. Equipment such as the vehicle shown here was created and tested at NASA Langley to make the mission a success. As of 2005, there has not been any manned spaceflight beyond low earth orbit since the end of the Apollo program. (NASA.)

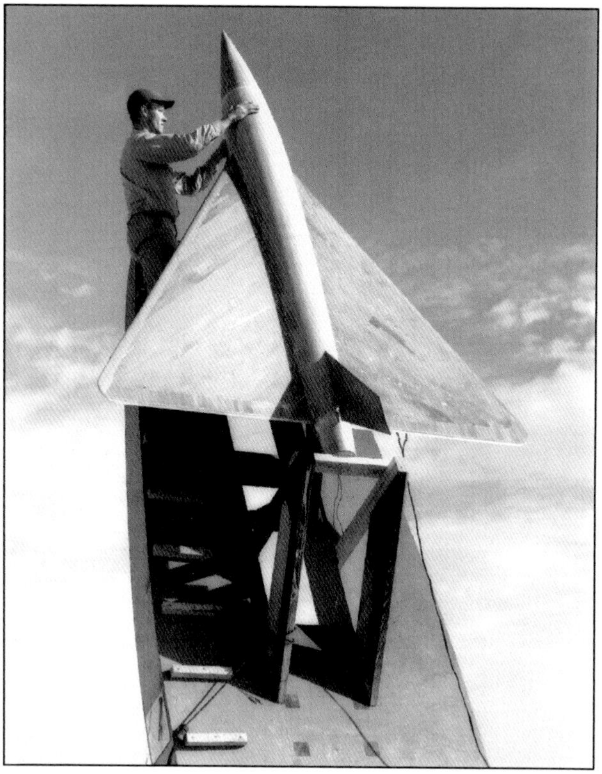

Research and Study at Wallops Island. The Wallops Island Flight Test Range, located on Virginia's Eastern Shore, is important to the mission of NASA Langley Research Center. In the above vintage photograph, technician Durwood Dereng prepares to pull the external power plug from an E17 drag-research model at Wallops Island. In the below 1958 photograph, impact tests conducted by Langley's Hydrodynamics Division use full-scale and model capsules based on the design from the Mercury Project to see the dynamic stability and aerodynamic heating of the capsule, as well as the pilot escape and parachute recovery systems. The biggest part of the Wallops program was the series of full-size capsules, launched with the Little Joe rocket booster, developed especially for Mercury. (NASA.)

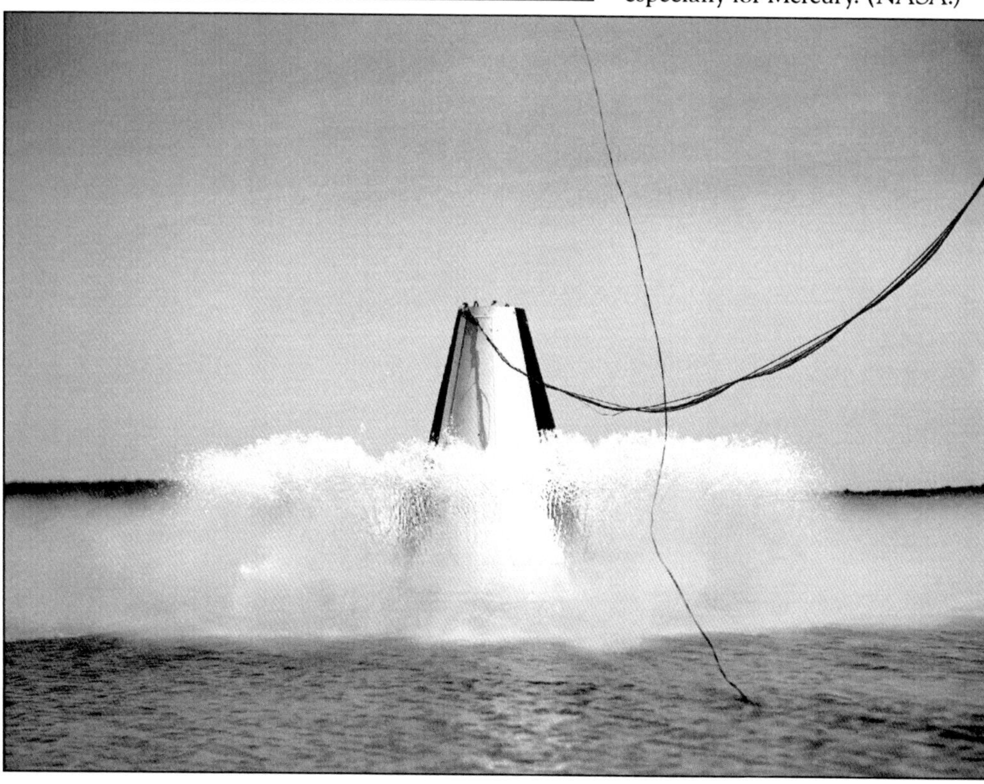

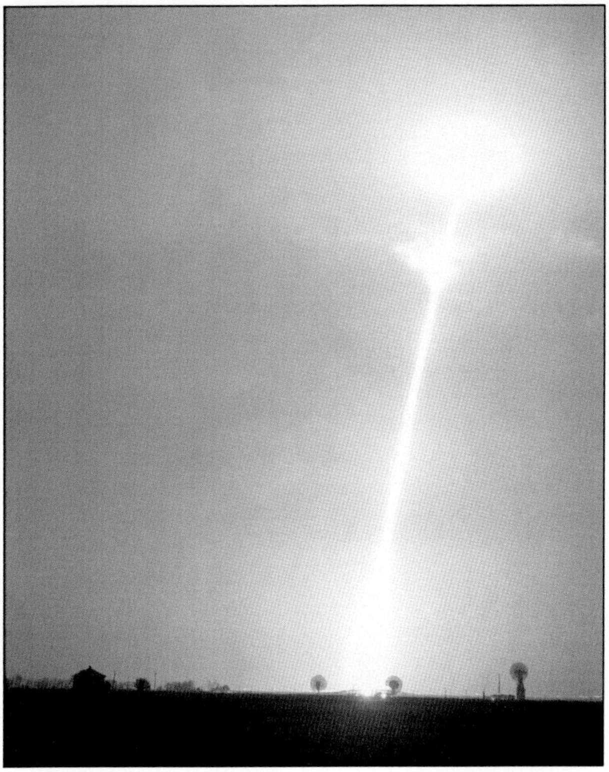

LIGHT MY FIRE. Seen streaking across the dark night sky on Virginia's Eastern Shore is the occasional rocket from NASA Langley's Wallops Island facility. The facility has been instrumental in carrying out the center's mission of space flight. In the February 1962 photograph at right, an ST-8 Scout rocket takes to the skies over Wallops carrying a reentry heating experiment. In the below August 1965 photograph, a rocket, readied for flight, is shown on the launcher in a horizontal position at Wallops Island. Many experiments, from the Mercury Project to the space shuttle, have been carried out here. (NASA.)

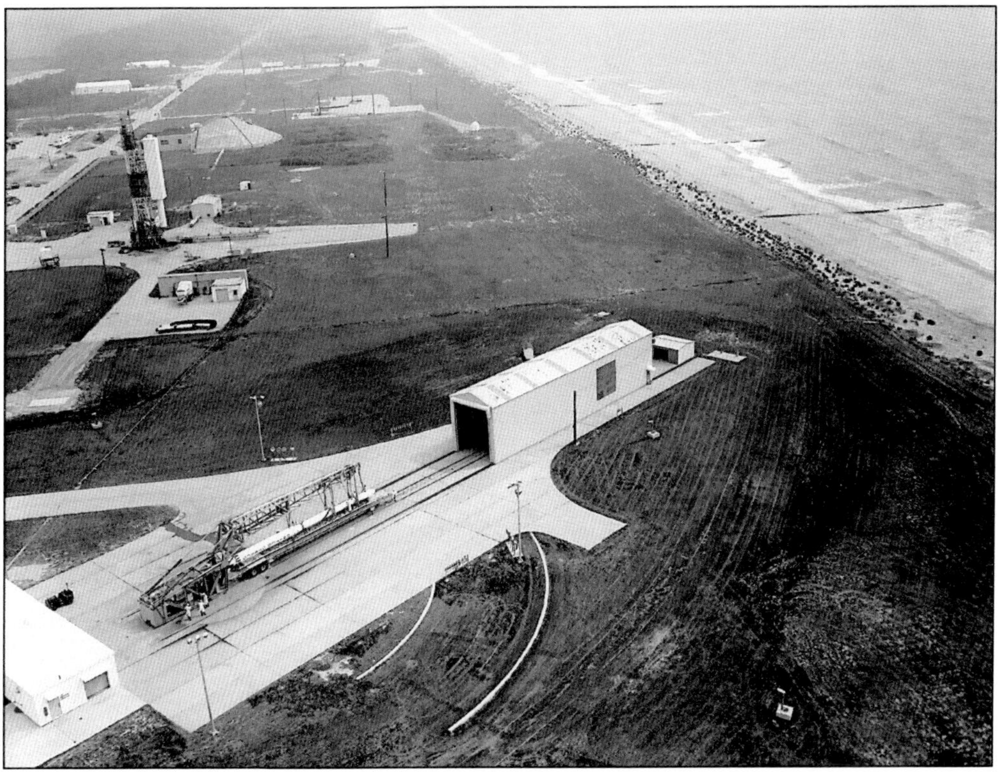

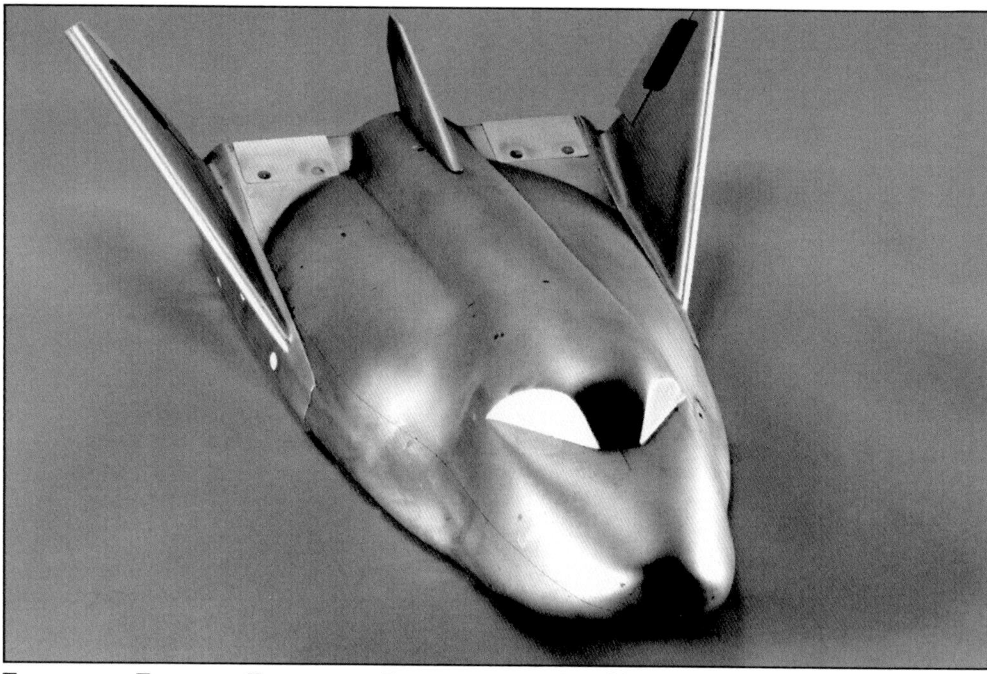

FLIGHTS OF FANTASY, FLIGHTS OF PRACTICALITY. In addition to space flight, flight within the atmosphere is also researched and tested at NASA Langley. The center has always been on the cutting edge in aeronautics: in the first half of the 20th century, groundbreaking work was done on aircraft design. After World War II, NACA began to work on supersonic flight; when the first supersonic flight took place in 1947 in the experimental X-1 aircraft piloted by Capt. Charles "Chuck" Yeager, it was monitored by NACA personnel. In the above 1988 photograph, a scaled model of the Langley Personal Launch System Vehicle is shown. In the below 1998 photograph, an instrumented Boeing 757 is pictured on the taxiway at Langley Air Force Base. (NASA.)

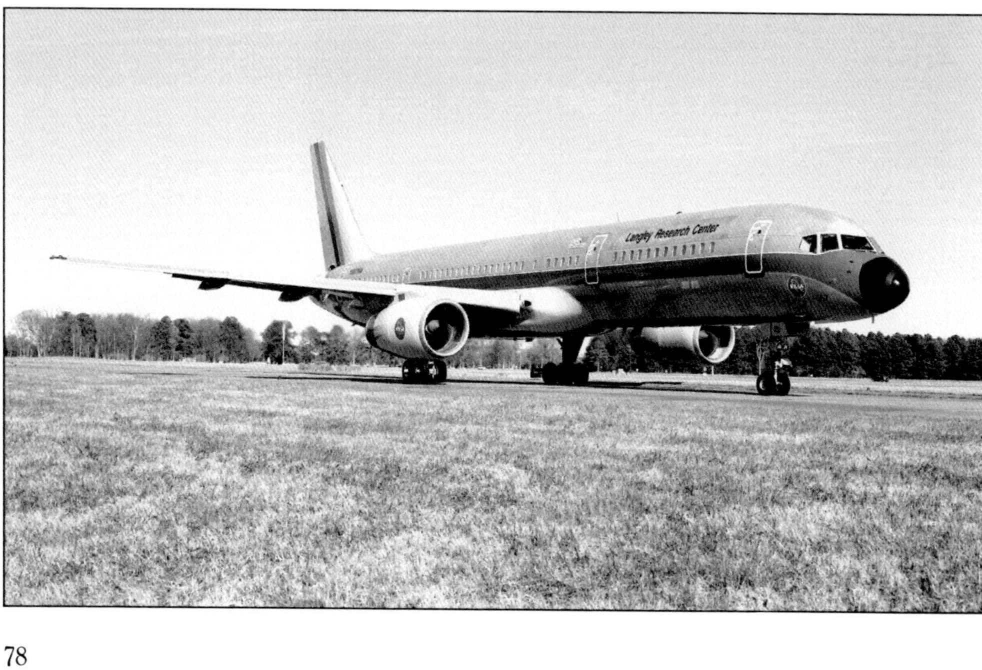

Four

Big Old Jet Airliner

Hampton Roads was on the aviation map early in the development of commercial air service; as early as 1926, the town had daily service to Washington, D.C., in three-propellered tin monoplanes.

This early service, operated by Philadelphia Rapid Transit (PRT) Air, actually gave Norfolk regular flight service before many major American cities.

By the 1930s, Eastern Air Transport, which later became Eastern Airlines, opened up service with a route to Richmond and connections north to New York City and south to Atlanta, Georgia, and Florida.

Today, the region has two commercial airports—Norfolk International Airport, which, unusually, is actually set in a botanical garden, and Newport News/Williamsburg International Airport, which began as Patrick Henry Field, growing from a World War II army installation.

Over the years, the airports have had several terminals. In fact, the Norfolk Airport once operated from a golf course shack.

Also, over time, the airports have had service from many different airlines, including names of some long gone—Pennsylvania Central Airlines (PCA), Capital, Eastern, Allegheny, Trans World, Pan Am, National, and Piedmont, to name a few.

But commercial aviation looks bright in the region. In addition to flights offered from every major carrier, Hampton Roads is also served by the two largest and most successful low-cost airlines, Air Tran and Southwest.

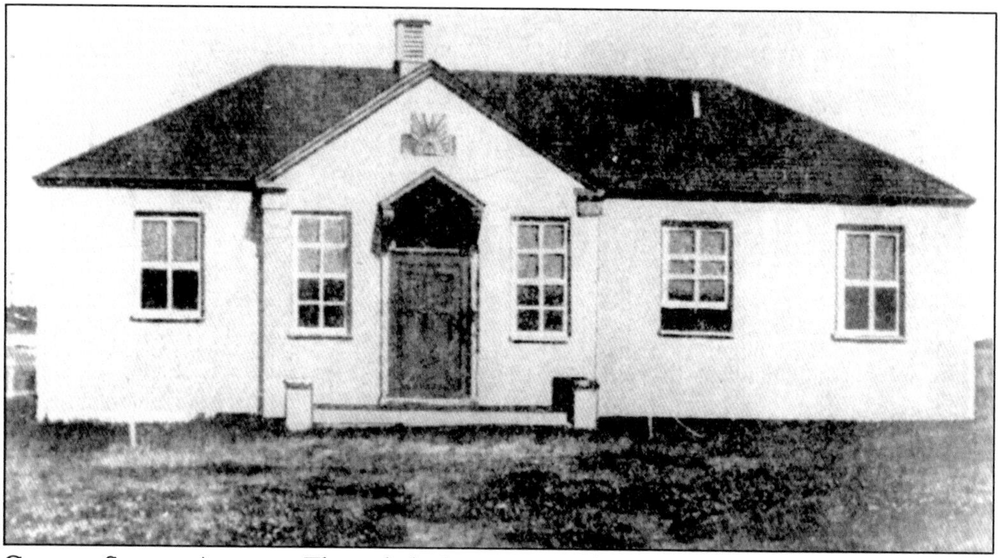

GRANBY STREET AIRPORT. This tidy little air terminal was built in 1932 on Granby Street, just north of the Ward's Corner neighborhood. Erected on the site of the former Grand Central Terminal, this building housed operations for Ludington Lines and Eastern Air Transport until military operations at the nearby naval base forced commercial service to move to another part of the city. (NPL.)

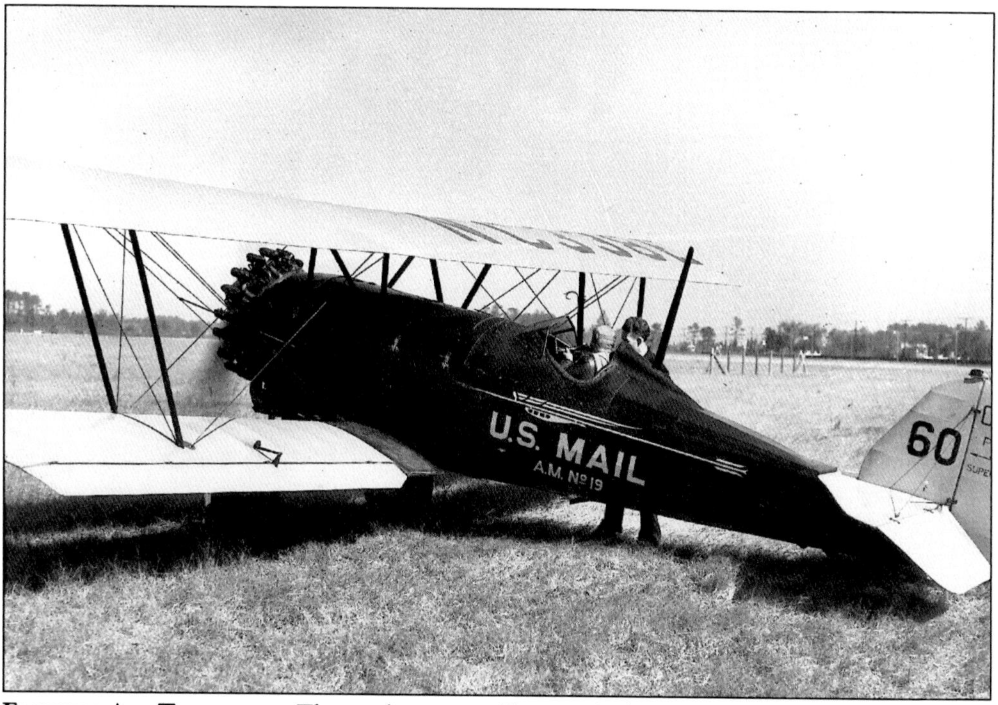

EASTERN AIR TRANSPORT. The predecessor to Eastern Airlines, Eastern Air Transport got its start in 1926. It began service to Norfolk in 1931 but discontinued it about a year later. One of their planes is shown in this October 1931 photograph. Note the reference to their mail contract, "U.S. Mail AM No. 19." Eastern served Norfolk at the Granby Street and Glenrock airports. (NPL.)

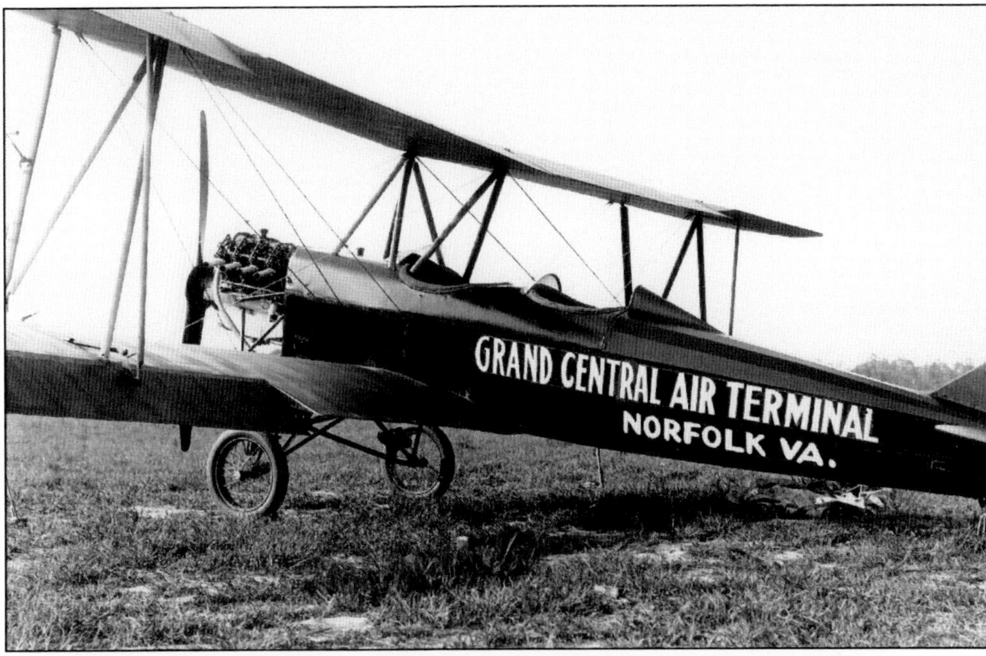

RETURN YOUR TRAY TABLE. . . . Here are some early flyers into Norfolk: the above August 1930 photograph is of a plane that publicizes the airport, Grand Central Air Terminal (probably owned by local aviator Ben Epstein). The second photograph, also from August 1930, shows an airplane at the Granby Street Airport publicizing the "Cities of Norfolk and Portsmouth." Interestingly Norfolk's first commercial air service may have been as early as 1921. About that time, some Baltimore, Maryland, businessmen, led by P. Ewing Easter, had the idea of operating a line from Baltimore to Norfolk, plus other points along the coast, in an Aeromarine HS. There is no hard evidence it got off the ground, and the interest reportedly folded by 1922. (NPL.)

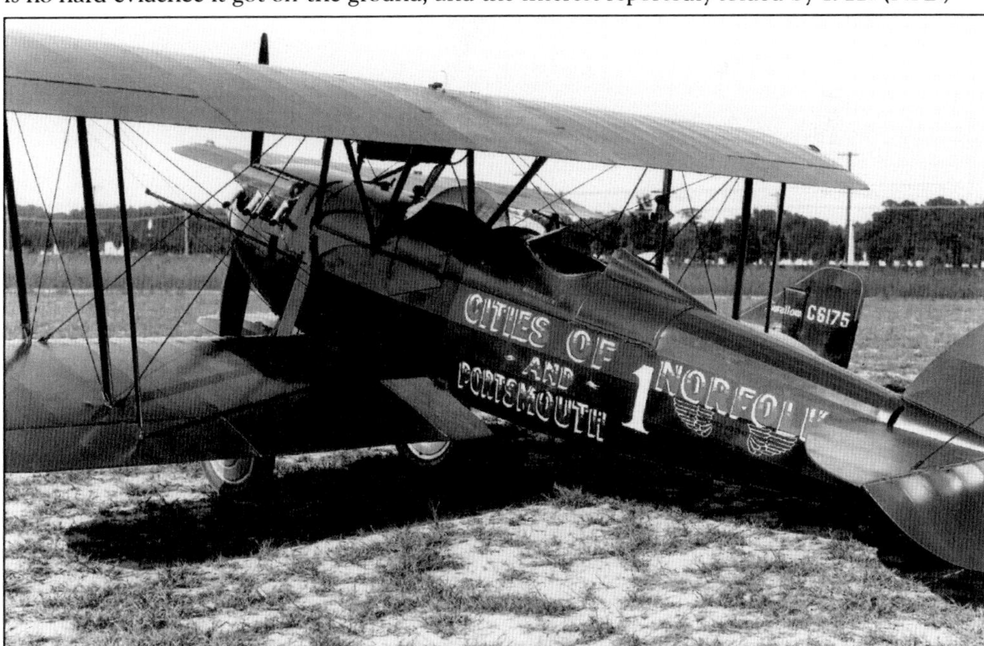

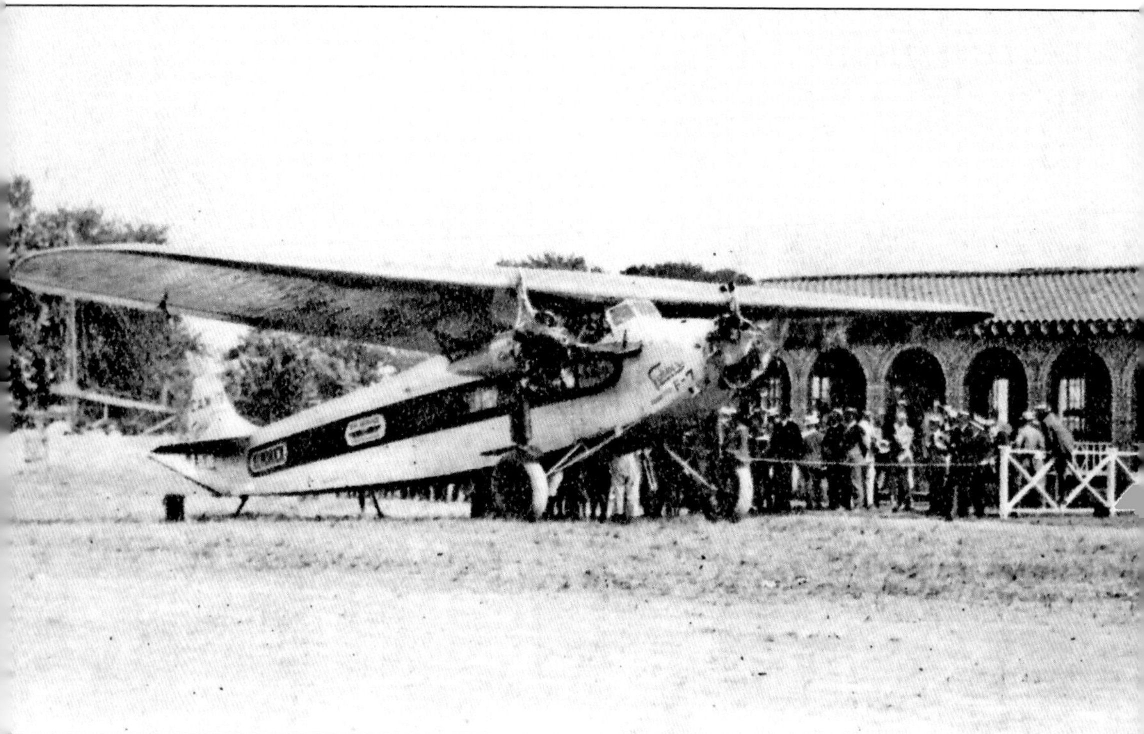

PRT Air Service. This mid-1920s airline-issued postcard shows one of Philadelphia Rapid Transit (PRT) Air's Fokker three-engine monoplanes loading passengers at Washington, D.C. The first passenger airline in America operating on regular daily schedule, it served Norfolk, briefly, in 1926. PRT Air operated flights to Washington (Hoover Flying Field), continuing to Philadelphia (navy yard), for just a few months; high costs forced its discontinuance. The daily flight from Norfolk, flying at an average speed of 90 miles per hour, took almost two hours to reach the nation's capital. The planes seated eight passengers and were equipped with lavatories. Windows opened for ventilation. Service was from a field north of the city off Granby Street, which would be void of commercial service for almost four years with the demise of PRT Air. However, the airlines gave residents a taste of the future of travel and gave the region commercial air service before many major metropolitan areas. (PEH.)

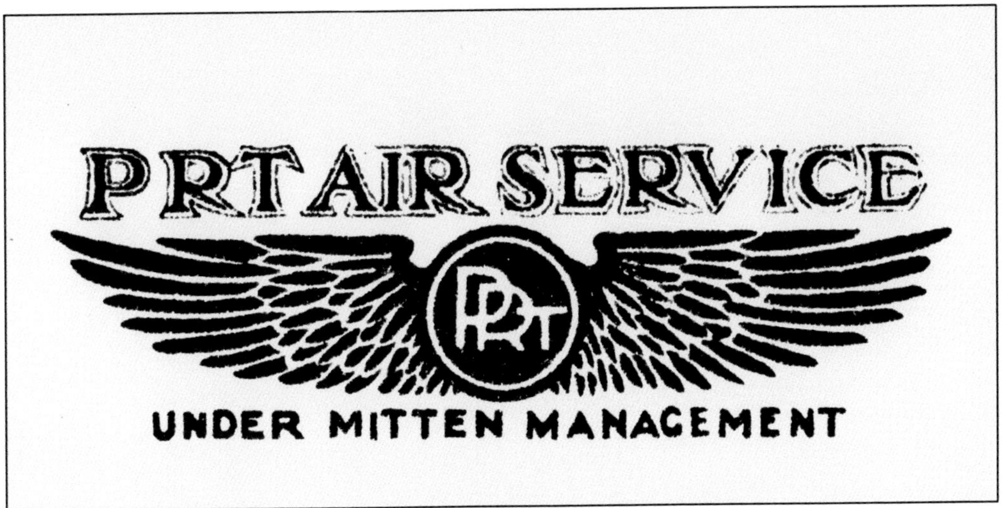

THE MITTEN LINE. PRT Air was owned by Thomas Mitten. The fledgling carrier started service in 1926, adding Norfolk on its route system shortly after it started flying. Lacking an airport, PRT Air used makeshift facilities at East Camp, north of Ward's Corner and now part of Naval Station Norfolk. The advertisement below sounded promising enough, but the carrier would fold within a few months. It cost $20 to fly one-way to Washington, D.C., on one of their three-engine Fokker planes; a round-trip was priced at $35. The first flight carried 3,000 letters and a bouquet of roses and dahlias for Pres. Calvin Coolidge in appreciation of an airmail contract for the area. (PEH.)

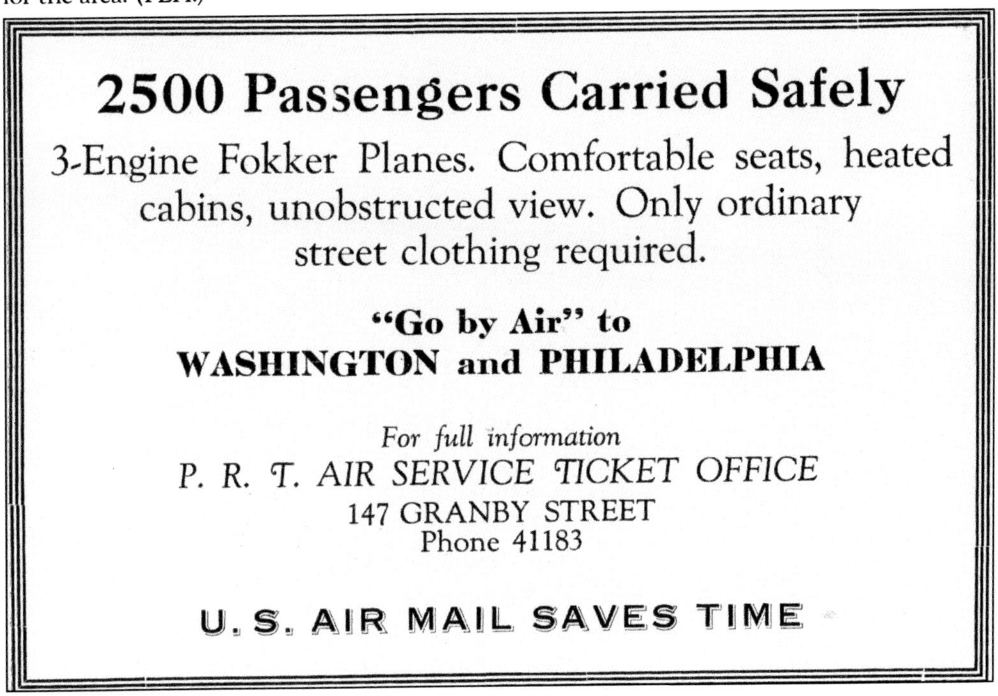

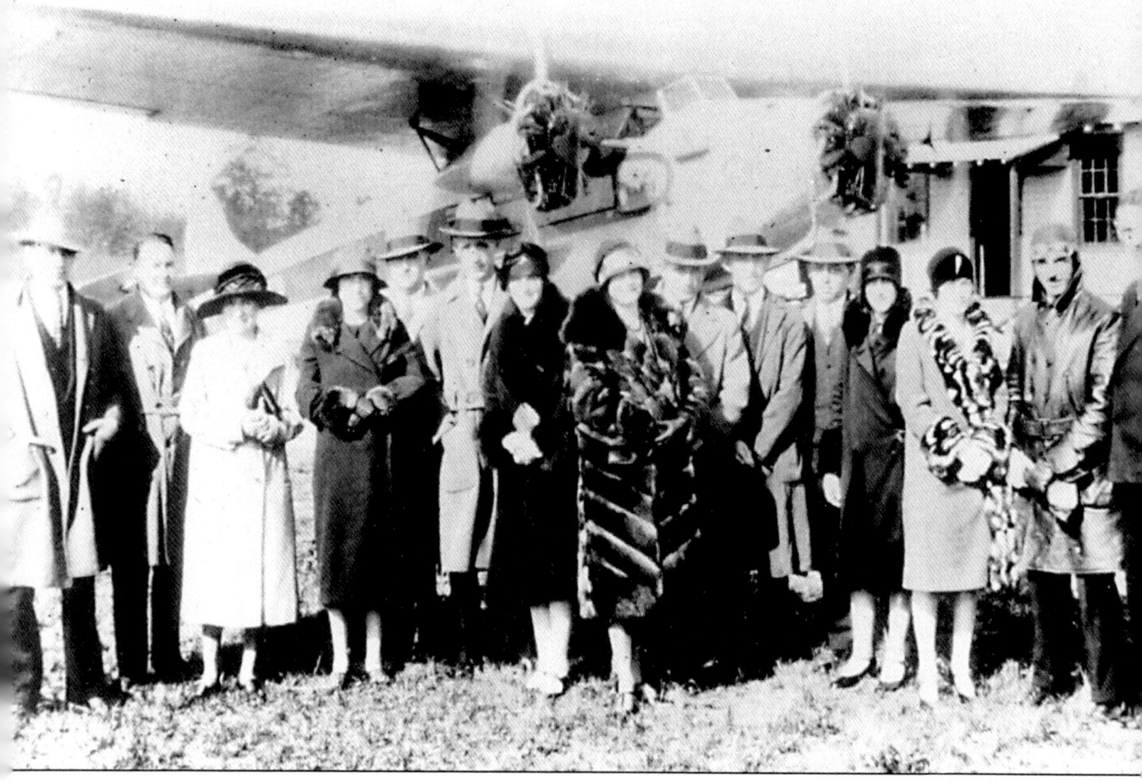

NOW BOARDING. Passengers line up with the captain of a PRT Air Fokker trimotor at the Granby Street Airport just before a flight, most likely in 1926. When PRT Air went out of business within a few months of starting service, it created a void in Hampton Roads. In fact, it would not be until 1929 that flights of substance again took place. That happened when World War I pilot and Norfolk resident Ben Epstein opened an air-taxi service between Norfolk and Richmond from the Granby Street Airport. The field would also be called Grand Central Air Terminal. In 1931 or 1932, a small stucco terminal was built to welcome passenger service from Ludington Lines and Eastern Air Transport. Epstein remembered the airport only as "a place to park your plane . . . [and] a place to get a cup of coffee." In 1932, the navy opposed expansion of the field because of the proximity to the Norfolk Naval Air Station, and commercial air operations were moved to the Glenrock Airport. Later, the navy took over the Granby Street site. (NIA.)

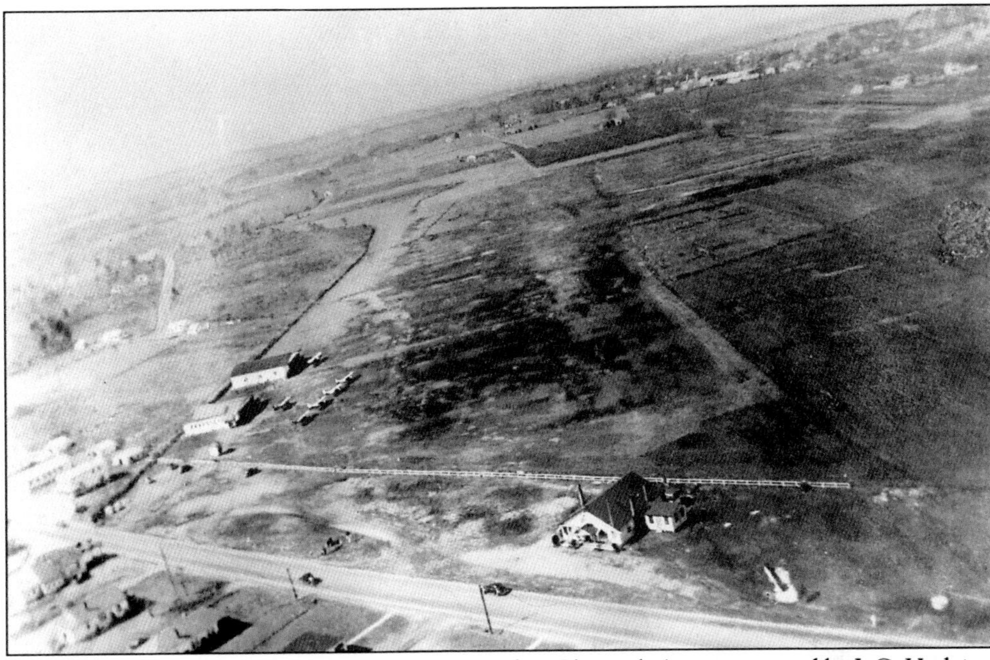

Glenrock Airport. Commercial service moved to Glenrock Airport, owned by J. C. Hudgins, northeast of downtown Norfolk, in 1932 when the navy opposed expansion of the Granby Street Airport. The above photograph shows an aerial view of the field on June 21, 1941. The site is today JANAF Shopping Center. In the below photograph, passengers board a Ludington aircraft on February 7, 1932, at an airport open house. By 1933, the Great Depression took its toll; Ludington Lines sold out to Eastern Air Transport, which, unable to make a profit in Norfolk, pulled their service in 1933. It would be another five years before air service returned to Hampton Roads. (NPL.)

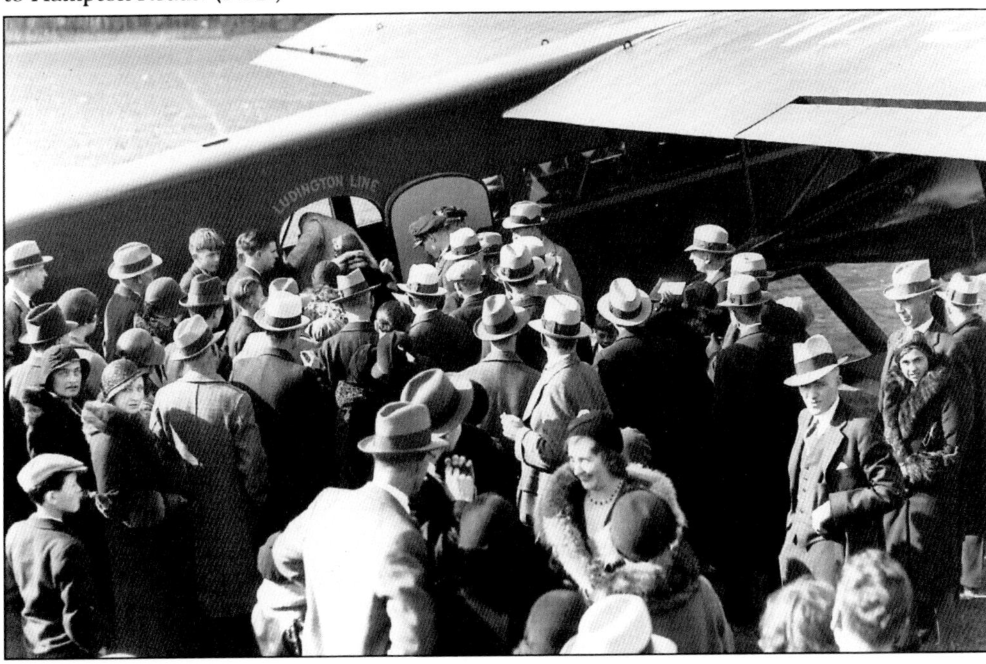

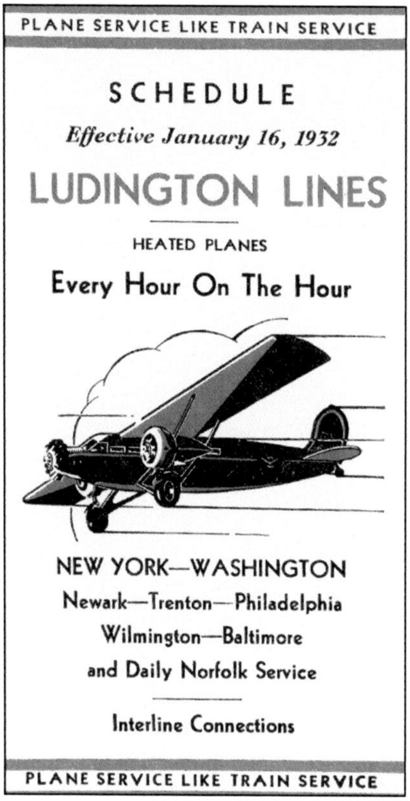

Plane Service Like Train Service. Starting as an agent to demonstrate Farman sports planes in 1922, the aeronautical company of Charles Townsend Ludington became Ludington Philadelphia Flying Service and, in 1929, Ludington Line. The above illustration shows the cover of their January 16, 1932, flight schedule, which included service to Norfolk's Glenrock Airport. The below illustration shows the actual timetable from that schedule, which includes a flag stop at Langley Field. Ludington was unable to secure a government mail contract and bled red ink. In 1933, Eastern Air Transport bought Ludington for $260,000, which included its seven Stinson aircraft. (PEH.)

WASHINGTON-NORFOLK DIVISION§

Baltimore ★ and Langley Field★

Bus Connection Available for Virginia Beach

SOUTHBOUND			NORTHBOUND ★		
Leave Washington Airport	Arrive Norfolk Airport	Arrive Hotel Monticello	Leave Hotel Monticello	Leave Norfolk Airport	Arrive Washington Airport
9.55 A.M.*	11.20 A.M.*	11.35 A.M.*	11.15 A.M.*	11.30 A.M.*	12.55 P.M.*
2.55 P.M.	4.20 P.M.	4.35 P.M.	4.15 P.M.	4.30 P.M.	5.55 P.M.

★9.20 A. M. and 2.20 P. M. Planes from Baltimore Connect at Washington. Northbound Connect at Washington for Points North.

Northbound Planes stop at Langley Field 11.35 A. M. and 4.35 P. M.; Southbound at 11.15 A. M. and 4.15 P. M. (on reservation). Add five minutes to schedule for stops.

* Daily Except Sunday.

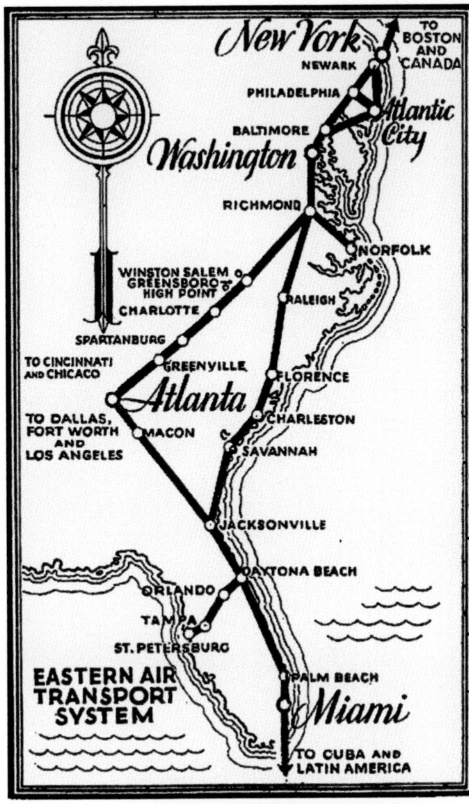

GOODBYE GLENROCK. With the effects of the Great Depression, in 1933 Ludington Lines, one of the two air carriers at Norfolk's Glenrock Airport, was forced to sell its interest to Eastern Air Transport, which also served the terminal. The above early-1930s route-system map shows Eastern's flights to Norfolk. Unable to make money in Hampton Roads, Eastern decided to leave the market. The below illustration is a postal cover carried on the airline's last flight from Norfolk on May 31, 1933. Eventually Glenrock Airport would fall out of favor, and when Pennsylvania Central Airlines (PCA) eyed service to Norfolk in 1938, the city converted a nearby golf course to create a municipal airport. (PEH.)

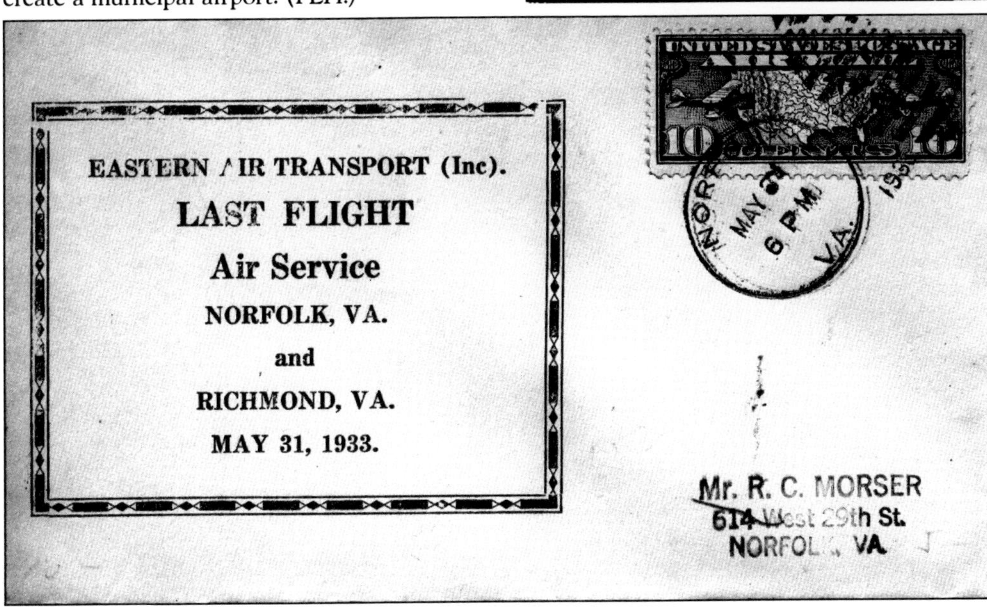

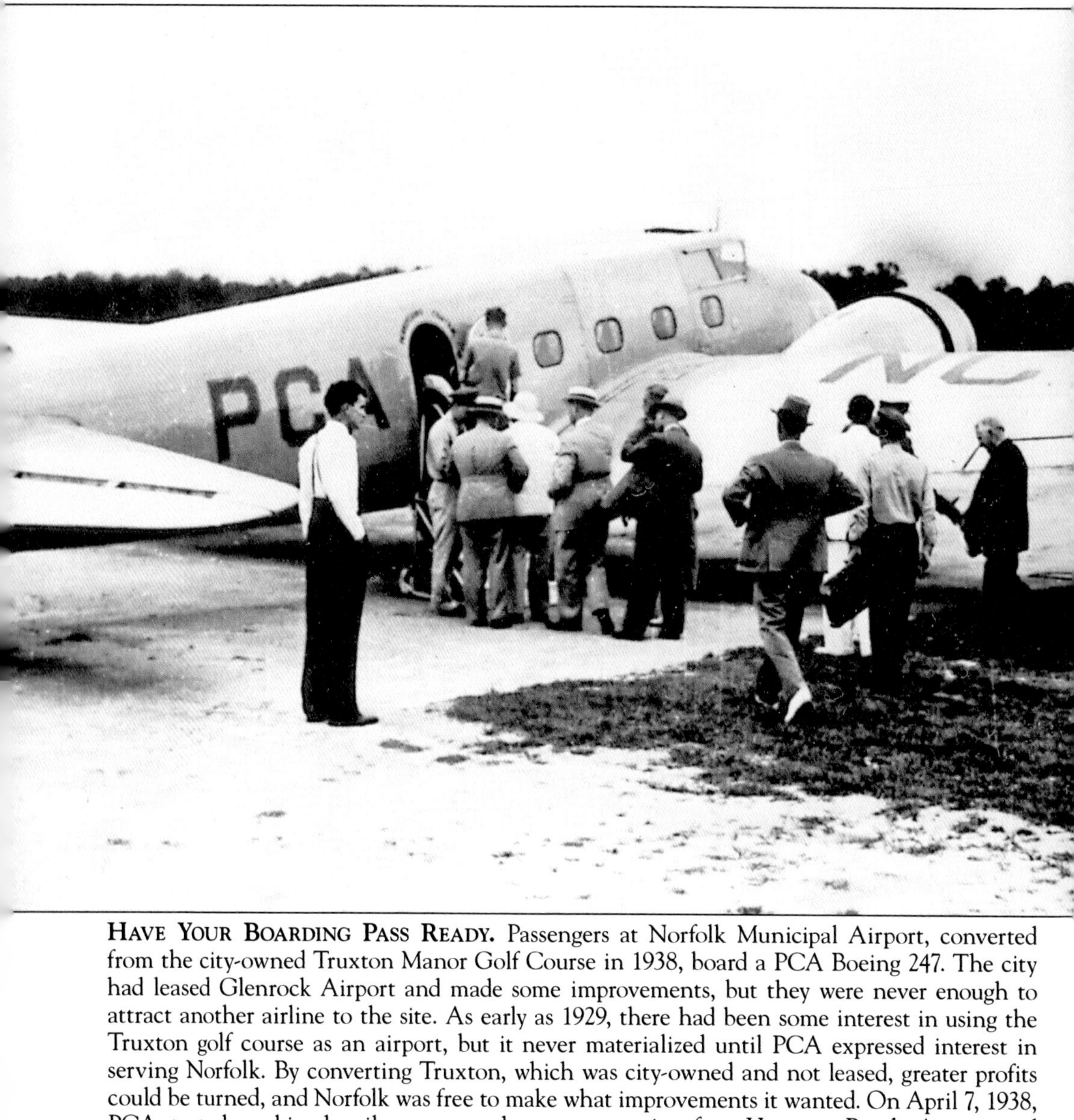

Have Your Boarding Pass Ready. Passengers at Norfolk Municipal Airport, converted from the city-owned Truxton Manor Golf Course in 1938, board a PCA Boeing 247. The city had leased Glenrock Airport and made some improvements, but they were never enough to attract another airline to the site. As early as 1929, there had been some interest in using the Truxton golf course as an airport, but it never materialized until PCA expressed interest in serving Norfolk. By converting Truxton, which was city-owned and not leased, greater profits could be turned, and Norfolk was free to make what improvements it wanted. On April 7, 1938, PCA started combined mail, express, and passenger services from Hampton Roads. A renovated clubhouse served as the passenger terminal until a permanent terminal could be built; it opened in 1940. (NIA.)

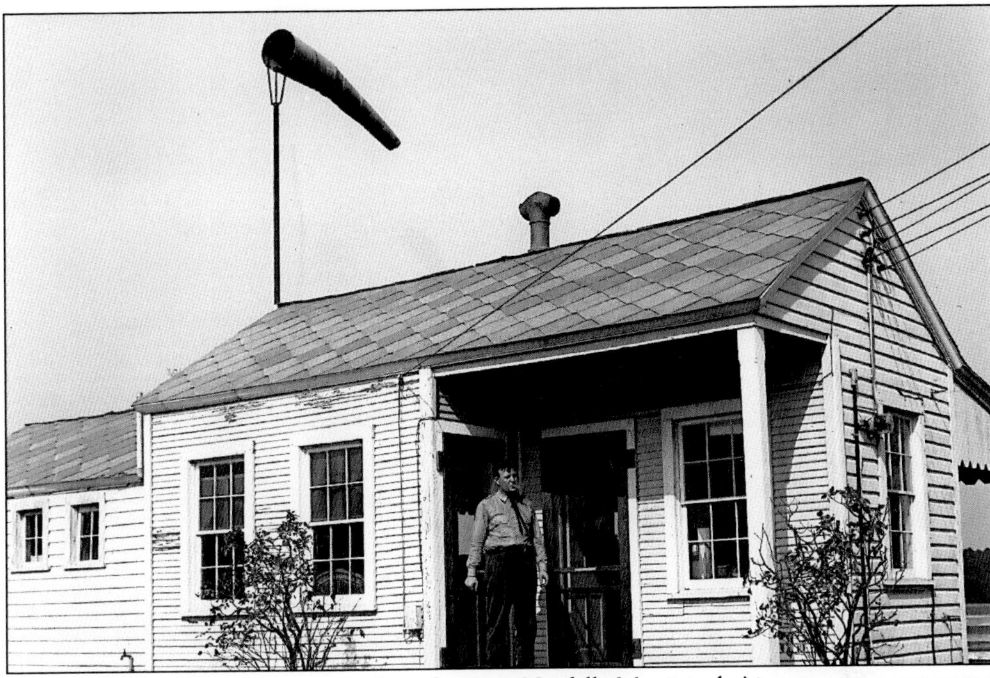

CADDY SHACK. The first terminal at the new Norfolk Municipal Airport was a renovated clubhouse left over from the former Truxton Manor Golf Course. Its exterior is shown in the above photograph. The below picture shows the temporary terminal's interior. The move into the former clubhouse was necessary to accommodate service begun in 1938 by Pennsylvania Central Airlines. With a Works Progress Administration (WPA) grant of $317,000, as well as city and state funds, a permanent terminal was built and opened in 1940. This is still the site of Norfolk's passenger airport. (NIA.)

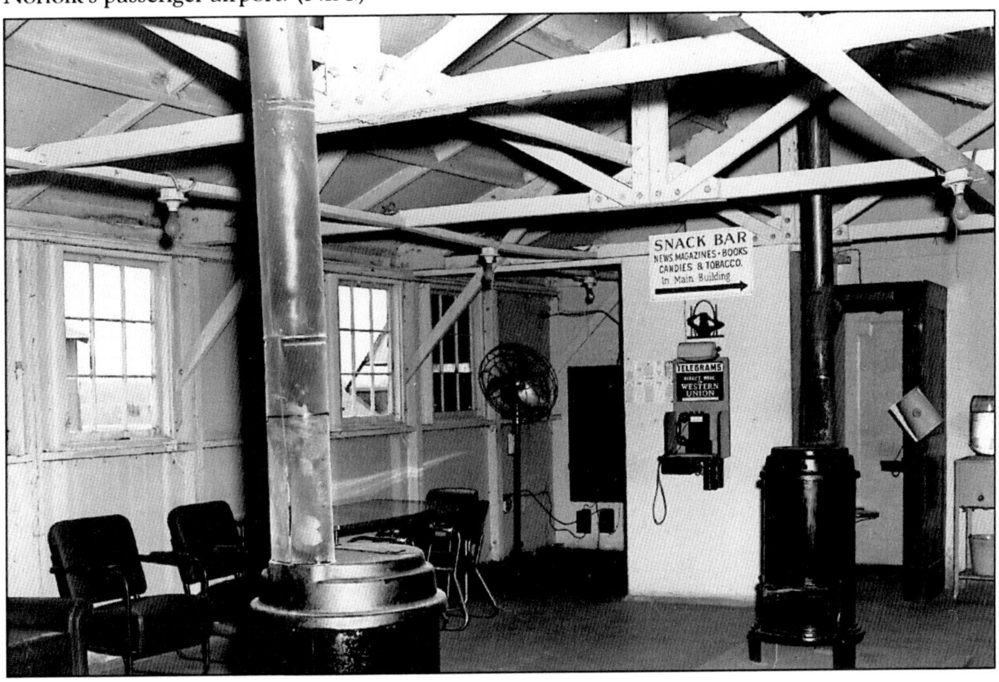

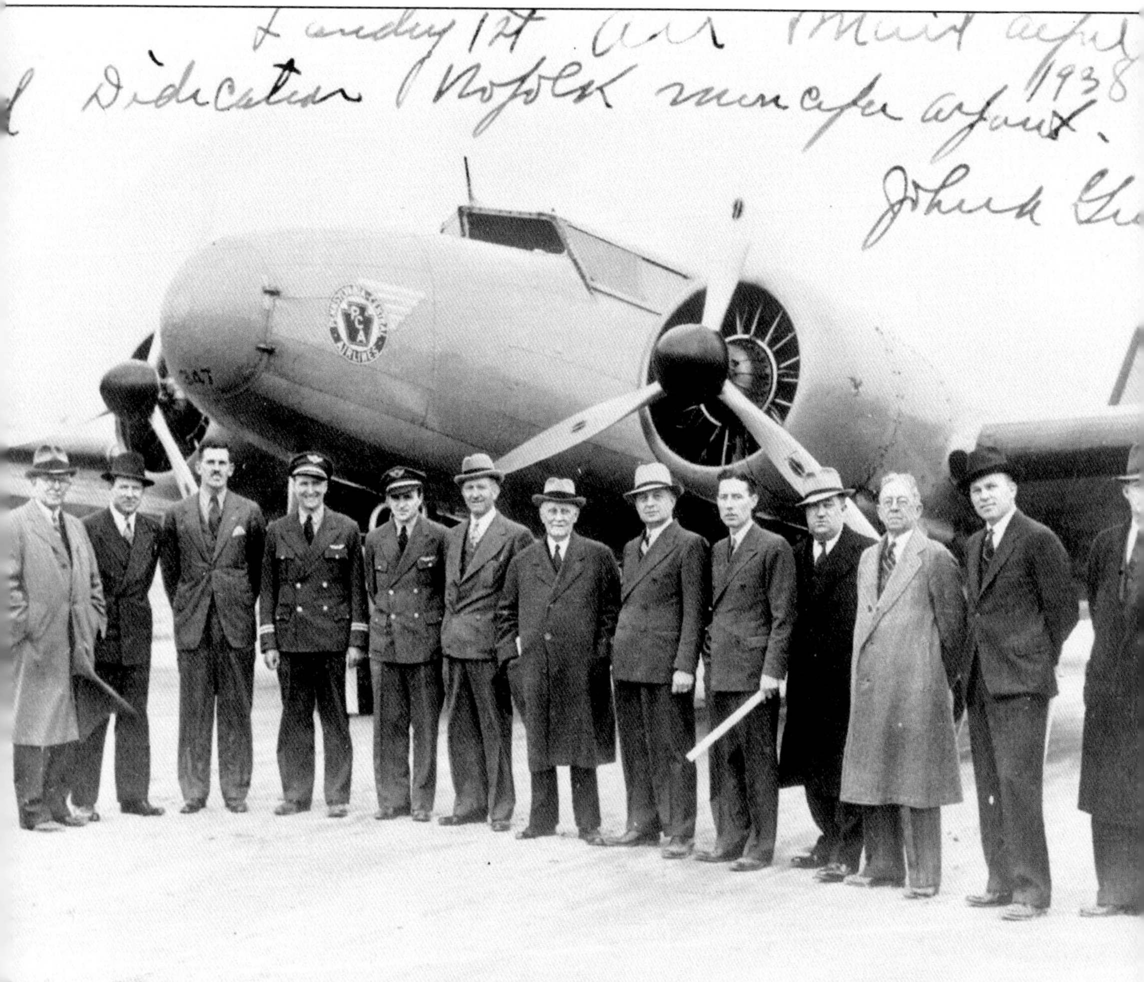

FAIRWAYS BECOME FLYWAYS. This group gathered on April 7, 1938, to inaugurate service from Norfolk on PCA and to dedicate the new Norfolk Municipal Airport. Behind the crowd is a PCA Boeing 237. The new airport, on the site of the former 465-acre Truxton Manor Golf Course, featured a 2,500-foot runway with obstruction lights. The flights from PCA brought back commercial airline service to Norfolk; it had been five years since Eastern Air Transport suspended service at Glenrock Airport. The first year in operation, the new Norfolk Municipal Airport carried 3,028 passengers. Last year, more than 600,000 folks flew into the current Norfolk International Airport, which is located on the same site as the 1938 flying field. (NPL.)

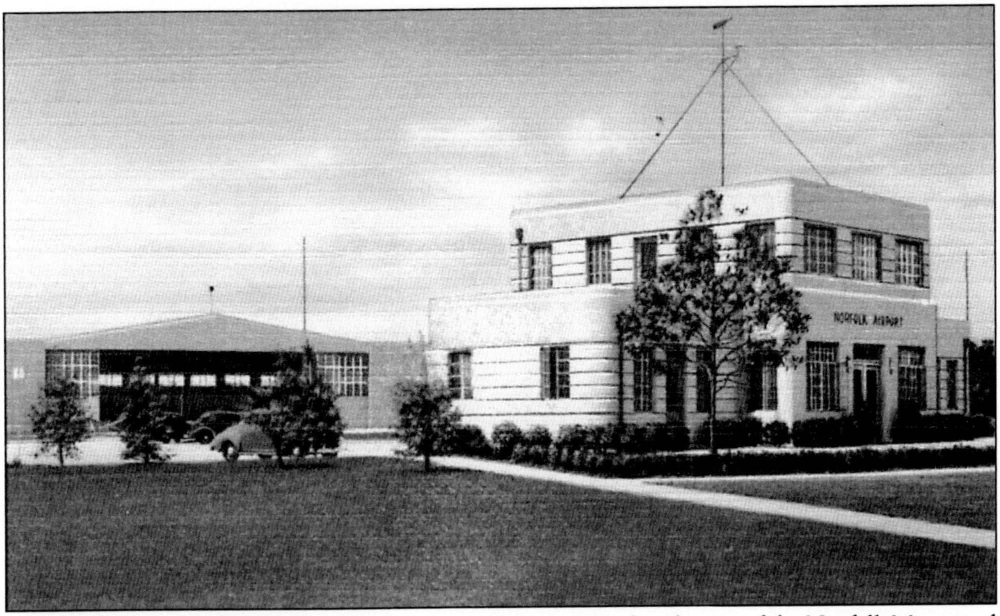

FIRST PERMANENT TERMINAL. The first permanent terminal at the site of the Norfolk Municipal Airport opened in 1940. The front of the building is shown in the above vintage postcard and the back in the below March 1940 photograph, which also shows a Pennsylvania Central Airlines Boeing 247. In just a few years, however, the use of the terminal would drastically change. Norfolk Municipal Airport became a vital resource for the war effort; the Army Air Corps assumed control of airport operations from 1942 to 1947, extending the runway and adding two more to handle the increased number of flights with larger aircraft. Some $4 million in expansions and improvements were made. When the troops returned from the war, the Army Air Corps returned the airport to the city. (PEH; NPL.)

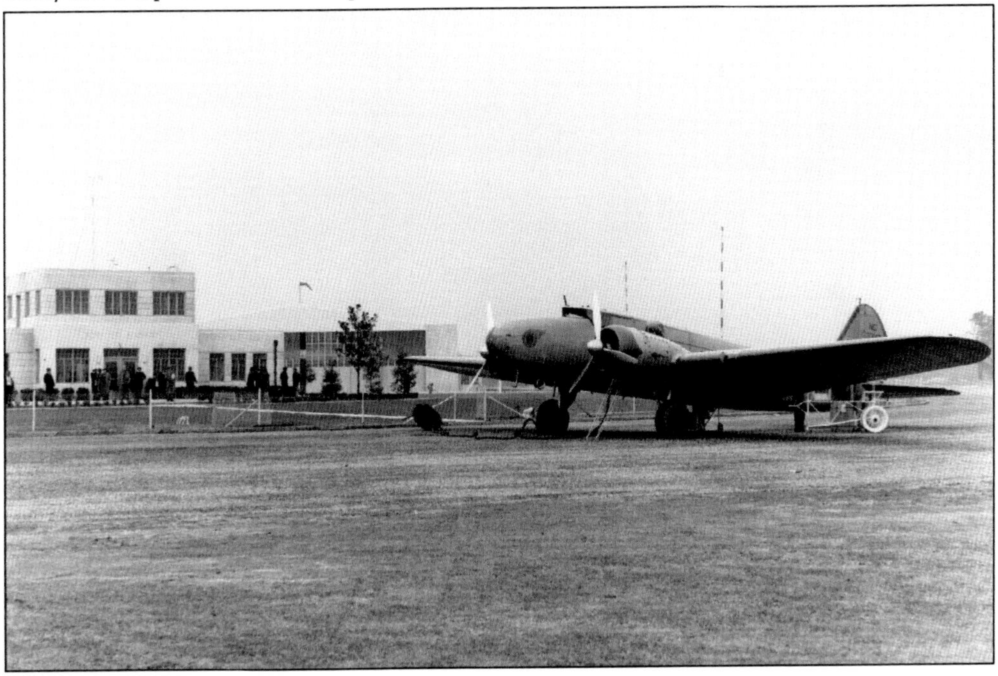

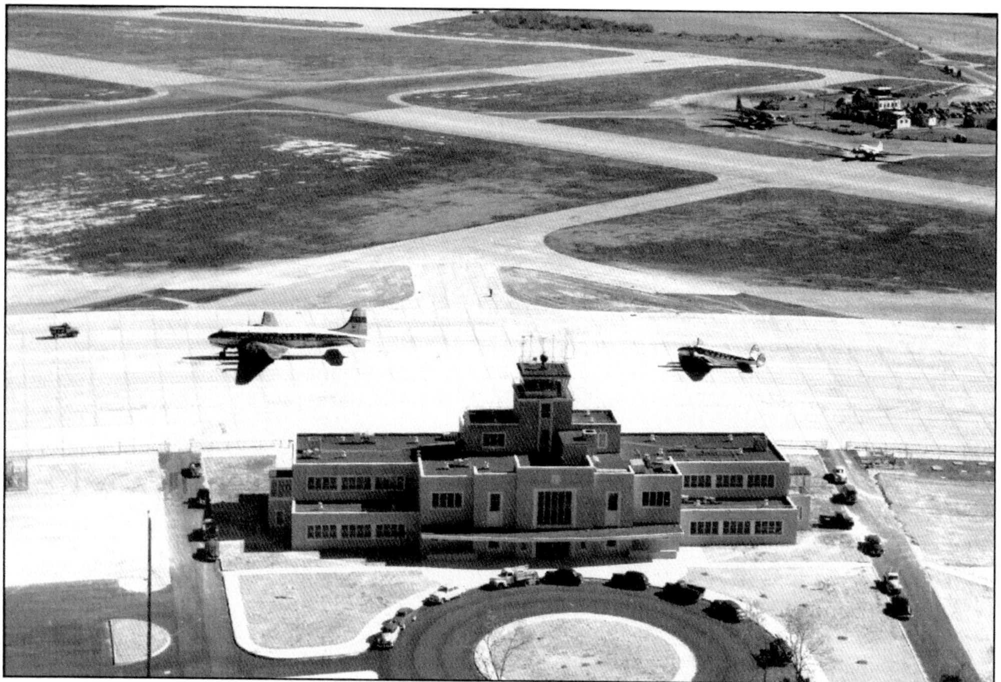

SOARING TO NEW HEIGHTS. Passenger traffic continued to grow after World War II; in 1940, 13,564 passengers passed through Norfolk Municipal. By 1950, that number had risen to 202,323, handled by National, Capital, and Piedmont Airlines. In 1948, construction on a new $1-million terminal was begun; the facility opened in 1951. In the above photograph, the new terminal is in the foreground, and two National Airlines planes are parked on the tarmac. In the background, the 1940 terminal appears to still be in use. The below photograph shows the 1951 terminal just prior to opening. In 1952, the older terminal was demolished to make way for new taxiways to speed up ground operations. When the facility opened in May 1951, radio and television star Arthur Godfrey was the master of ceremonies. (NPL; NIA.)

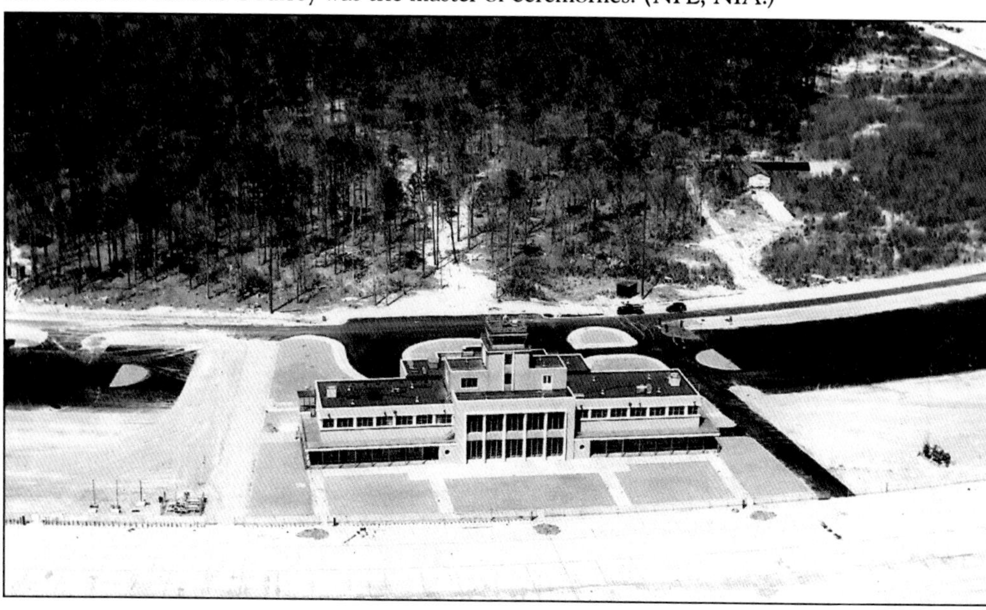

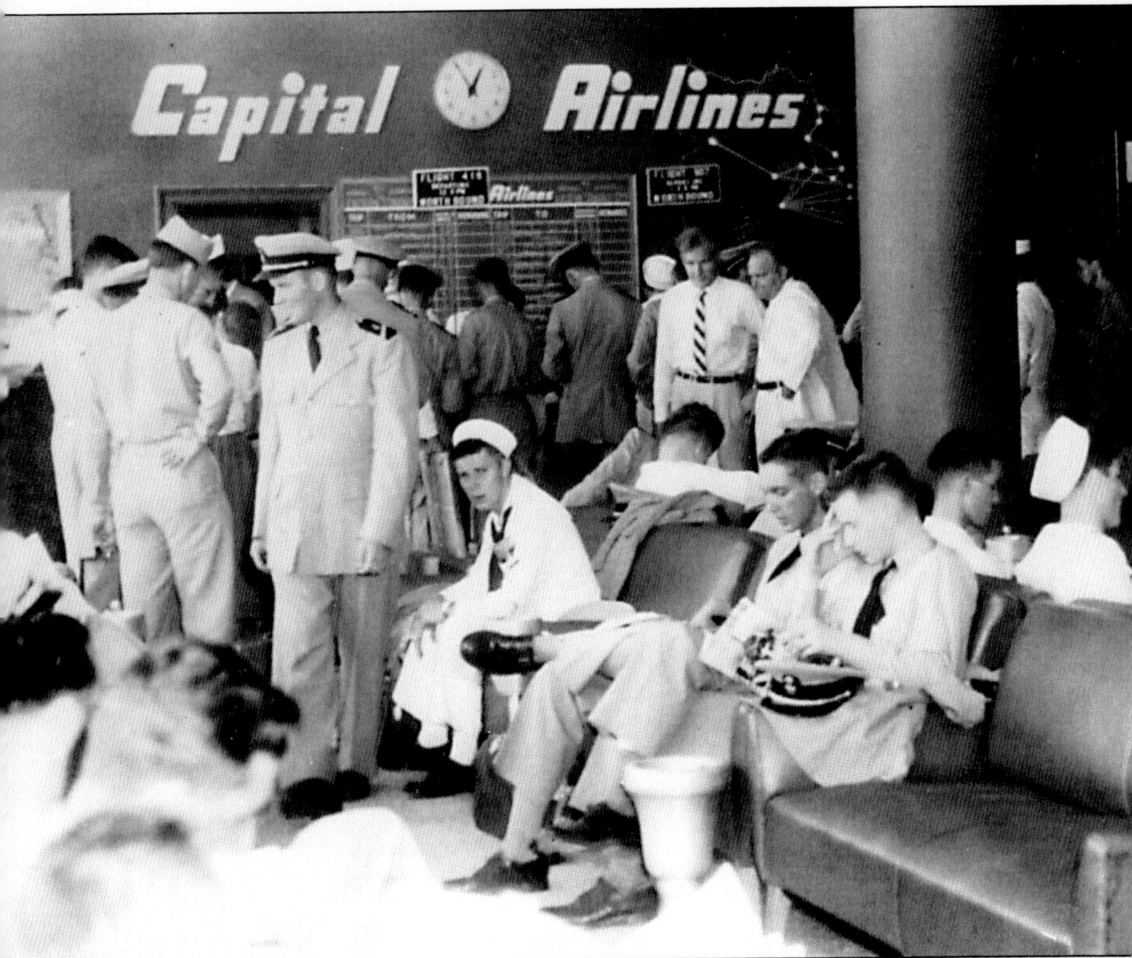

PLENTY TO SEE WHILE WAITING. This mid-1950s photograph shows the Capital Airlines gate area at Norfolk Municipal Airport. The new facility opened in 1951 and was a tremendous improvement over the 1940 terminal. Inside, the main lobby stretched 63 feet to a wall of glass looking out onto the field. Capital, National, and Piedmont Airlines shared the ticket counter space in the lobby. Green leather sofas and chairs lined up before the glass on the field side of the lobby. Featured in the lobby was a barber shop and coffee shop. On the second floor, the Azalea Room, a dining room seating 200 persons, gave diners a panoramic view on one side of the air field and on the other of the Azalea Gardens (today's Norfolk Botanical Gardens). Also on the second level were airport offices; on the third and fourth floors were radar and radio equipment. Another nice feature of the facility was the air-conditioning throughout. (NPL.)

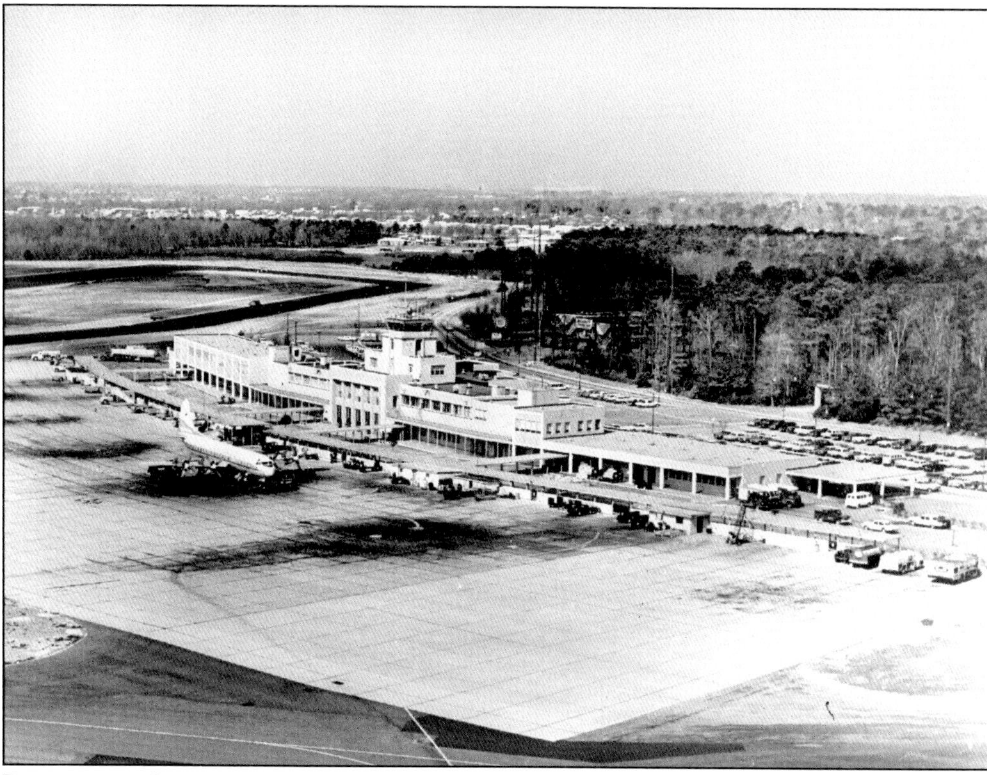

PROGRESS IN JUST OVER 50 YEARS. By the time these photographs were taken, showing the tarmac side of the 1951 terminal building, it had only been a little more than five decades since the famous Wright brothers' flight in Kitty Hawk, North Carolina, in 1903. During that time, advancements in aviation, many accomplished right here in Hampton Roads, had given rise to commercial airliners seating nearly 100 passengers. In the top photograph, a National Airlines Lockheed Electra is visible. In the bottom photograph, the same plane is to the right; the nose of a United Airlines Viscount (obtained with their purchase of Capital Airlines) can be seen. (NPL.)

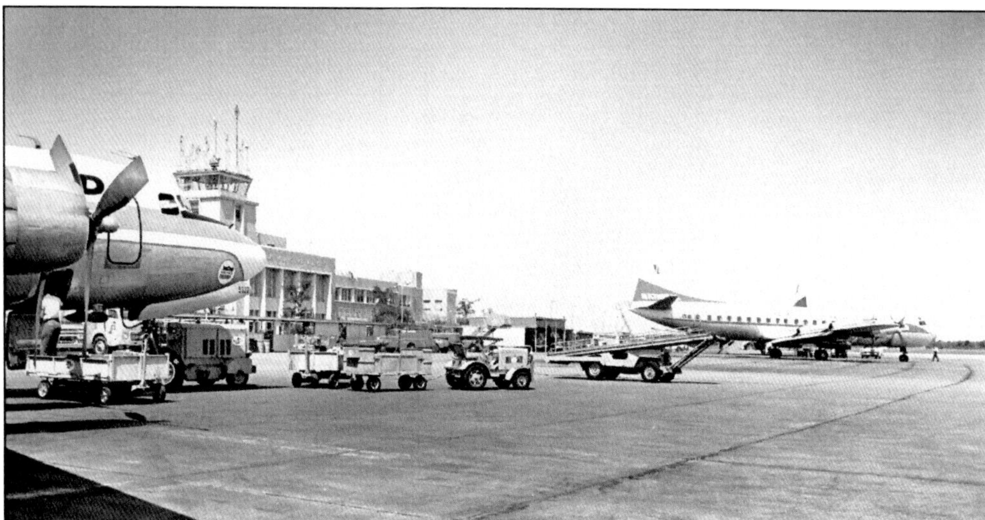

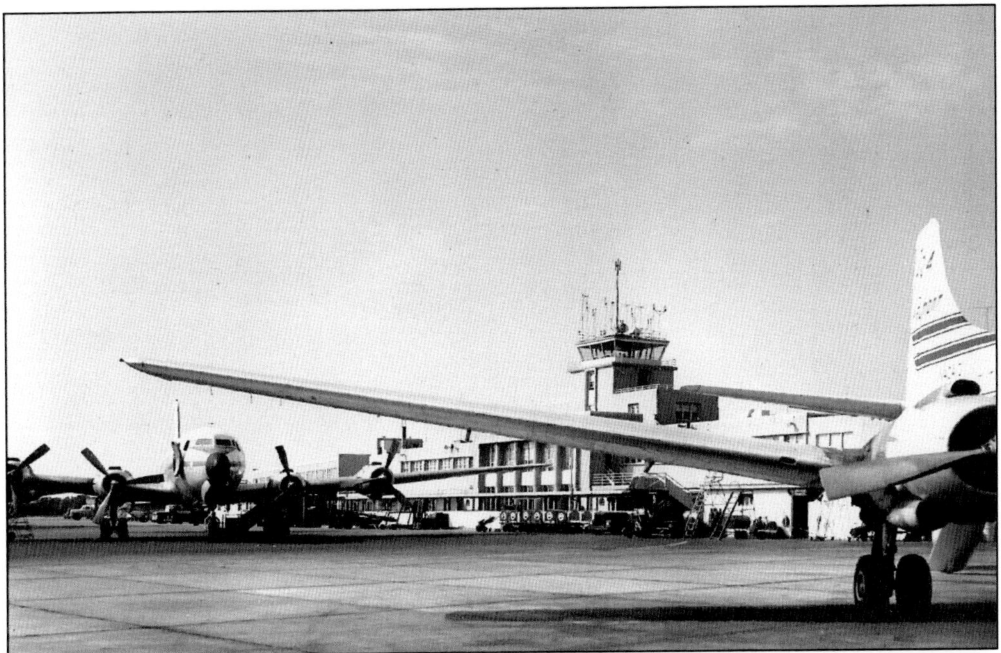

WE ARE NUMBER 30 FOR TAKE-OFF. As evident in these two *c.* 1960 photographs, Norfolk Municipal Airport (it would become Norfolk Regional Airport in 1968) was a very busy place on the tarmac as well as in the terminal. By 1959, passenger numbers were 384,622. In 1959, $3 million in improvements were completed for the field, including enlargement of the terminal by 30,000 square feet with the addition of two new wings, expanded car parking, additional ramp space, a new access road, a lengthening of the main runway to 6,000 feet to serve short- and medium-range jets, a resurfacing of existing runways, and additional new taxiways. The work would have to suffice for travelers for the next 15 years until a new terminal opened. (NPL.)

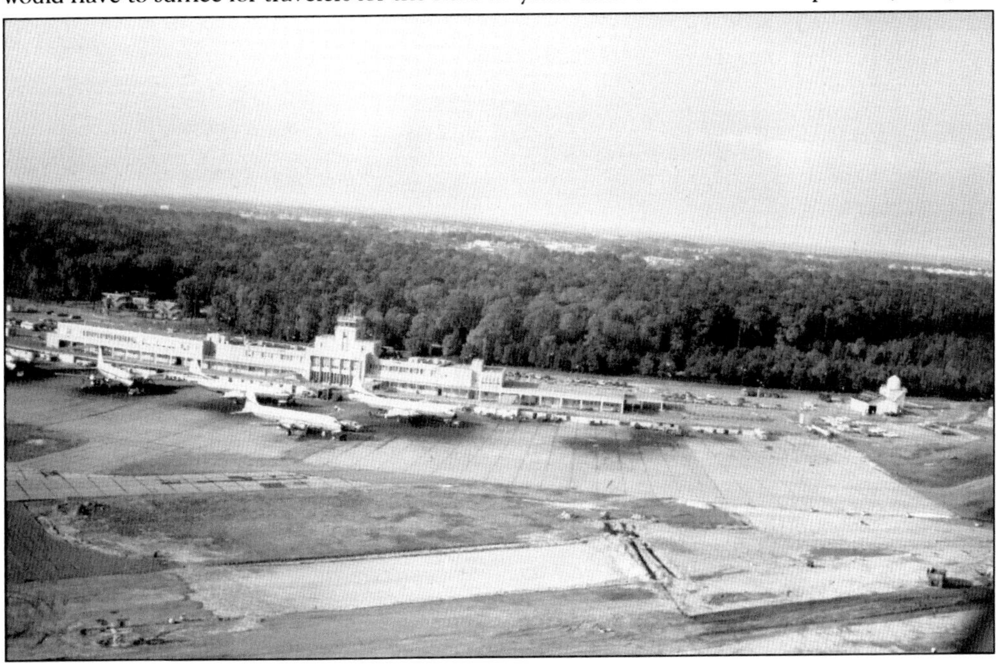

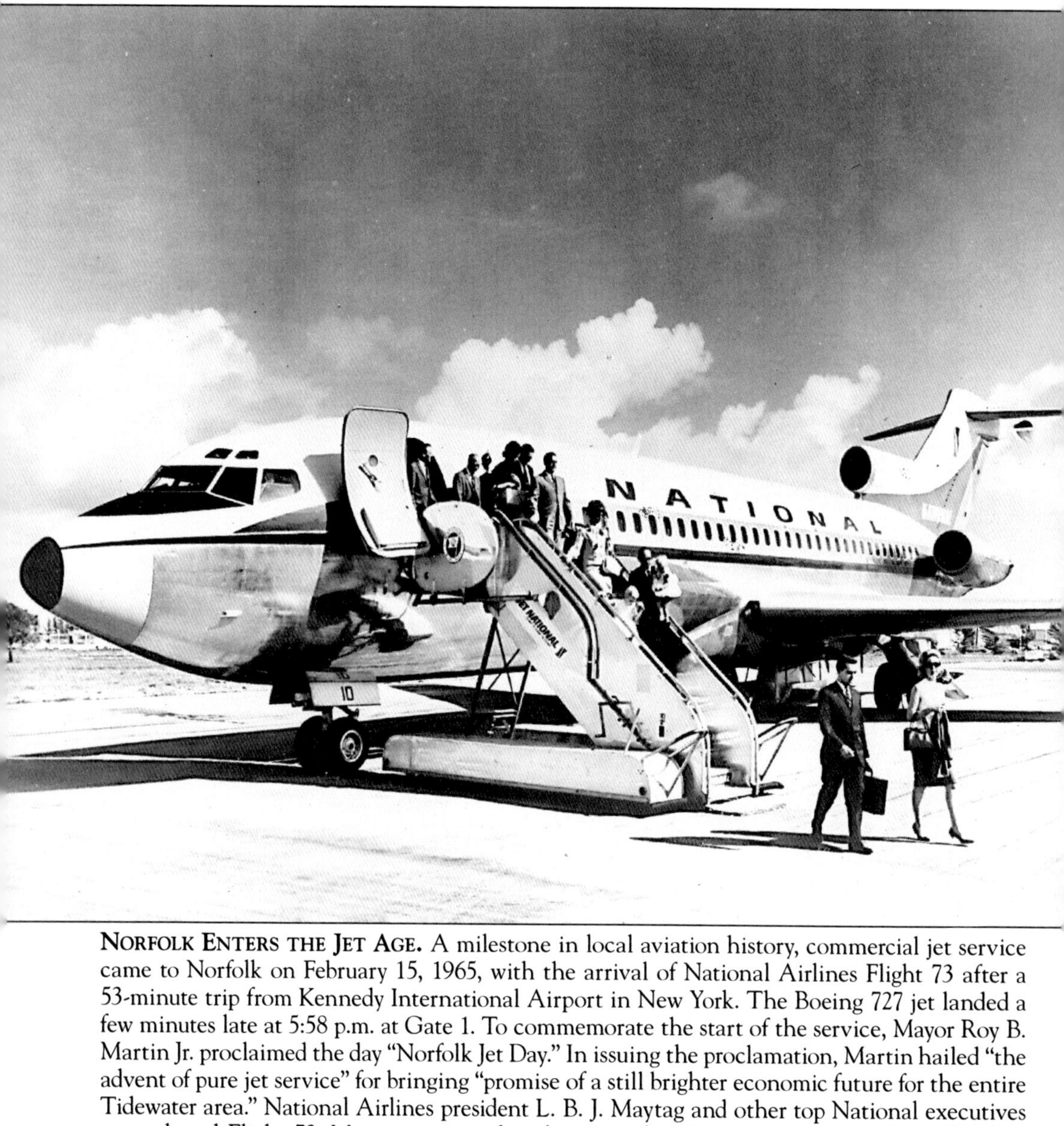

NORFOLK ENTERS THE JET AGE. A milestone in local aviation history, commercial jet service came to Norfolk on February 15, 1965, with the arrival of National Airlines Flight 73 after a 53-minute trip from Kennedy International Airport in New York. The Boeing 727 jet landed a few minutes late at 5:58 p.m. at Gate 1. To commemorate the start of the service, Mayor Roy B. Martin Jr. proclaimed the day "Norfolk Jet Day." In issuing the proclamation, Martin hailed "the advent of pure jet service" for bringing "promise of a still brighter economic future for the entire Tidewater area." National Airlines president L. B. J. Maytag and other top National executives were aboard Flight 73. Maytag presented a plaque to the city commemorating Norfolk's first commercial jet flight. The plane turned around as Flight 74 and, less than an hour later, departed for a return trip to New York. The following year, United Airlines started Boeing 727 jet service from Norfolk to Chicago, Illinois. (NIA.)

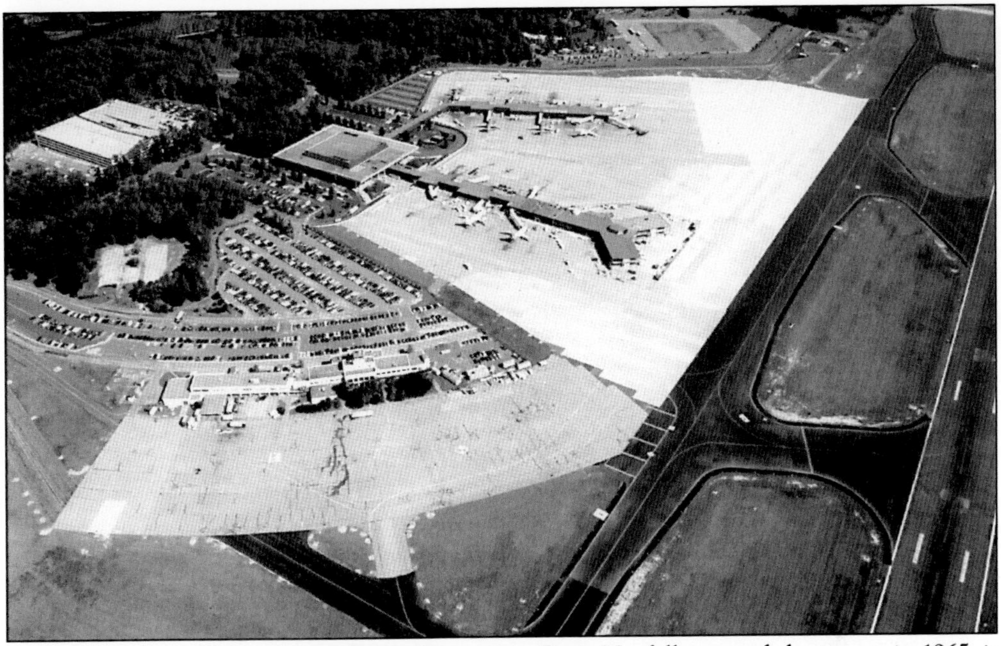

A Cure for the Terminally Over-Crowded. Once Norfolk entered the jet age in 1965, it became apparent a larger airport terminal would be needed. Construction began in October 1971 on a new facility. Opened in 1974, Norfolk International Airport solved many of the crowding issues associated with the 1951 terminal and gave room to grow. In the above photograph, the 1951 terminal is to the left and the new, $30-million facility, just prior to opening, is to the right. The below photograph also shows the new terminal just prior to opening; it was dedicated January 19, 1974. It is the only airport located within a botanical garden. To help it fit in with the surroundings, 8,000 azaleas, camellias, and rhododendrons were planted. The airlines at the time were Allegheny, National, Piedmont, and United. (NIA.)

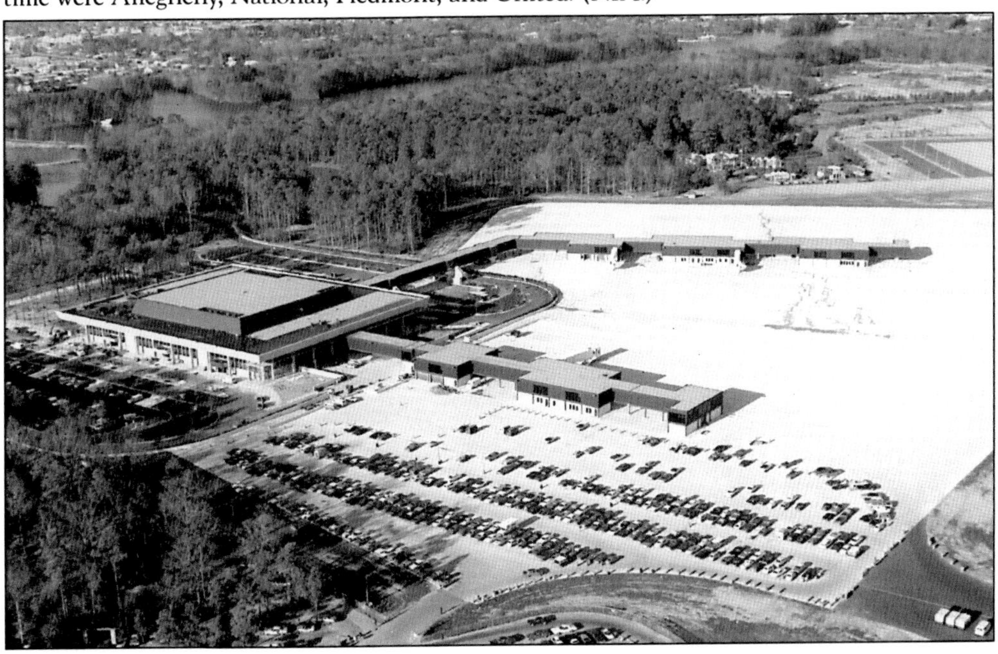

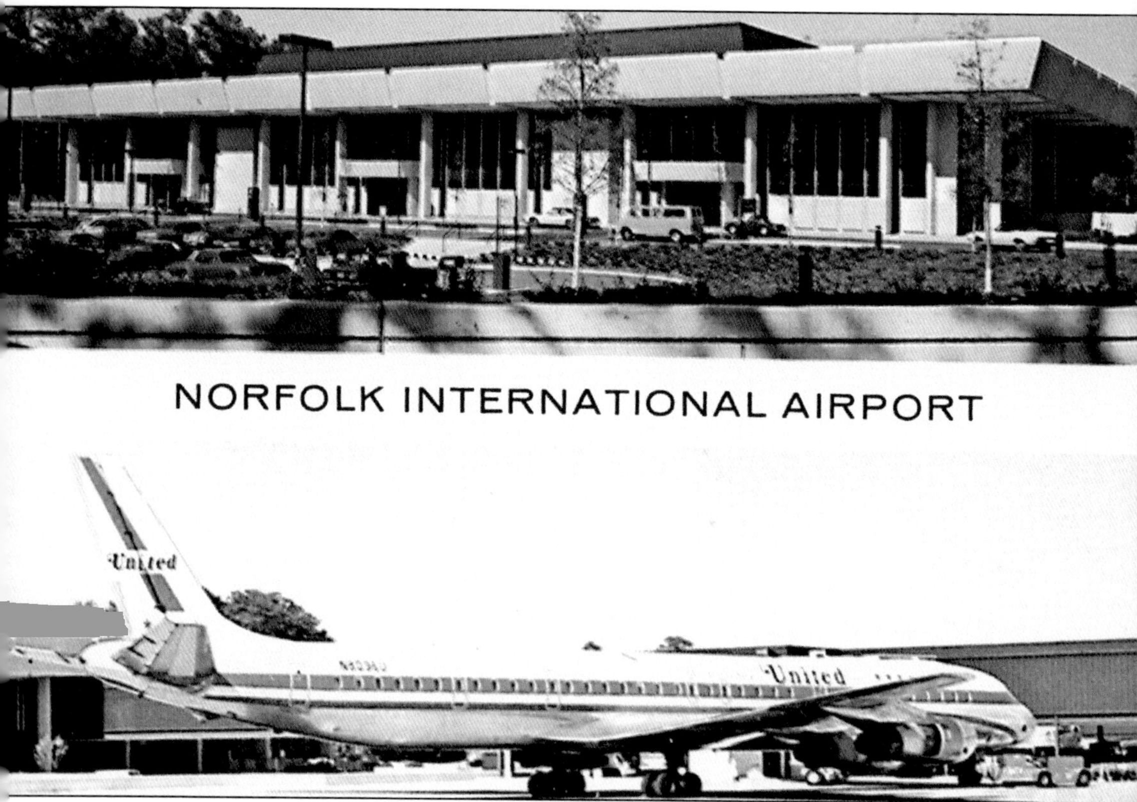

NORFOLK INTERNATIONAL AIRPORT. Soon after the expansion of the 1951 terminal by adding two concourses in 1959, it became apparent the current air terminal would need to be replaced. Passenger numbers had grown from 3,028 in 1938 to 640,954 in 1965. Also, larger and larger jets were taxing the existing airport. In 1974, a new terminal opened, shown in this postcard, and additional land was secured for further expansion. In 1976, the name of the facility was changed from Norfolk Regional Airport to Norfolk International Airport to reflect the addition of federal customs facilities. A unique feature of the airport is that it is actually located in Norfolk Botanical Gardens; the lush landscaping is apparent to passengers as they approach or leave the terminal. In 1991, Norfolk International underwent a concourse expansion and added 10 additional gates. In 2002, a new, 243,000-square foot arrivals building was opened and the main terminal building was refurbished. (PEH.)

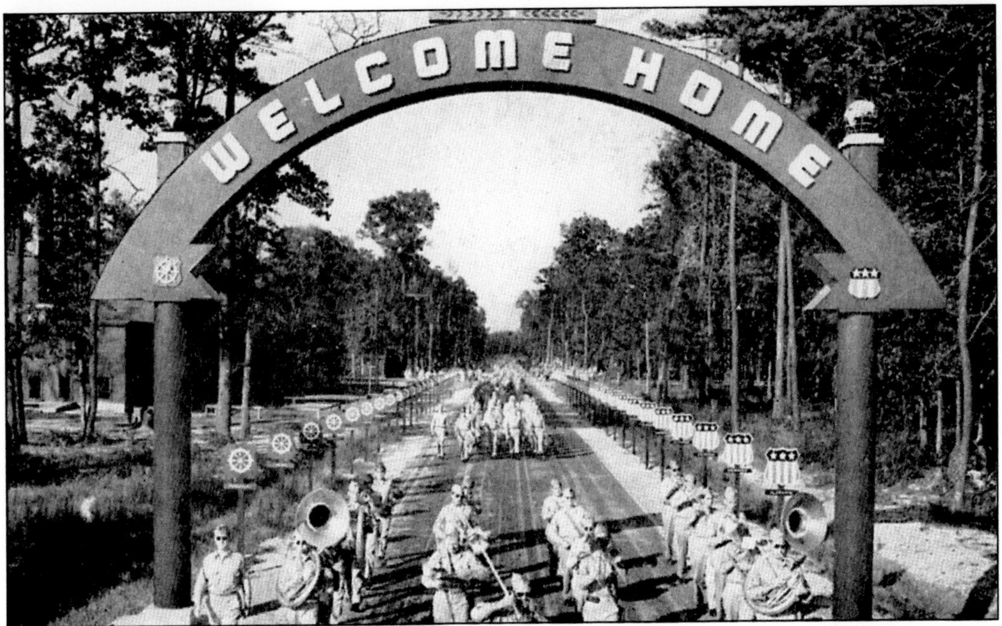

CAMP PATRICK HENRY. Operating from December 1, 1942, through January 31, 1945, on 1,700 acres of land in Newport News, Camp Patrick Henry was a staging area for up to 85,000 personnel at a time, with a shuttle rail service shipside to the Hampton Roads Port of Embarkation. It was also used as a repository to welcome returning soldiers. Almost 1.5 million people passed through the camp, which is today the site of the Newport News/Williamsburg International Airport. The above photograph is the camp entrance; the below photograph is an aerial shot of the facility. Although nothing of Camp Patrick Henry remains, its legacy lives on with the three-letter airport code designation, PHF—Patrick Henry Field. (PEH; NNWI.)

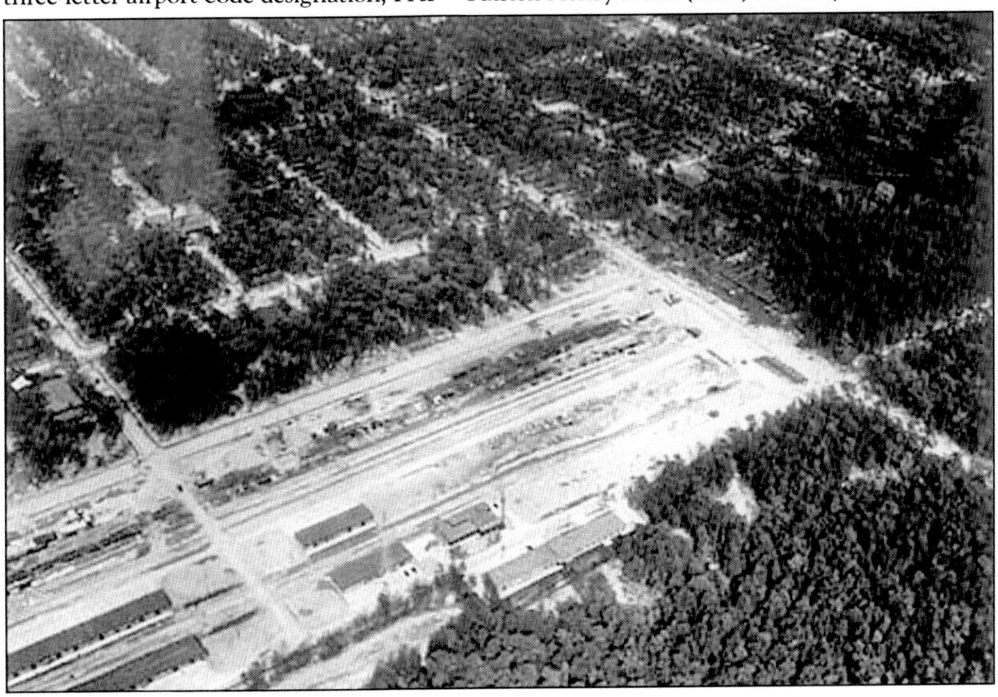

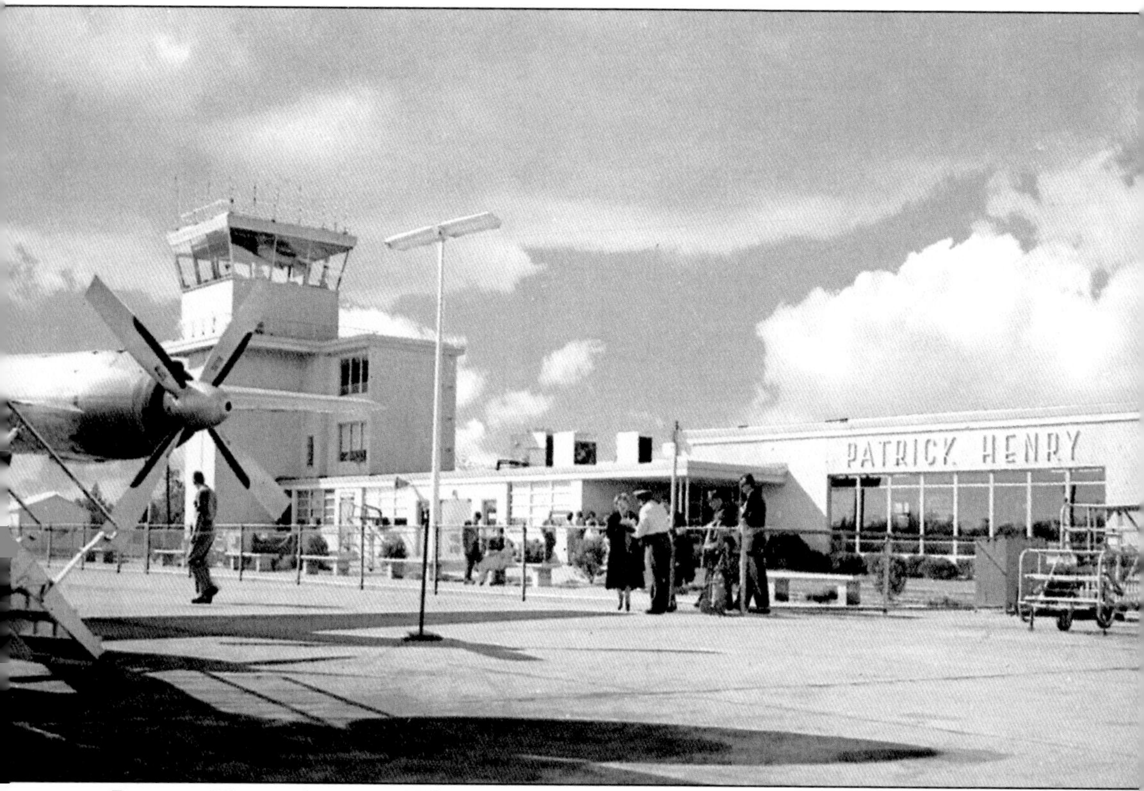

PATRICK HENRY AIRPORT. When Camp Patrick Henry was deactivated shortly after the end of World War II, the land sat vacant. In 1947, an agreement was reached to cede 924 acres from the U.S. War Asset Administration to the Peninsula Airport Commission to establish an airport for the region. Commercial airline service began with flights by Piedmont Airlines and Capital Airlines in November 1949. The airport opened with two 3,500-foot runways. A passenger terminal was built but was gutted by a fire in 1951; it was replaced by a new terminal in 1955. Subsequent runway expansions allowed use by larger aircraft, which included service by United Airlines and National Airlines. A modern new terminal was opened in 1992, and today, carriers include Air Tran, Delta, and US Airways. This photograph shows a propjet unloading at the 1955 terminal. (PEH.)

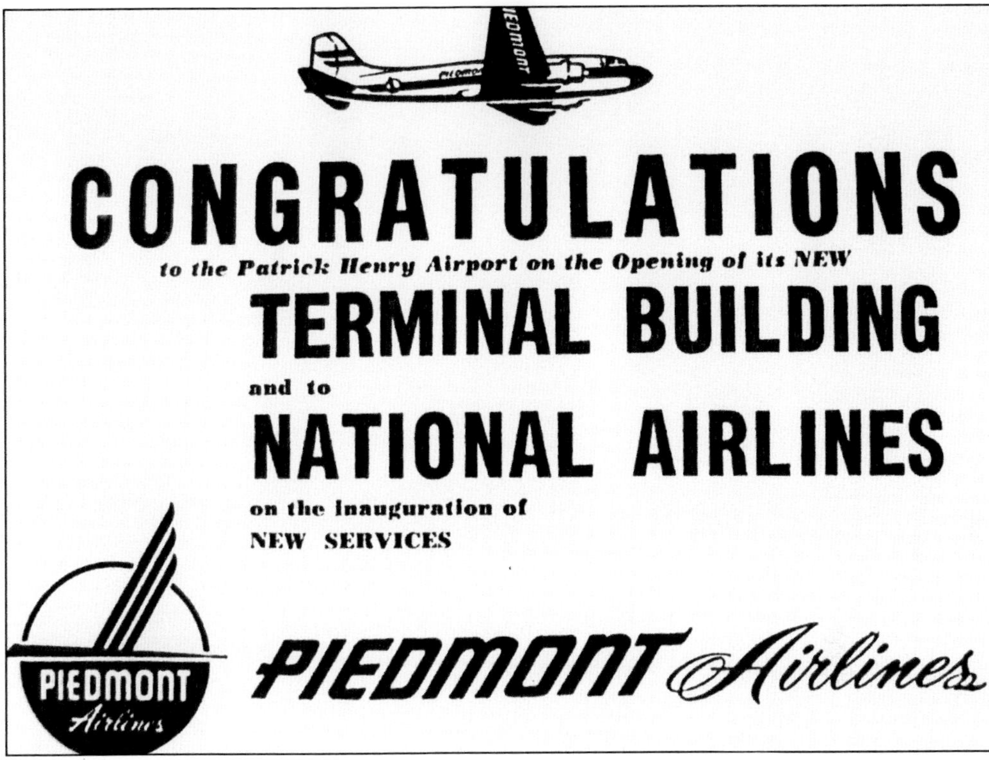

CONGRATULATIONS. Piedmont Airlines took out this advertisement congratulating folks on the peninsula on the opening of Patrick Henry Airport in November 1949. At the time, service was provided by Piedmont (a forerunner of US Airways) and National Airlines (later part of Pan Am; now defunct). In 1990, the name changed to Newport News/Williamsburg International Airport. In 1992, a modern new terminal was opened. (PEH.)

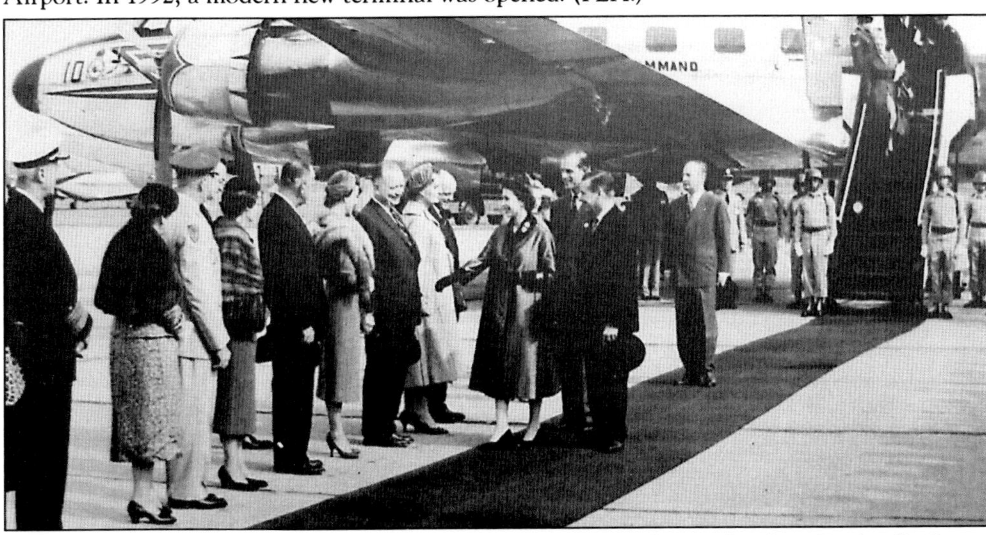

LONG LIVE THE QUEEN. Quite a buzz was created in October 1957 when England's Queen Elizabeth II and Prince Philip flew into Patrick Henry Airport on the occasion of the Jamestown Festival 350th Celebration. The queen, in the center of this photograph, arrived on a Royal Canadian Air Force plane. (Newport News Public Library.)

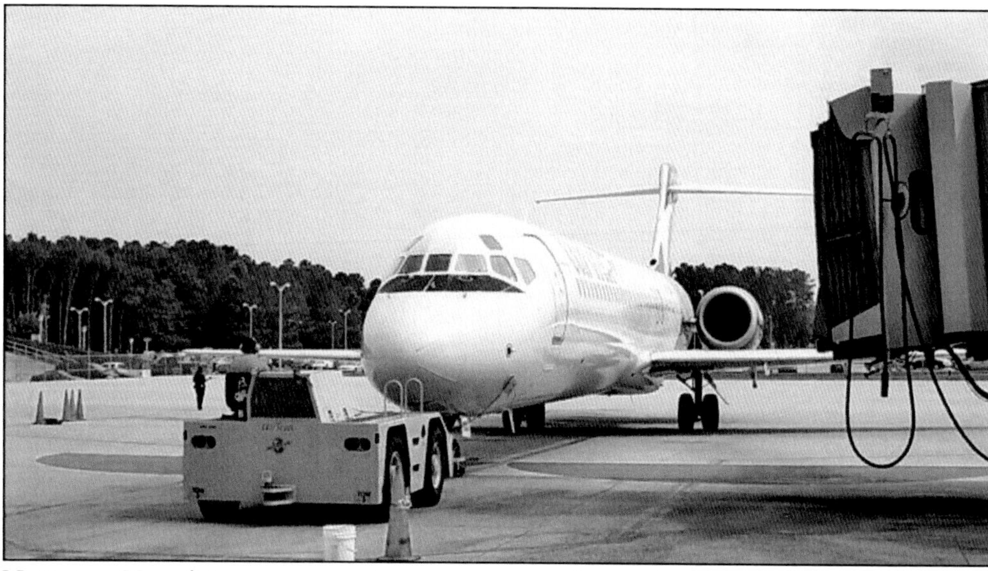

Newport News/Williamsburg International. Today the only thing that remains of Patrick Henry Field is the three-letter airport code: PHF. In 1990, ground was broken on a modern new terminal. When it opened in 1992, the smaller facility, around since 1955, was converted to general aviation use. In addition to service by Delta Airlines and US Airways, flights to Boston, New York City, Atlanta, and Orlando are offered by Air Tran Airways; one of the discount carrier's Boeing 717s is shown in the above photograph. In the photograph below, a fife-and-drum corp celebrate Air Tran's inaugural service to Boston. (NNWI.)

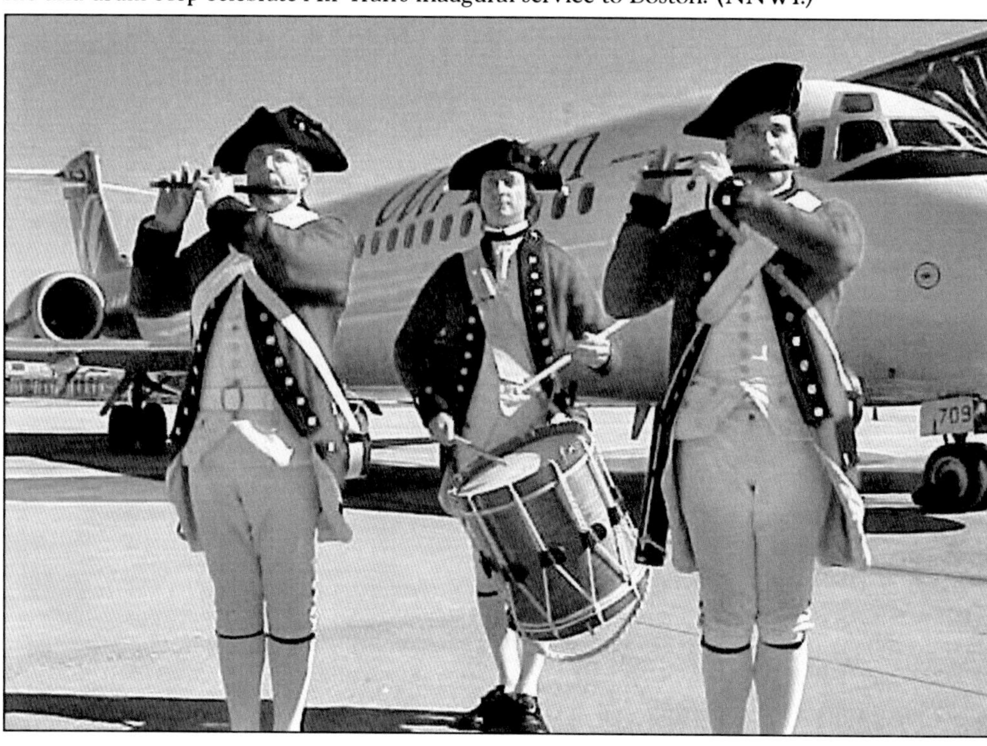

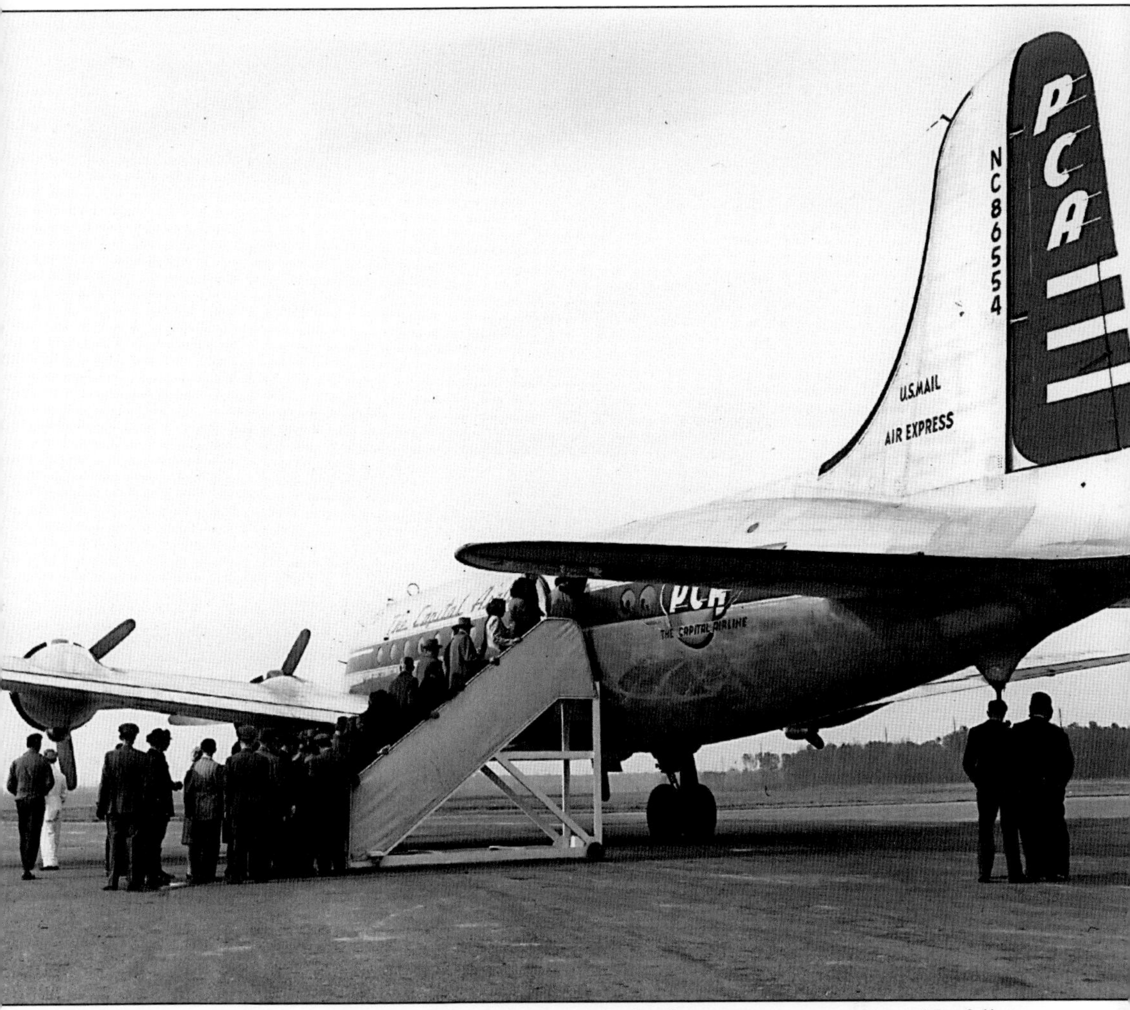

Pennsylvania Central Airlines. This PCA DC-4 is discharging its passengers at Norfolk in the mid-1940s. PCA began flying from Norfolk on April 7, 1938, with combined mail, express, and passenger service. It would not last too long, however; Norfolk Airport was leased by the Army Air Force from 1942 until 1946; after that time PCA returned. The history of Pennsylvania Central goes back to Clifford Ball Airlines in 1926, which later became Pennsylvania Airlines and merged with Central Airlines in 1936. In 1941, the carrier moved its headquarters from Pittsburgh, Pennsylvania, to Washington National Airport in Arlington, and in 1948, PCA changed its name to Capital Airlines. Capital would continue to serve Norfolk until 1961, when the carrier was bought by United Airlines. Today, United still serves Norfolk International Airport. (NPL.)

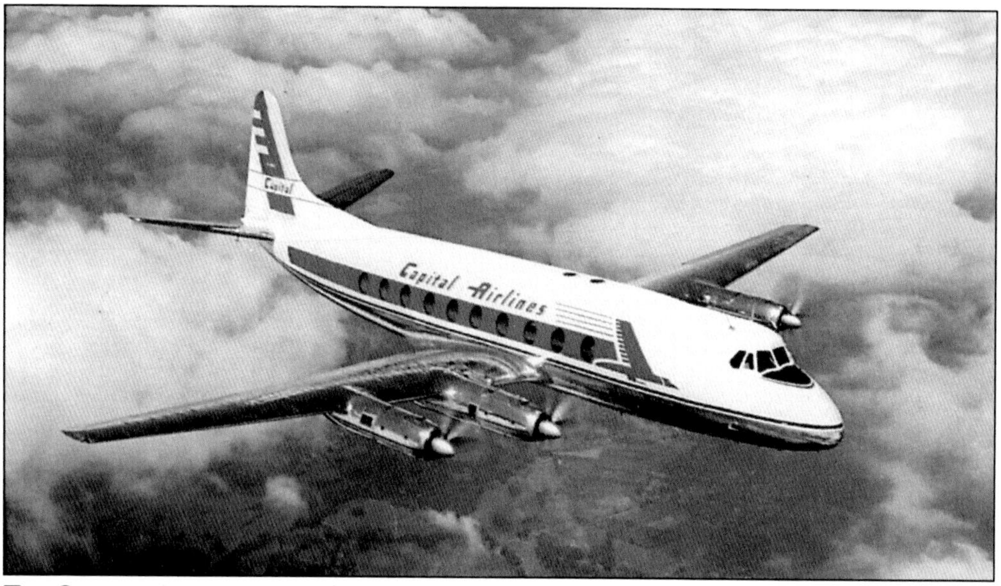

THE CAPITAL AIRLINE. Pennsylvania Central Airlines changed its name to Capital Airlines to reflect their burgeoning route system. The airline began service to Norfolk in 1938. In the above photograph, one of the carrier's Viscount "Capitaliners" is shown in flight. Capital became the first U.S. operator of the British-built Vickers Viscounts, the first passenger turboprop. In the below photograph, the airline's route system in 1947 is examined. From Norfolk, Capital operated routes north, connecting in Washington, D.C., and routes west into North Carolina and points south. After a series of accidents and labor difficulties, the airline began having financial difficulties. On July 1, 1961, it was purchased by United Airlines. (PEH.)

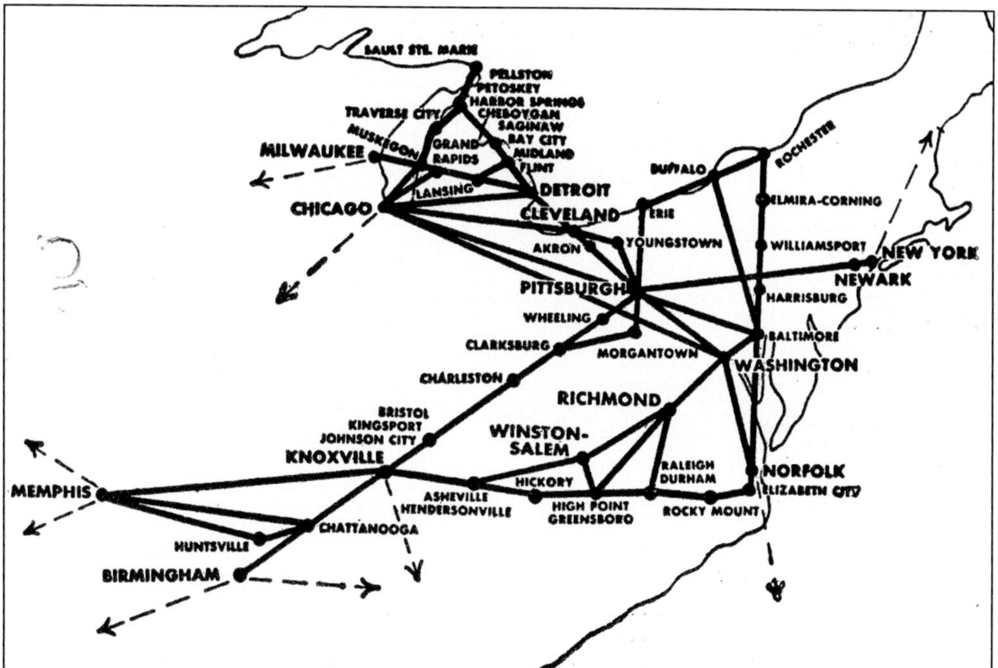

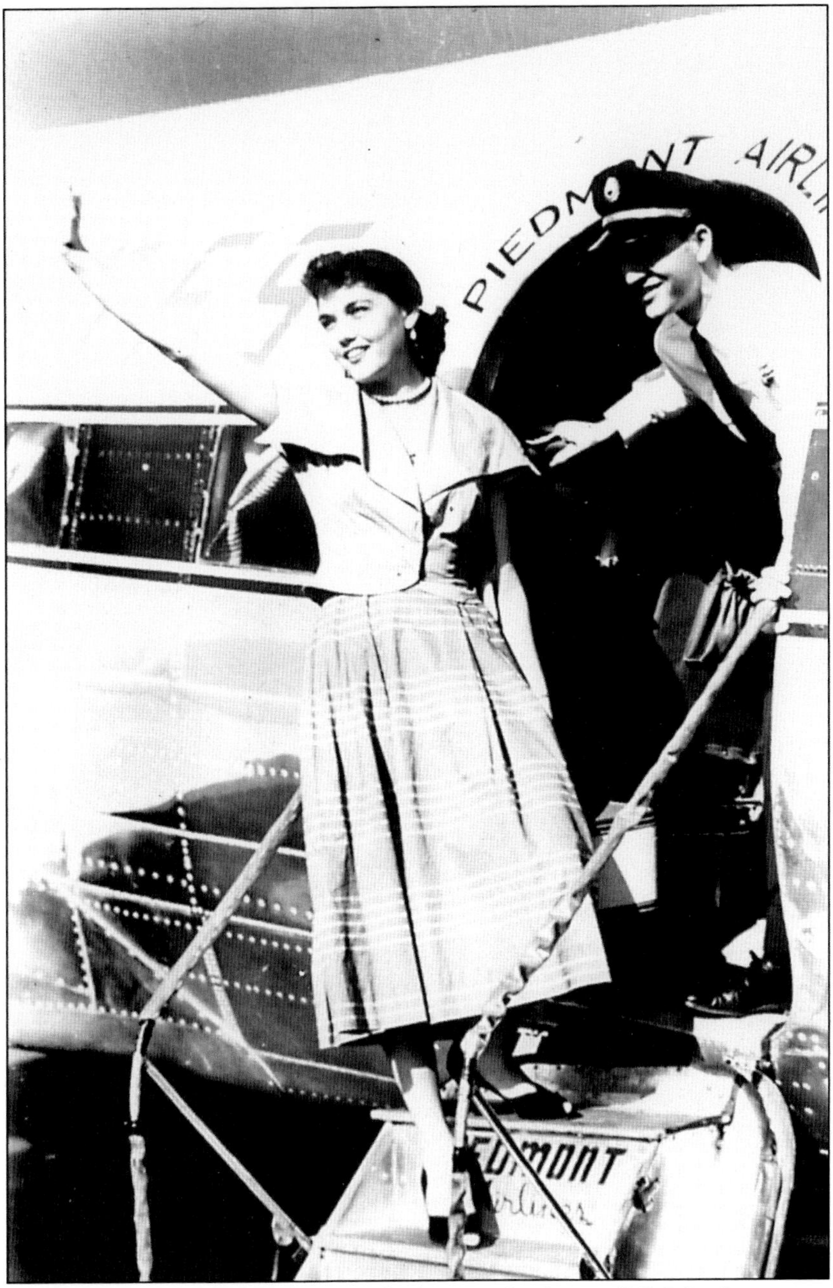

WELCOME ABOARD. This 1948 photograph shows a Piedmont DC-3 loading passengers in Norfolk. This was new service for the region: Piedmont began flying to Norfolk in May 1948 (just three months after it began inaugural service) and continued until 1989, when it was purchased by USAir (now US Airways). In 1949, the airline also served Patrick Henry Field in Newport News. The DC-3 was the workhorse of Piedmont, which made frequent stops in small towns across the region. Later the carrier added Martin 4-0-4 aircraft and, in 1967, entered the jet age with Boeing 727s. After airline deregulation in 1978, Piedmont grew from the smallest of U.S. carriers to the sixth-largest airline with more than 200 jet aircraft flying 25 million passengers annually from Los Angeles to London, with Norfolk in between. (NPL.)

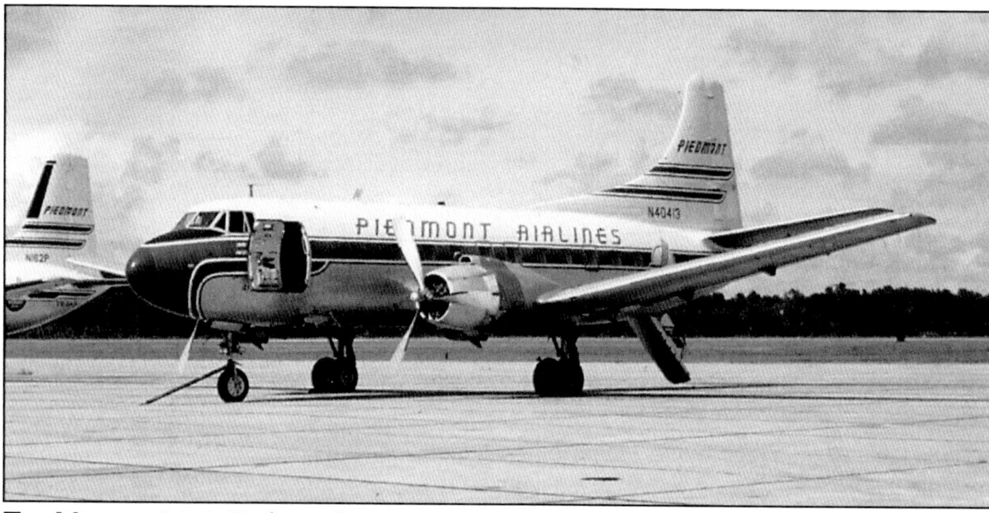

The Martin 4-0-4. Piedmont began service in 1948 utilizing the tried-and-true DC-3, which it flew until 1963. Propeller aircraft used also included the Martin 4-0-4, delivered in 1958 from TWA; these were replaced in 1969 with the Japanese-designed and -built NAMC YS-11. Although jet service was introduced in the late 1960s, prop service was essential for the small towns Piedmonts served. (PEH.)

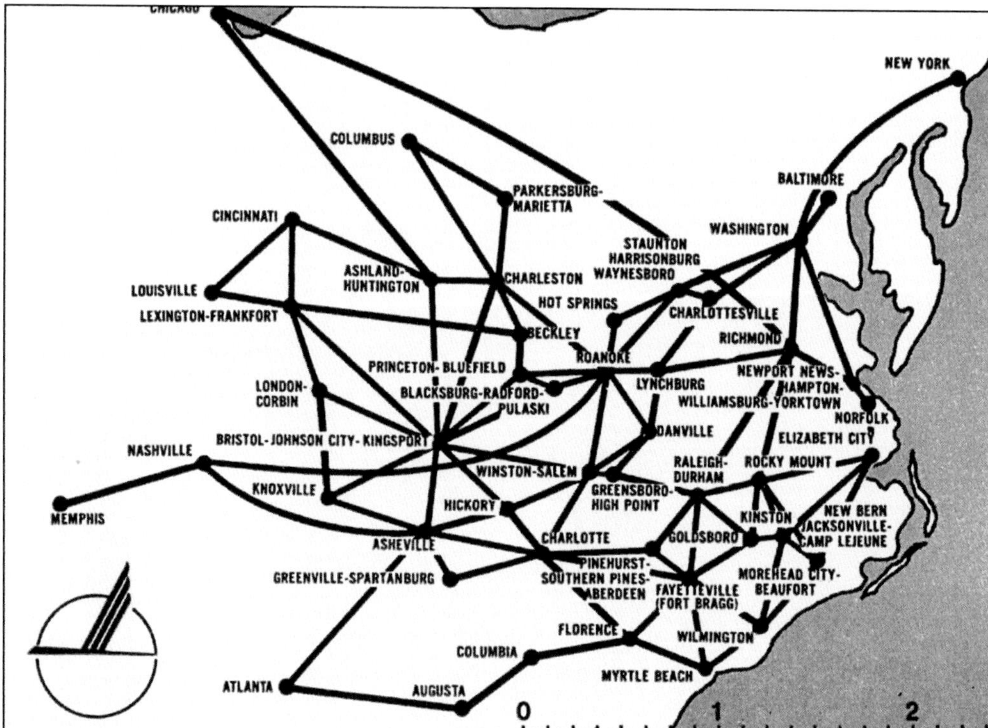

Piedmont's Routes in 1970. Affectionately called Peat-moss Airlines because of the rural, folksy flavor of the carrier, Piedmont, at least until deregulation in 1978, mostly flew to smaller markets. For years, it was the dominant carrier at Norfolk Airport and flew from Patrick Henry Airport in Newport News too. The route of the Pacemakers is shown here from a 1970 flight schedule. (PEH.)

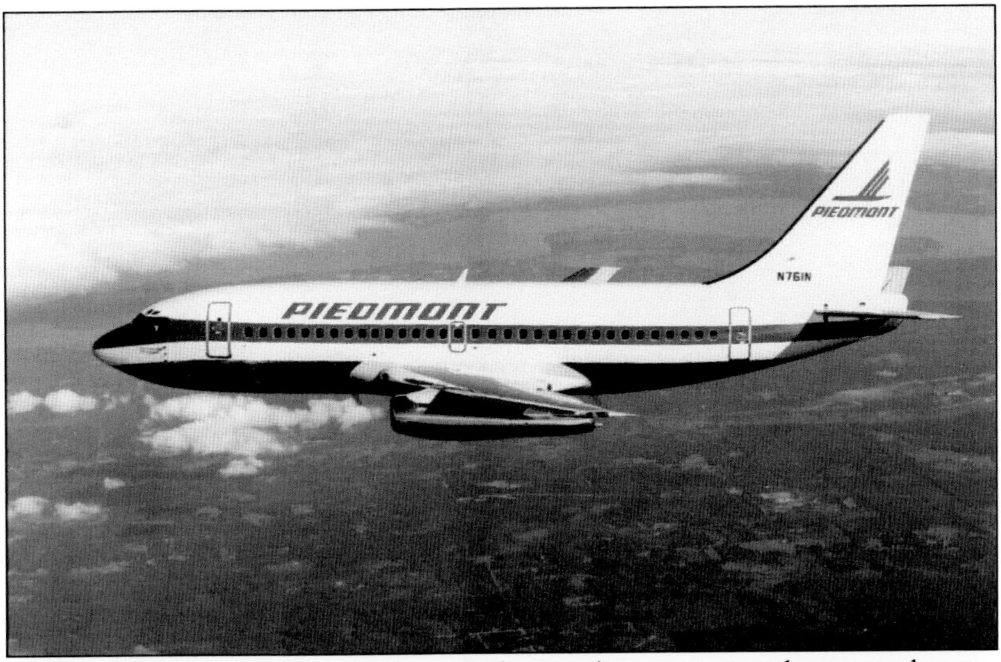

PIEDMONT BOEING 737. This aircraft, in Piedmont colors, was seen perhaps more than any other at Norfolk Airport. Piedmont entered the jet age in 1967 with the addition of Boeing 727s. The next year, the carrier added the Boeing 737, which became, like the DC-3 before it, the workhorse of the fleet. (PEH.)

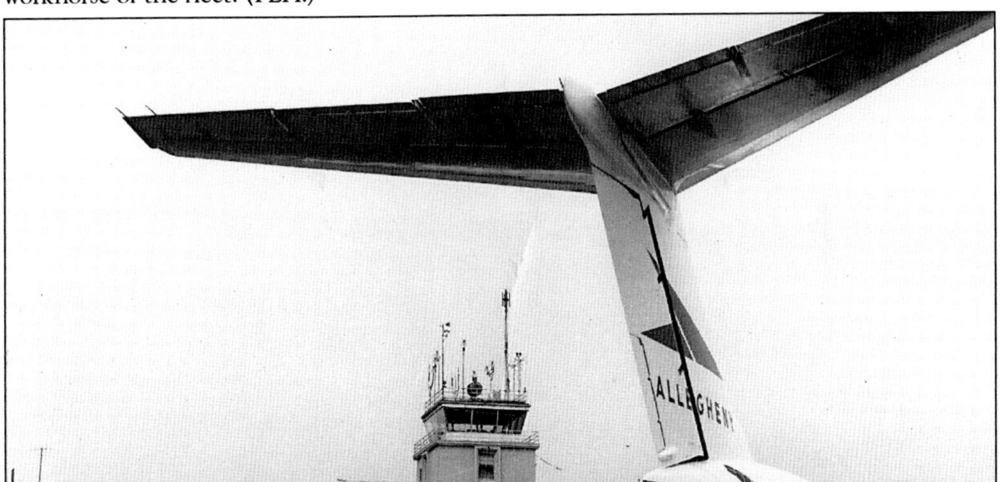

ALLEGHENY AIRLINES. This DC-9 is shown parked in front of Norfolk's 1951 terminal in the late 1960s. Allegheny began in 1939 as All American Aviation and changed its name to Allegheny in 1953. In 1979, the carrier changed its name to USAir (now US Airways) and later bought Piedmont Airlines. Allegheny began service from Norfolk in August 1966. (NPL.)

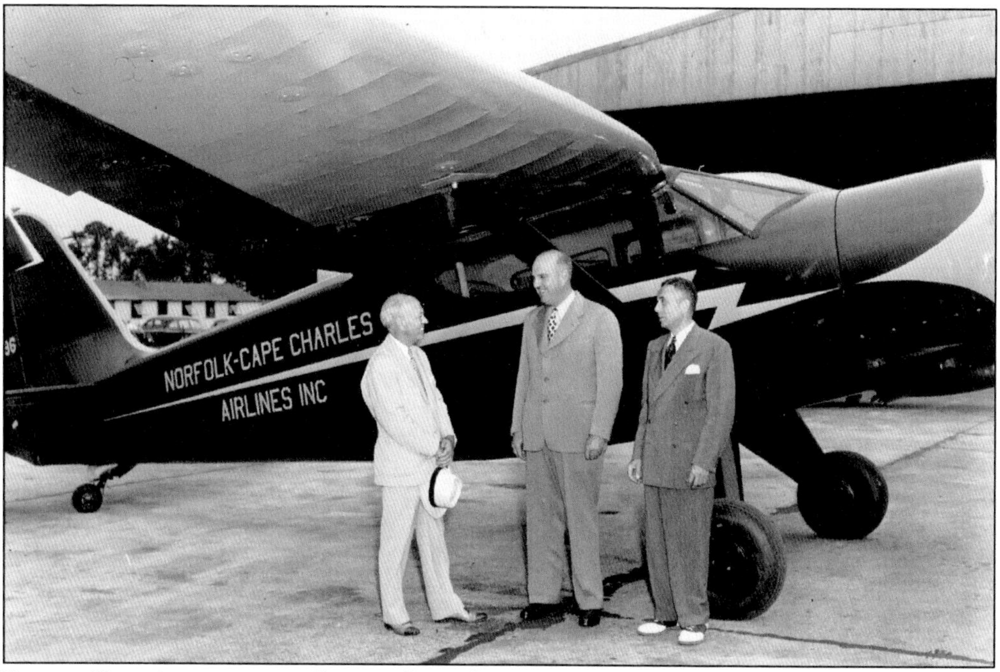

FLYING YOU AROUND THE STATE. Over the years, Hampton Roads has been serviced by several small local carriers, such as Norfolk–Cape Charles Airlines, shown in the above August 1947 photograph, and Air Virginia. One of Air Virginia's British Aerospace HS-748 prop planes is shown in the below photograph. At times, there has even been service between Norfolk International Airport and Newport News/Williamsburg International Airport, but the 15-minute flight was more for passengers continuing on to other destinations rather than those actually traveling between the two cities. Here's another interesting note: Ludington Lines operated a "flag" service between Norfolk and Langley Field in 1932. If passengers were at Langley Field, the plane would stop before continuing on to Washington, D.C. (NIA; PEH.)

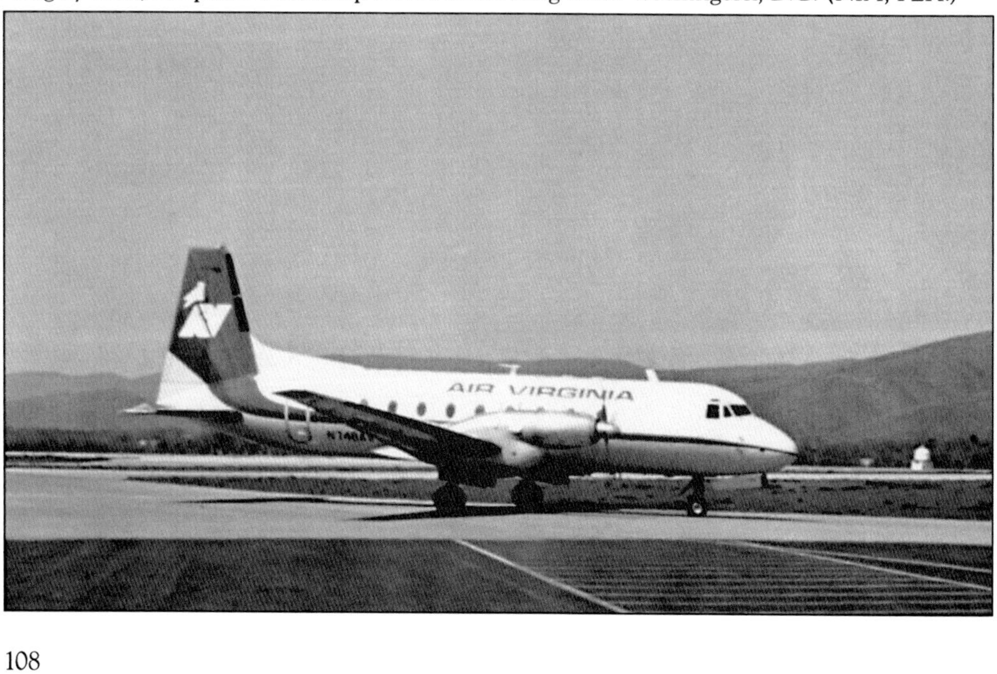

POWER TO THE PEOPLE. Sounding more like a Communist bus system than a low-fare airline, People Express was, all the same, revolutionary. When the airline first took to the skies on April 30, 1981, service was from Newark to just three cities, Norfolk being one of them. At the time, there was nothing quite like People Express, which was truly no frills but very low cost. In the above photograph, part of a flight schedule, showing the low fares from Norfolk to New York City, is illustrated. In the below photograph, the hub-and-spoke system from Newark to Norfolk and other destinations is apparent. Unfortunately, success became too much and the carrier rapidly grew, causing financial and labor problems. It was purchased by Continental Airlines in 1987. (PEH.)

PEOPLExpress

From:

NORFOLK/ VIRGINIA BEACH, VA

Norfolk Reservations—(804) 625-6029
Peninsula Area Reservations—(804) 877-2272

To New York, NY/Newark, NJ

All Flights Arrive North Terminal, Newark Int'l Airport

7:25a	8:25a	141	Daily	0	$35	$23
10:35a	11:35a	143	Daily	0	$35	$23
1:35p	2:35p	145	Daily	0	$35	$23
4:30p	5:30p	144	Daily	0	$35	$23
7:25p	8:30p	147	Daily	0	$23	$23
10:30p	11:30p	149	Daily	0	$23	$23

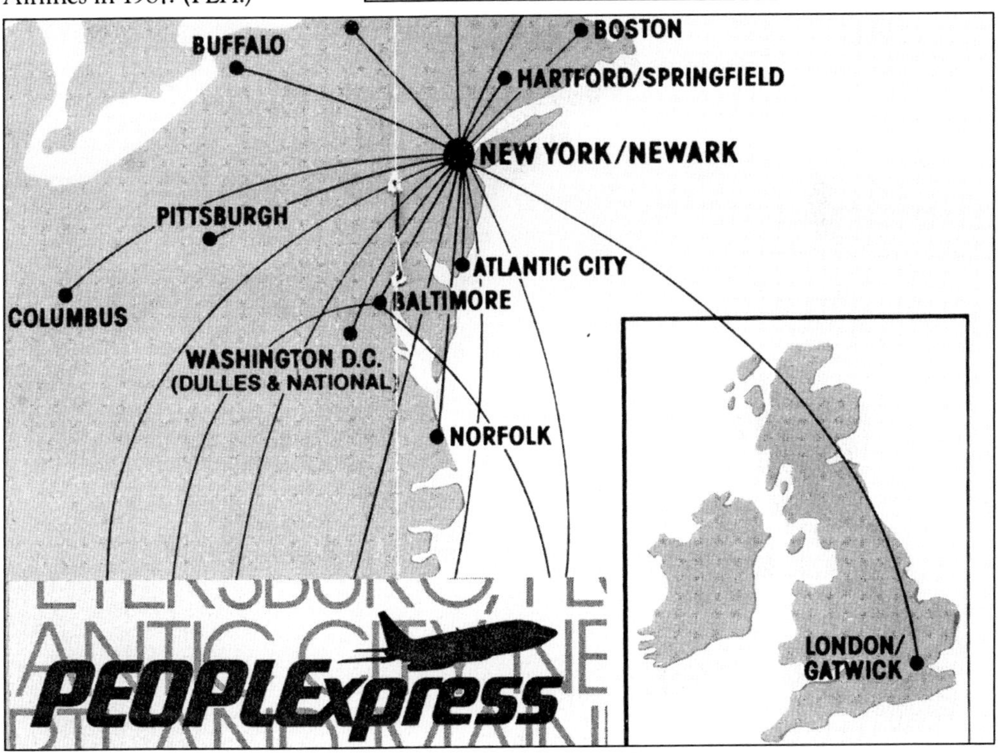

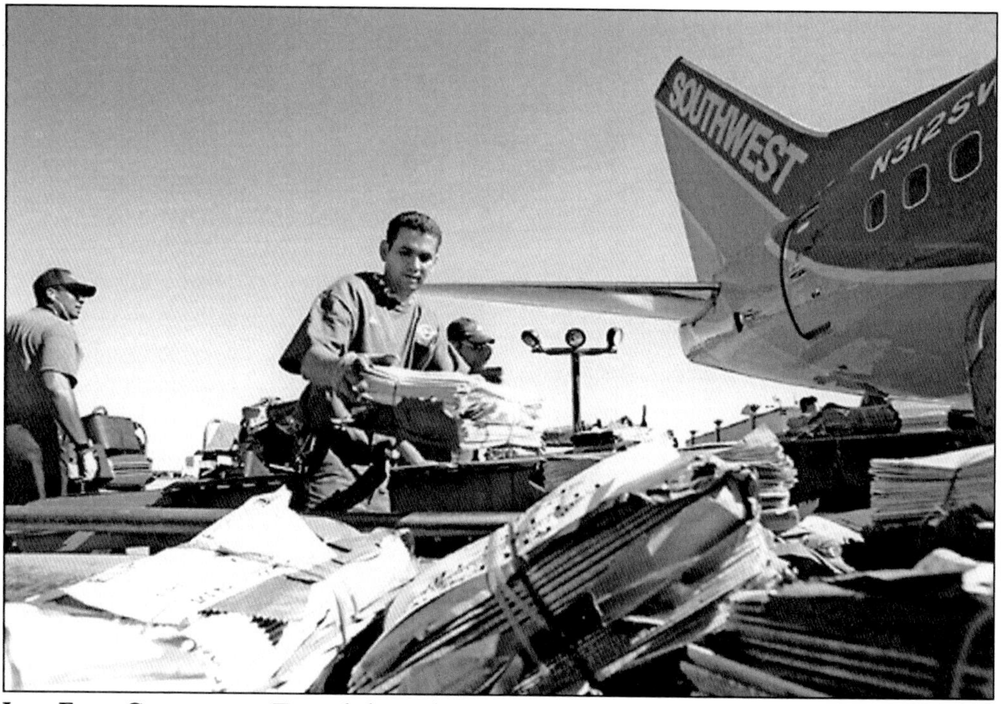

LOW-FARE CHAMPIONS. Two of the industry's top-ranked low-cost carriers serve Hampton Roads. Southwest Airlines (http://www.southwest.com) flies from Norfolk International Airport to Baltimore, Chicago, Las Vegas, Jacksonville, and Orlando. In the above picture, one reason for their success—streamlined efficiency—is demonstrated by ramp agents. One of their Boeing 737 airplanes is shown. Air Tran Airways (http://www.airtran.com) flies from Newport News/Williamsburg International Airport to Boston, New York City, Atlanta, and Orlando. One of their Boeing 717 airplanes is shown in the below photograph. (Above: Southwest Airlines, photograph by David Woo; below: Air Tran Airways.)

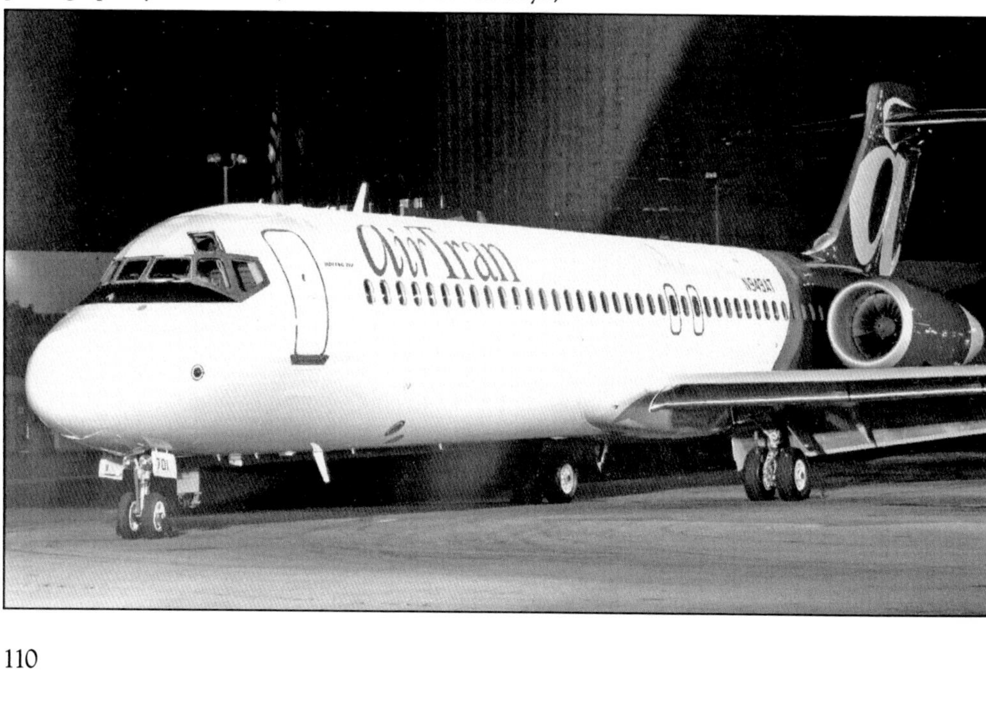

Five

Flying High

Hampton Roads is a military town, from air, sea and land. Look to the skies over Hampton Roads, and you are likely to see a number of aircraft, ranging from Coast Guard helicopters to Air Force F-15 Eagles and Navy F/A-18s. You might even see a rocket being launched into space from Wallops Island, just up the Eastern Shore.

From the marshy land that became Langley Air Force Base and the NASA Langley Research Center to the mudflats that became Naval Air Station Oceana, military aviation is widespread across the region.

And that presence continues to grow.

At NASA Langley Research Center, scientists do daily research in aeronautics. At Naval Station Norfolk, flight operations occur on the average of every six minutes; it is the world's largest naval base. At NAS Oceana, more than 200,000 flight operations happen annually, making it the world's largest air station.

Military aviation has come a long way in Hampton Roads from Eugene Ely's first flight in his Curtiss biplane off the deck of a naval ship and from the bombardment of battleships off the Virginia Capes by Billy Mitchell.

On the horizon are new-generation stealth fighters that look like something from Area 51; experimental craft that can take off like a conventional airplane but reach the limits of outer space; and fighter jets that operate on glass cockpit technology while flying at supersonic speeds.

It's an aspect of the armed forces that is really taking off.

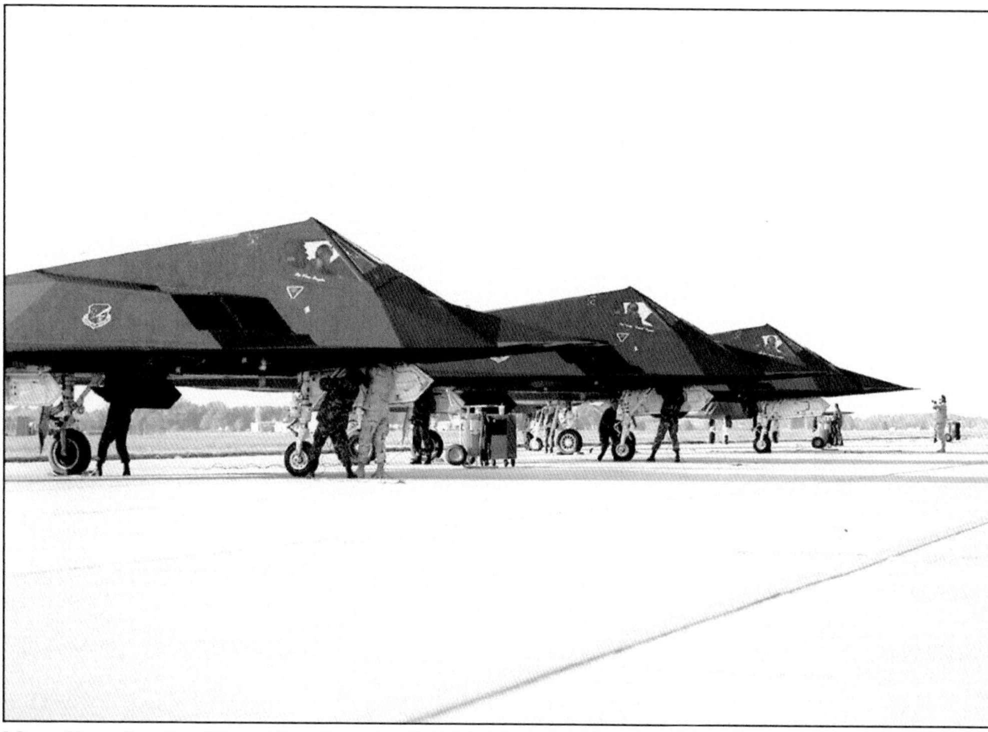

Now You See It, Now You Don't. F-117A Nighthawk aircraft park along the flight line at Langley Air Force Base. The F-117A is the world's first operational aircraft designed to exploit low-observable stealth technology. It does so by the use of various radar-absorbent materials, grid covers on the intakes, and the use of narrow-slot "platypus" exhausts surrounded by heat-absorbing tiles. (Air Force photograph by S.Sgt. Vince Parker.)

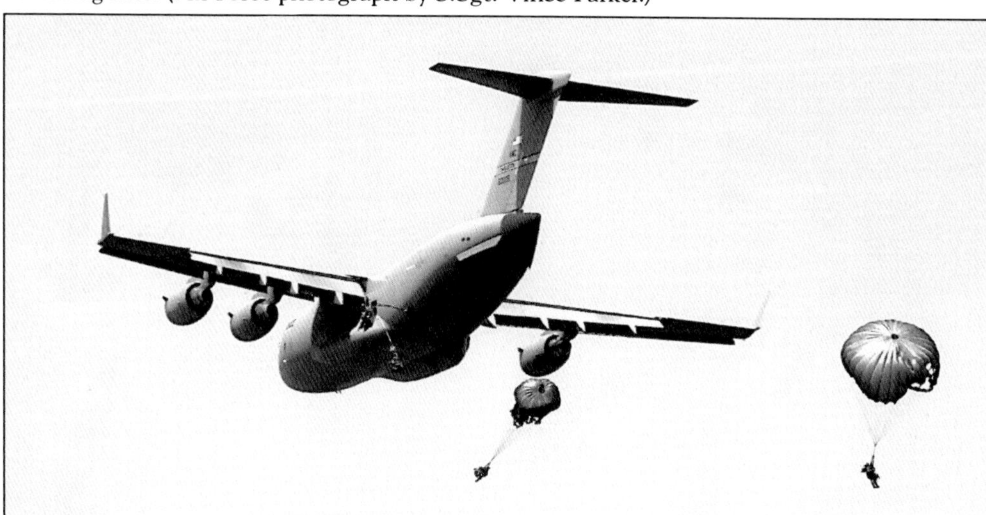

Look, Up in the Sky. Red Horse paratroopers jump out of a C-17 Globemaster III during the 2004 Langley Air Show. The popular event, held each spring, showcases a variety of military aircraft, as does the Oceana Air Show, held at Naval Air Station Oceana each fall. Both feature demonstrations and performances as well as static displays. (Air Force photograph by S.Sgt. Dawn M. Bolen.)

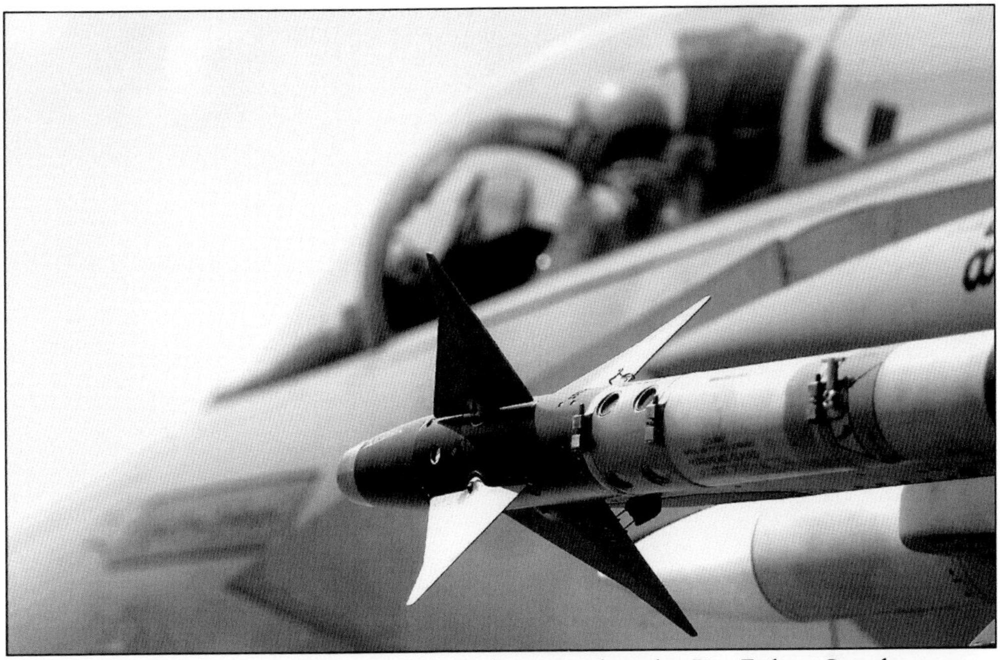

FLY HIGHER THAN AN EAGLE. An F-15 Eagle assigned to the 71st Fighter Squadron moves into position for take-off before a sortie supporting Operation Noble Eagle at Langley Air Force Base. The F-15 is a frequent sight at Langley. It has an unequaled combination of performance, firepower, and avionics. (Air Force photograph by T.Sgt. Ben Bloker.)

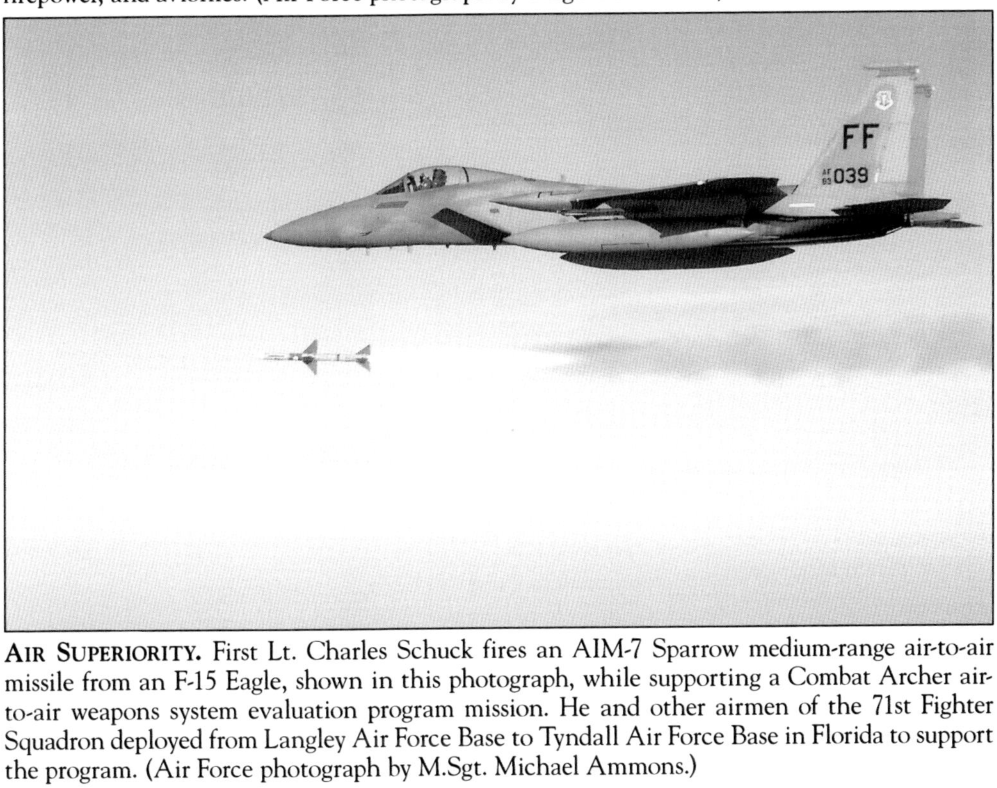

AIR SUPERIORITY. First Lt. Charles Schuck fires an AIM-7 Sparrow medium-range air-to-air missile from an F-15 Eagle, shown in this photograph, while supporting a Combat Archer air-to-air weapons system evaluation program mission. He and other airmen of the 71st Fighter Squadron deployed from Langley Air Force Base to Tyndall Air Force Base in Florida to support the program. (Air Force photograph by M.Sgt. Michael Ammons.)

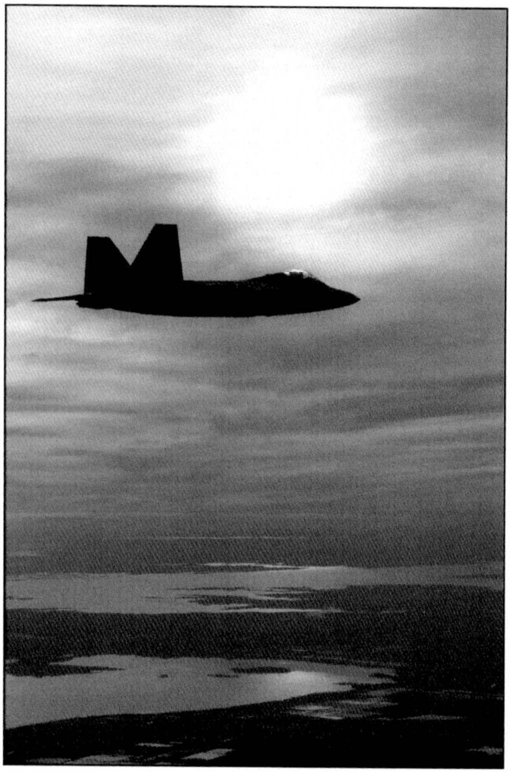

A New Bird in the Sky. Now seen over Hampton Roads are the new F/A-22 Raptors, as shown in this photograph. Langley Air Force Base was slotted to be the home of the first operational squadron of the F/A-22s. The fast, agile, and stealthy F/A-22s are meant to be successors to the F-15. New technology assures the Raptor air superiority. (Air Force photograph by T.Sgt. Ben Bloker.)

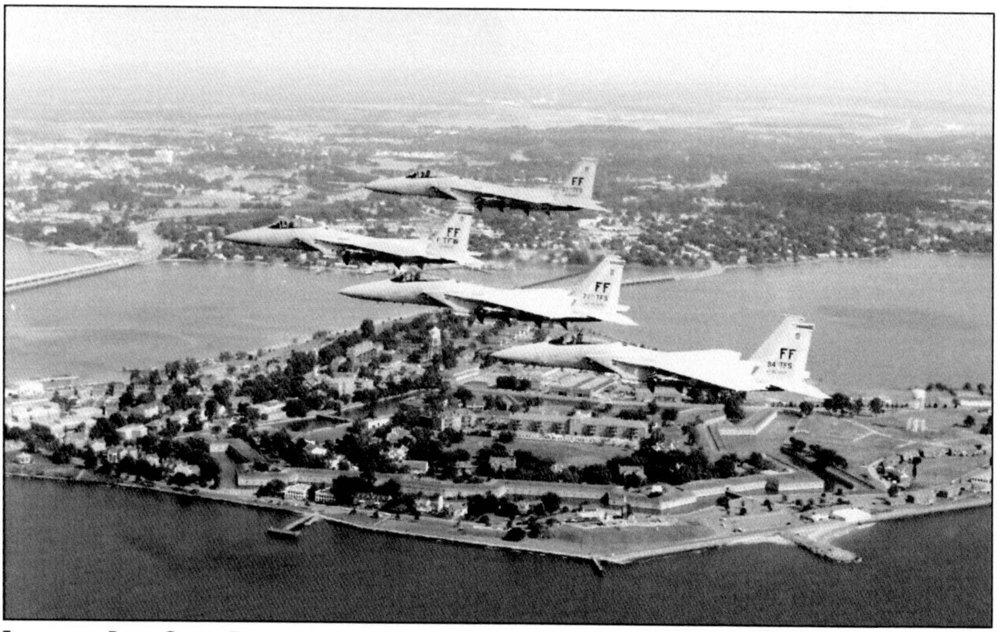

Langley Jets Over Fort Monroe. Langley Air Force Base is among the oldest continuously active air bases in the United States. Langley is home to the First Fighter Wing, with a mission of maintaining combat capability for rapid global deployment to conduct air superiority operations. It does so with the F-15 Eagle. Covering some 2,900 acres, Langley is home to more than 10,000 military personnel and civilian employees. (VASC.)

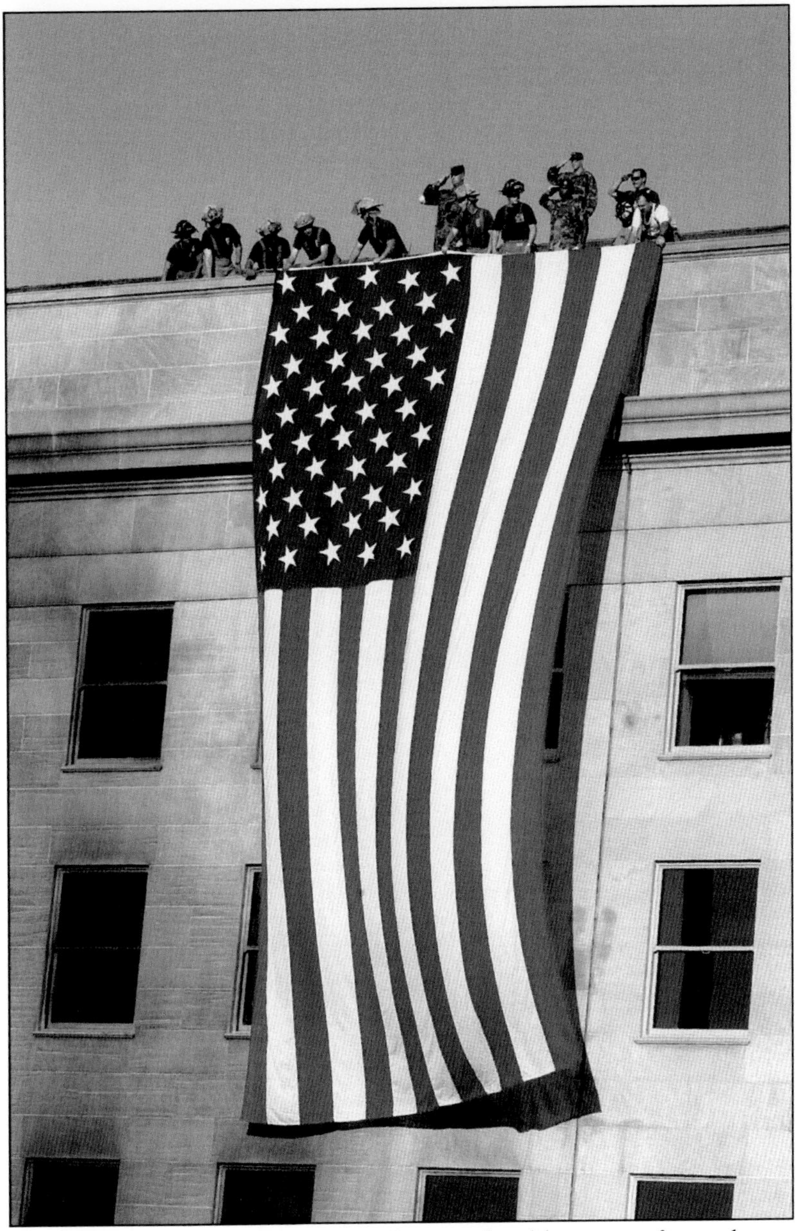

Remembering September 11. Military members rendered honors as fire and rescue workers unfurled a huge American flag over the side of the Pentagon during research and recovery work following the September 11 terrorist attack. American Airlines Flight 77, which had left Washington's Dulles International Airport, was hijacked and flown into the side of the building at 9:37 a.m. Langley Air Force Base played a role in the events of that day: when it was apparent the American flight had been hijacked, three F-16 jets flown by the 119th Air National Guard Fighter Wing from Langley Air Force Base were ordered to try to intercept the American flight. Unfortunately, by the time they reached Northern Virginia, the jet had already crashed into the Pentagon. The F-16s were then switched to intercept United Airlines Flight 93, but that plane had crashed into a field in rural Pennsylvania when they arrived. (U.S. Navy photograph by Michael W. Pendergrass.)

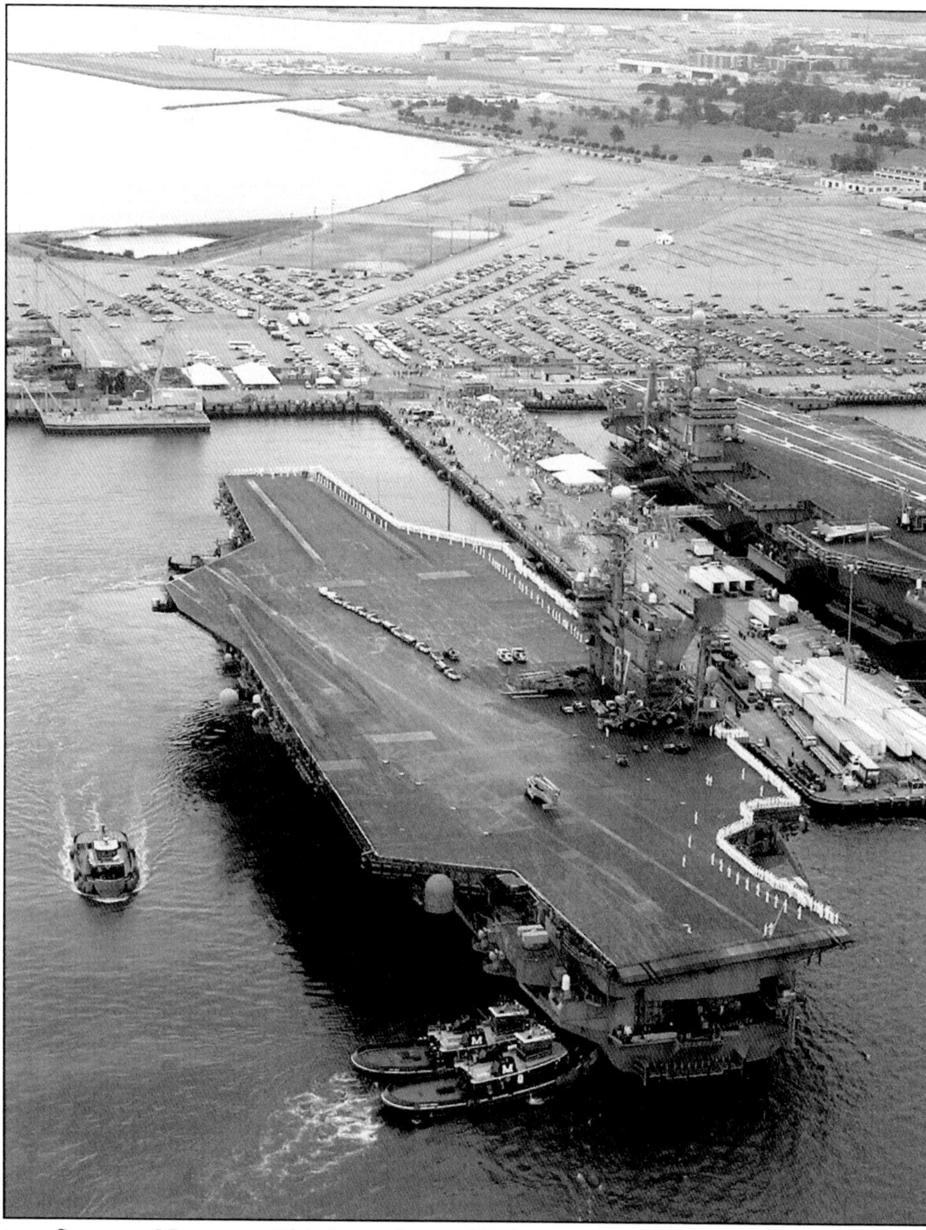

NAVAL STATION NORFOLK. This base, the world's largest naval station, occupies about 4,300 acres in the Sewell's Point area of Norfolk. When the 75 ships and 134 aircraft homeported at Naval Station Norfolk (like the aircraft carrier shown in this photograph) are not at sea, they are alongside one of the 13 piers or inside one of the 11 aircraft hangers on site for repair, refitting, or training. Naval Station Norfolk is homeport to aircraft carriers; cruisers; destroyers; large amphibious ships; submarines; a variety of supply and logistics ships; C-2, C-9, C-12, and E-2 fixed-wing aircraft; and H-3, H-46, H-53, and H-60 helicopters. Not only is the port busy, but the skies over the base are, too: air operations conducts more than 100,000 flight operations annually, or one every six minutes. Naval Station Norfolk started training aviators at Naval Air Detachment, Curtiss Field in Newport News in May 1917; about five months later, the detachment was moved to this facility, which had room for expansion. (HRNM.)

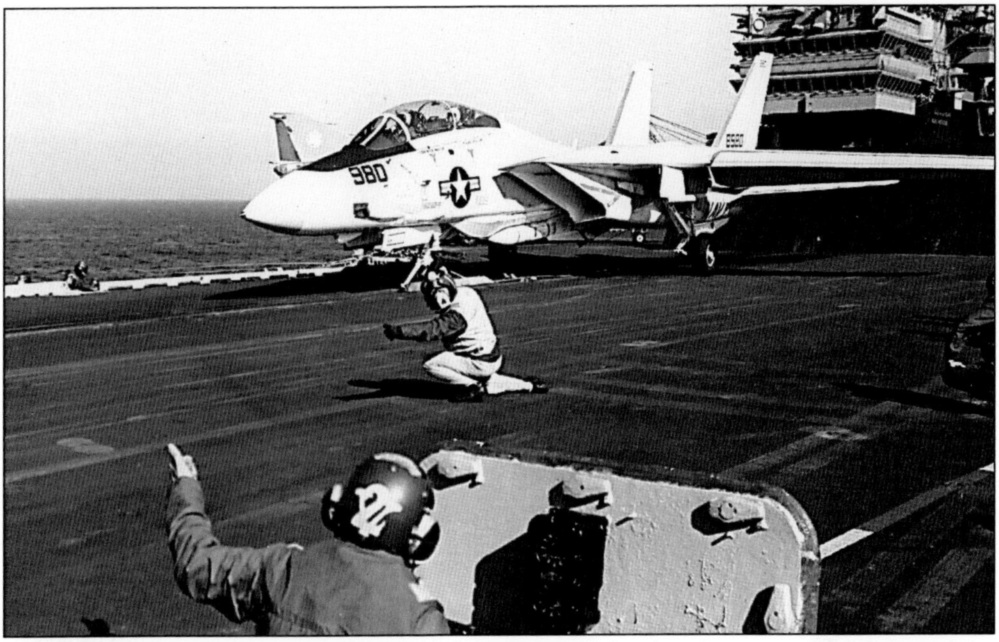

LET 'ER RIP. The thumbs are up and the launch is a go for this Grumman F-14 Tomcat from the aircraft carrier *Forrestal*, operating off the Virginia Capes. A number of aircraft carriers call Naval Station Norfolk port, with their flight wing being attached to various air stations, such as NAS Oceana. (HRNM.)

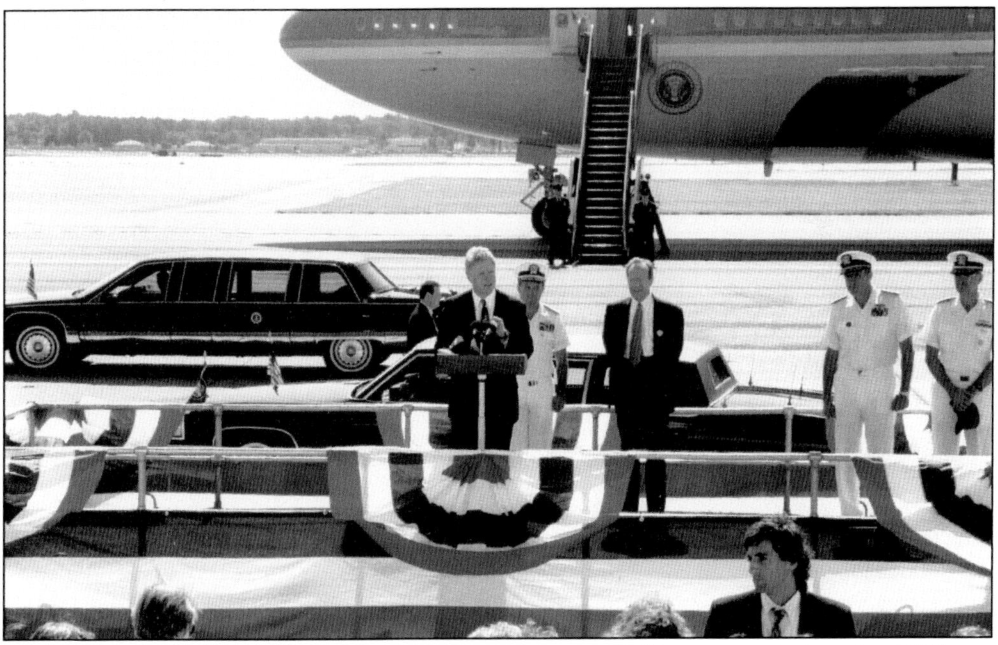

HAIL TO THE CHIEF. Naval Station Norfolk receives many VIP guests, including this 1995 visit by Pres. Bill Clinton. The air facilities at the base are large enough to handle any size aircraft, such as Air Force One, a Boeing 747. More than 150,000 passengers and 264,000 tons of mail and cargo depart annually on Air Mobility Command aircraft and other chartered flights from the field. (HRNM.)

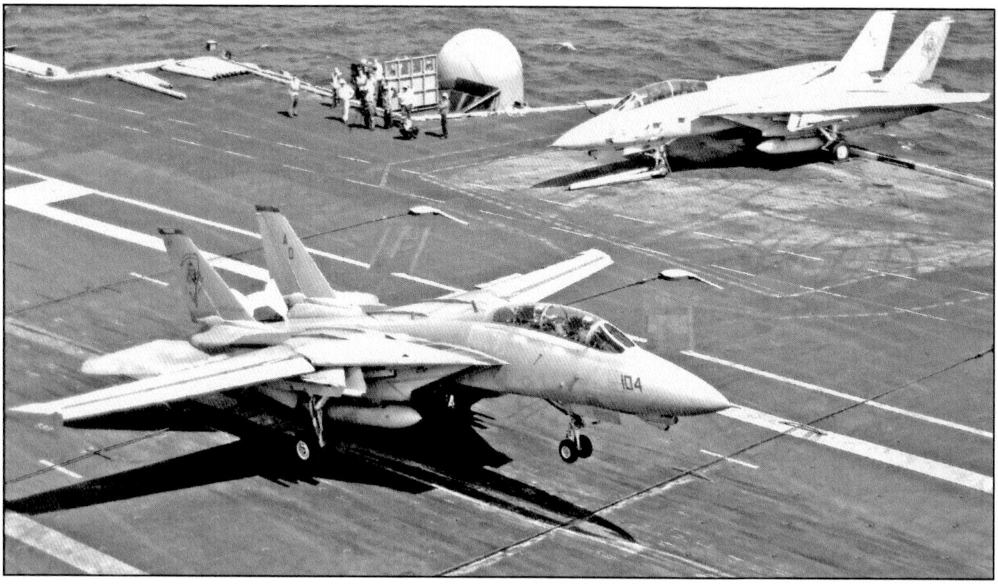

NAVAL AIR STATION OCEANA. Around since 1940, NAS Oceana continues to be an aviation powerhouse in Hampton Roads. In fact, this Master Jet Base has grown to become one of the largest and most advanced air stations in the world. From the four runways at this Virginia Beach facility, some 219,000 training operations are flown annually. A number of aircraft, such as the ones pictured here, call NAS Oceana home, including F-14 Tomcats, F/A-18 Hornets, F/A-18E/F Super Hornets, and H-3 Sea King helicopters. Also under the command of NAS Oceana is Naval Auxiliary Landing Field Fentress in Chesapeake, Naval Station Norfolk Chambers Field, and the Navy Dare County Range in North Carolina. (NASO.)

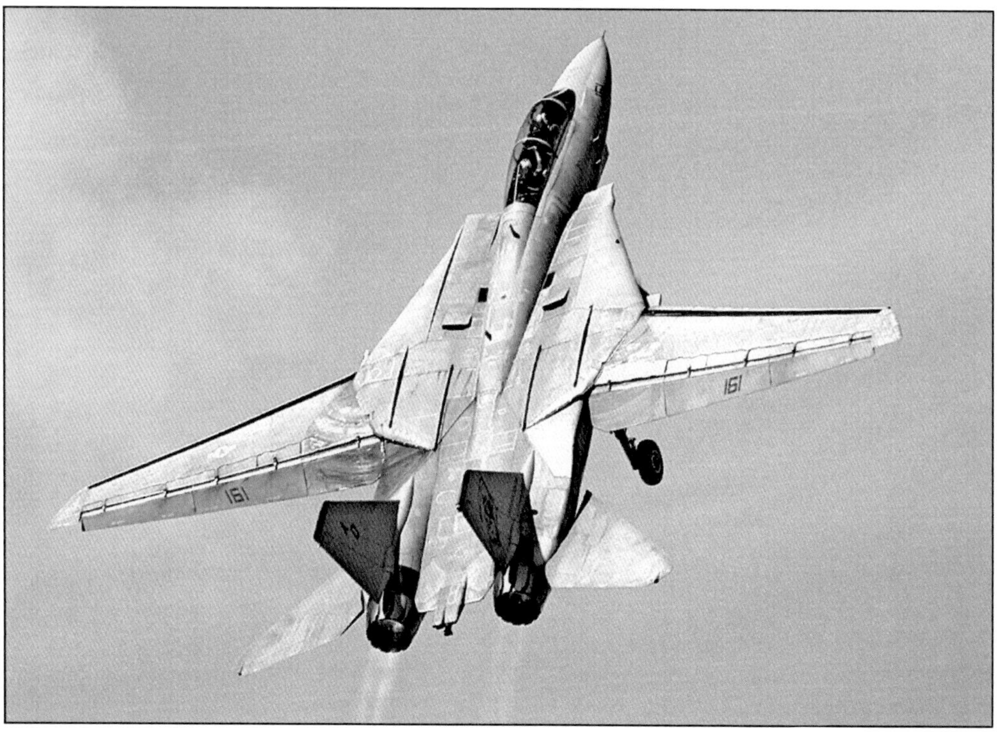

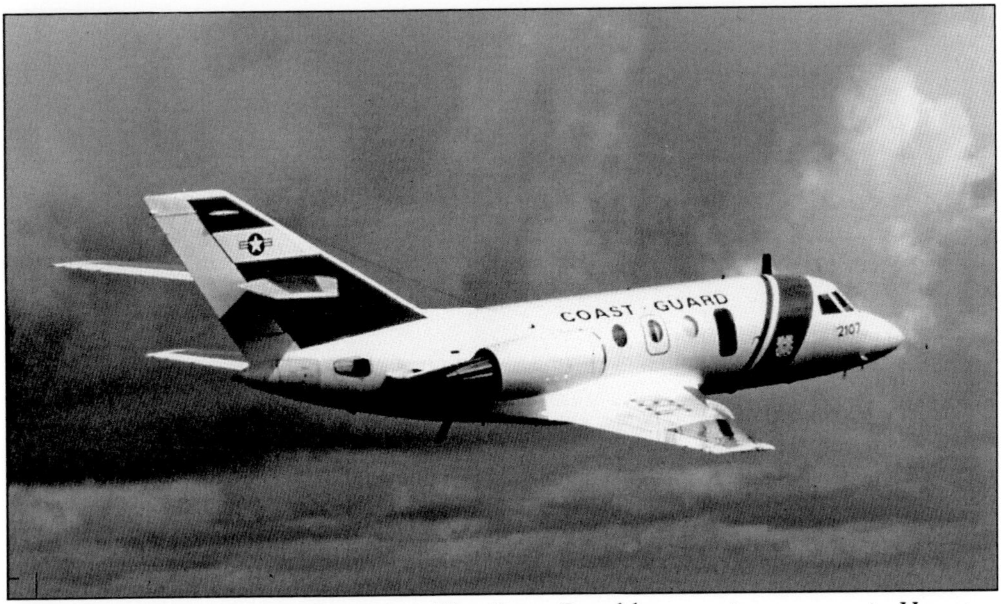

FIFTH U.S. COAST GUARD DISTRICT. The Coast Guard has a major presence in Hampton Roads; the Fifth District is headquartered in Portsmouth. From these offices, units are managed and supported to encompass not only Virginia, but also North Carolina, Maryland, Delaware, and parts of New Jersey and Pennsylvania. Within the district, there are numerous fields of operation utilizing 10 helicopters, four C-130 aircraft, and more. Some aircraft, like that shown above, are used for transport and patrol. Other, like the helicopter in the below photograph, carry out search-and-rescue mission. There are more than 4,300 active-duty Coasties and some 810 reservists within the Fifth District. (Old Coast Guard Station.)

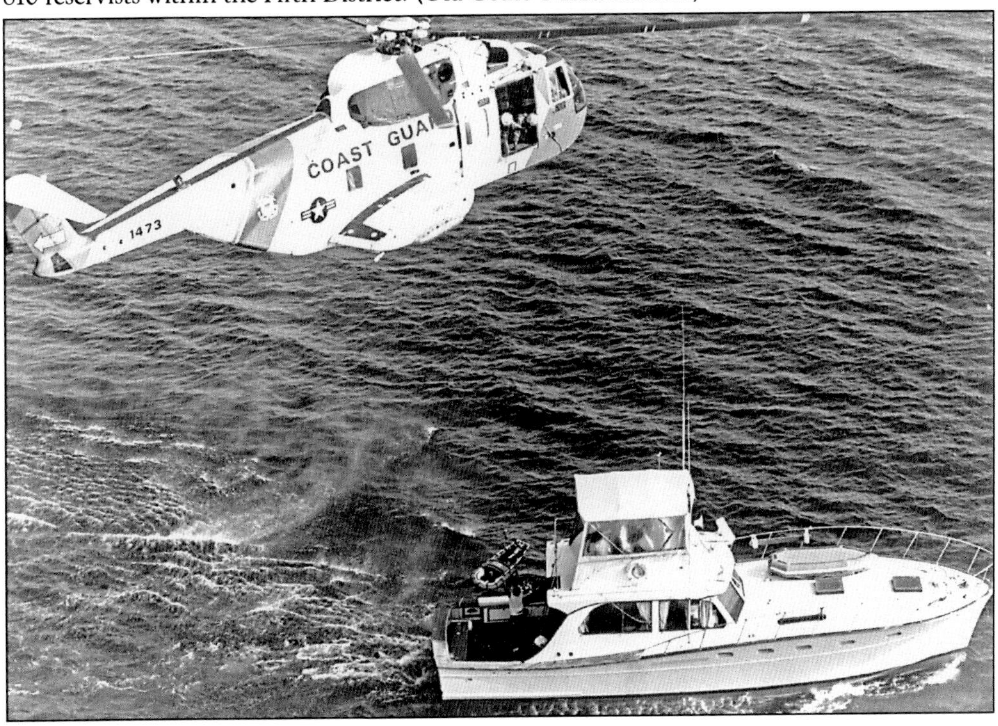

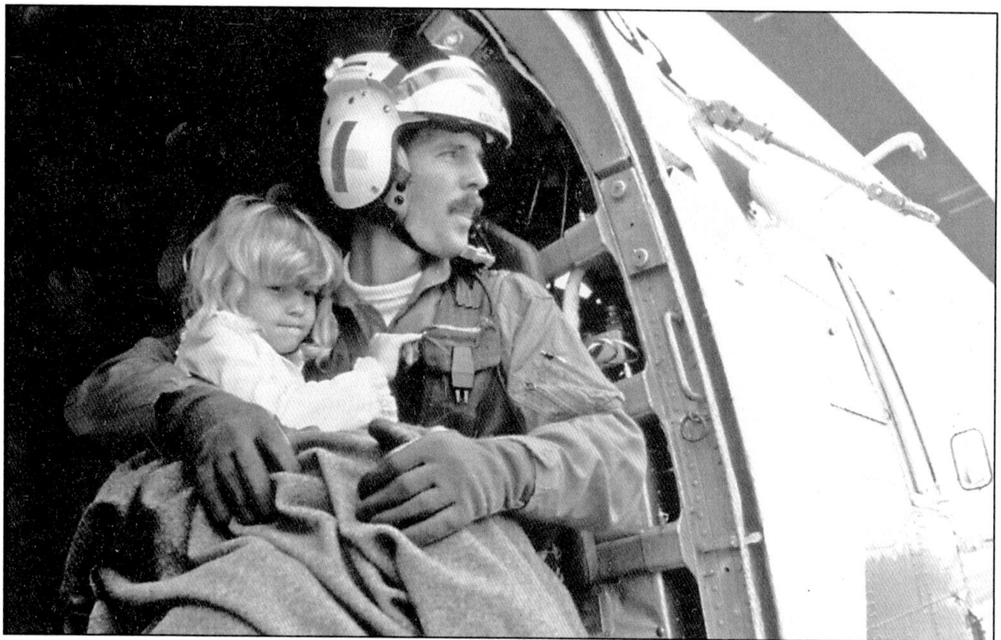

GUARDING THE COAST, AND MORE. One of the nation's five armed services, the Coast Guard's mission is to protect the public, environment, and U.S. economic interests in the nation's ports and waterways, along the coast, on international waters, and in other maritime regions. The Coast Guard is largely thought of for the many search-and-rescue missions it operates, as shown in the above photograph. It also patrols coastlines in defense of the country, especially post-9/11, as shown in the below photograph of a Coastie helicopter over Virginia Beach. The Coast Guard's Fifth District is headquartered in Hampton Roads, and there is a large presence at a number of area bases and fields; this includes Air Station Elizabeth City (North Carolina), which operates a number of aircraft, such as the HH-60 Jayhawk and HC-130 Hercules. (Old Coast Guard Station.)

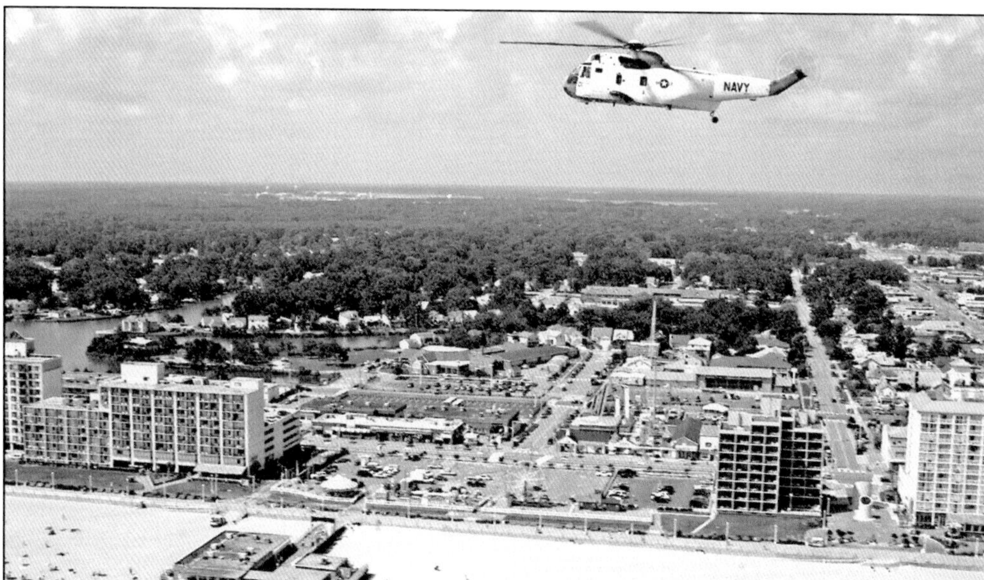

Six

How to Contact

Aviation is all around in Hampton Roads: all one needs to do is look to the skies and perhaps spy a commercial airliner leaving Norfolk International Airport or the Newport News/Williamsburg International Airport.

Maybe you would see an F-15 Eagle or one of the new F/A-22 Raptors streaking over Langley Air Force Base or a F/A-18E/F Super Hornet from Naval Air Station Oceana flying over the Virginia Beach oceanfront.

Across the region, there are a number of museums, monuments, and other venues dedicated in whole or in part to the legacy of flight in Hampton Roads.

Museums like the Virginia Air and Space Center richly chronicle commercial and military aviation advancements in the Commonwealth, especially the race for space and the amazing work done at NASA Langley Research Center. Other museums, like the Hampton Roads Naval Museum and Old Coast Guard Station, also touch on the importance of flight in the region.

Both commercial airports have areas where jets can be observed, and there are places for plane spotters to see aircraft movement at Oceana as well.

Here are some places to check out to keep your head in the clouds.

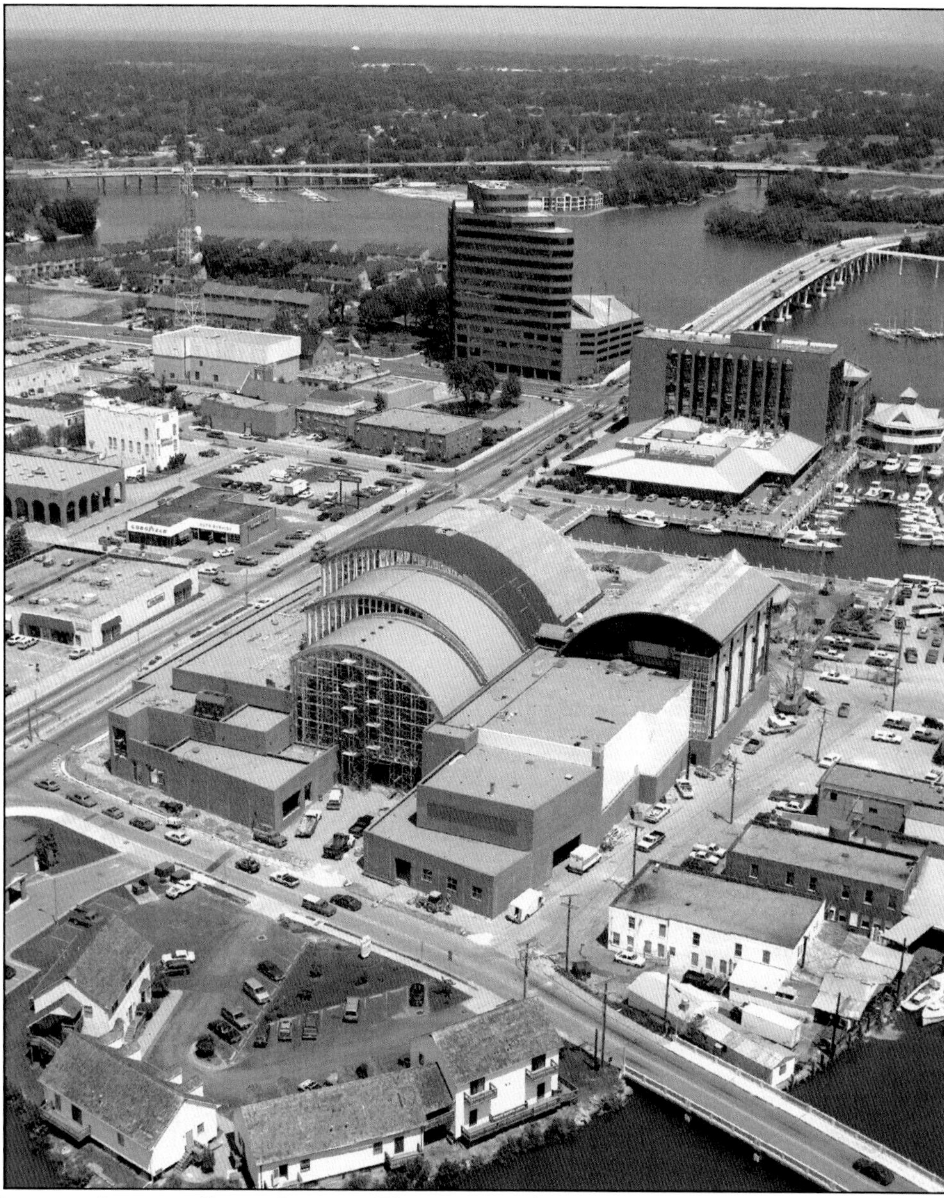

VIRGINIA AIR AND SPACE CENTER. This museum features dozens of hands-on air and space exhibits, an interactive aviation gallery that spans 100 years of flight, more than 30 historic aircraft, unique space flight artifacts, and more. Visitors can take the control of a flight simulator, climb aboard a World War II bomber, see the Apollo 12 Command Module that went to the moon (it returned to earth on November 24, 1969), observe a Mars meteorite, walk though an Air Tran DC-9 passenger jet suspended from the ceiling, and examine a replica of the 1903 Wright flyer. In addition to those displays, the Virginia Air and Space Center also offers a 3-D IMAX theater. The visitor center for NASA Langley Research Center and Langley Air Force Base, it is a must-see for aviation buffs. There is also an extensive gift shop on site. The center is open year-round, and admission for adults runs $8.75. The Virginia Air and Space Center is located in downtown Hampton at 600 Settlers Landing Road. The phone number is (757) 727-0900. The Web site is http://www.vasc.org.

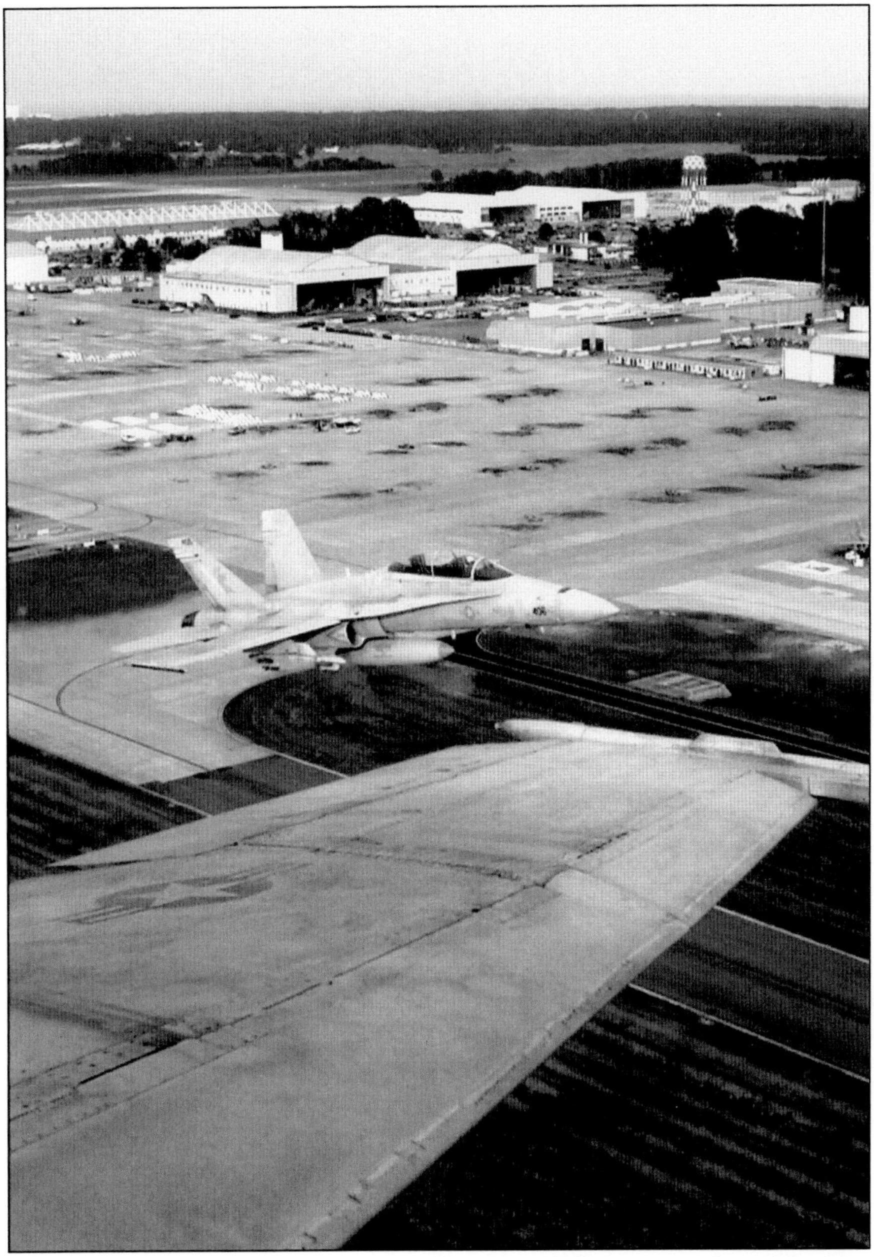

HAMPTON ROADS TRANSIT TOURS. Although not generally open to the public, Naval Air Station (NAS) Oceana and Norfolk Naval Air Station are open for tours seasonally through Hampton Roads Transit (HRT), the region's public transportation system. The NAS Oceana tour gives visitors a look at the more than 300 jet aircraft that call NAS Oceana home, including F-14 Tomcats and F/A-18 Hornets. Tours run June through September and cost $7.50 for adults. The Norfolk Naval Air Station tour takes visitors dockside to the home of the Atlantic Fleet for a look at aircraft carriers, destroyers, submarines, and other U.S. Navy aircraft and vessels. Tours run March through December and cost $7.50 for adults. The phone number for HRT is (757) 222-6100. The Web site is http://www.hrtransit.org/trolleytours.html. (U.S. Navy photograph by Photographer's Mate 1C Matthew J. Thomas.)

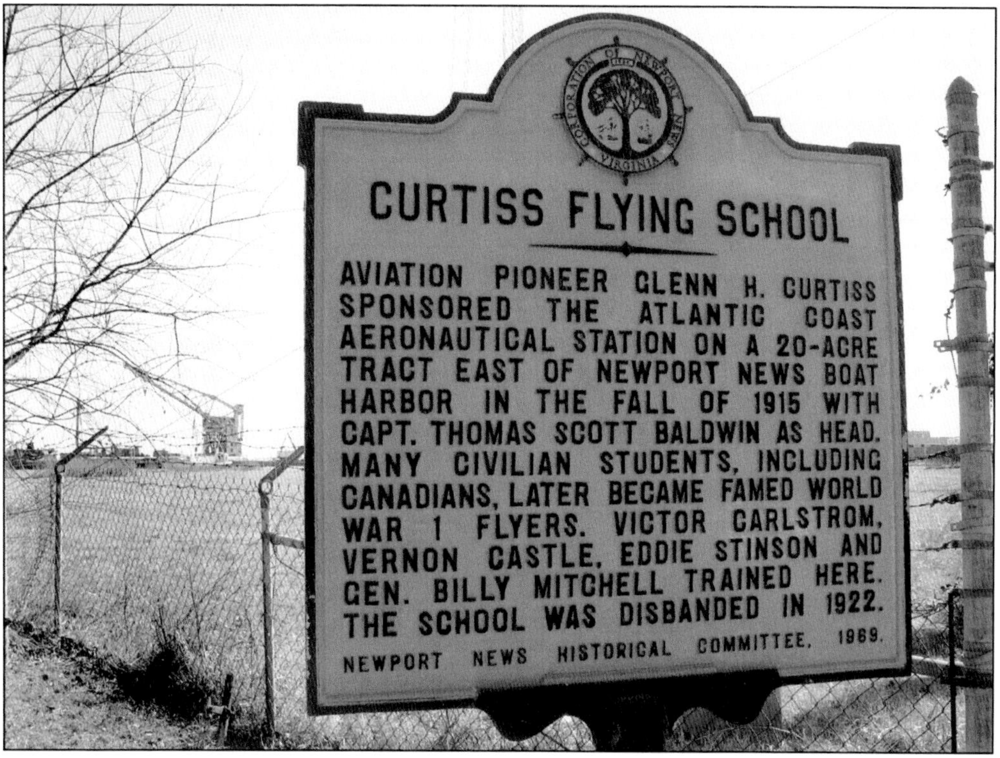

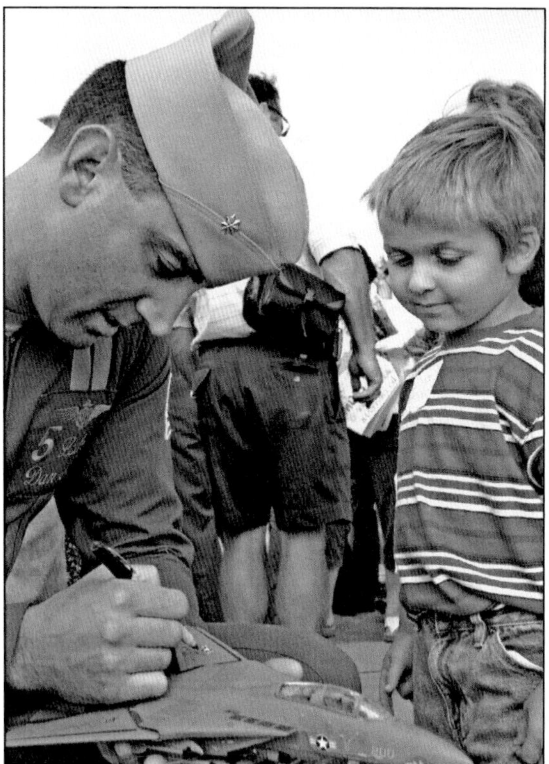

CURTISS FLYING SCHOOL. This monument is located on the site of the former Atlantic Coast Aeronautical Station, operated from 1915 until 1922 by aviation pioneer Glenn H. Curtiss on a 20-acre tract east of Newport News. The school was an important part of American history; some of the country's first aviation heroes got their start here. Today nothing remains except this sign, located in an industrial area at the southern end of Jefferson Avenue in Newport News near Lincoln Park. (PEH.)

AIR SHOWS OVER HAMPTON ROADS. Lt. Comdr. Dan Martin of the Blue Angels signs an F-14 Tomcat toy at the NAS Oceana Air Show (http://www.oceanaairshow.com), held each fall. Each spring, Air Power Over Hampton Roads takes place at Langley Air Force Base (http://www.langleyafbairshow.com) and includes an appearance by the Thunderbirds. (U.S. Navy photograph by Photographer's Mate 2C Anthony M. Koch.)

Places to Visit

Air Power Over Hampton Roads/Langley Air Show. See page 124 for more information.
(757) 764-5232
http://www.langleyafbairshow.com

Air Power Park and Museum. This park and museum has jets, missiles, rockets, and space artifacts in an outdoor display near Langley Air Force Base.
413 West Mercury Boulevard, Hampton
(757) 727-1163

Hampton Roads Transit Tour of Naval Station Norfolk. See page 123 for more information.
Naval Station Tour Center
9079 Hampton Boulevard, Norfolk
(757) 222-6100
http://www.hrtransit.org/trolleytours.html

Hampton Roads Transit Tour of NAS Oceana. See page 123 for more information.
Tourist kiosk: Atlantic Avenue and Twenty-Fourth Streets, Virginia Beach
(757) 222-6100
http://www.hrtransit.org/trolleytours.html

Hampton Roads Naval Museum. Located within Nauticus, the National Maritime Center in downtown Norfolk, this museum chronicles 225 years of naval history in the Hampton Roads region, including naval aviation.
1 Waterside Drive
(757) 322-2987
http://www.hrnm.navy.mil/

Murfreesboro Historical Association. Among the many displays offered by this group is a replica of the 1873 James Henry Gatling aeroplane. This replica, completed by students at nearby Chowan College under the direction of Shurley Vann, was built based on eyewitness accounts and newspaper clippings, since no photograph of the original craft exists.
116 East Main Street
(252) 398-5922
http://www.murfreesboronc.com

NAS Oceana Air Show. See page 124 for more information.
(757) 433-3131
http://www.oceanaairshow.com

NAS Oceana Flame of Hope Observation Park. Located on Oceana Boulevard about a half-mile from the base entrance, on the east side of the air station, this small park includes a POW/MIA memorial and an area to watch aircraft take off and land.

Newport News/Williamsburg International Airport. Due to Transportation Security Administration restrictions, access to gates is restricted to ticketed passengers only. However, there are places to observe airplanes near the General Aviation Terminal adjacent to the FAA control tower and inside the passenger terminal building, through windows, on the walkway to the concourse, and in the baggage claim area.
(757) 877-0221
http://www.nnwairport.com

Norfolk International Airport. Due to Transportation Security Administration restrictions, access to gates is restricted to ticketed passengers only. However, there is a small parking lot designated for airplane observation near the cargo terminal on Robin Hood Road, just off Military Highway. There is also a small space with benches to sit and observe aircraft from within the adjacent Norfolk Botanical Gardens, near the Baker Hall Visitor Center. Views of aircraft from the terminal building are limited.
(757) 857-3351
http://www.norfolkairport.com

Old Coast Guard Station. This historic Virginia Beach structure, built in 1903, has two floors of exhibits concerning the Coast Guard, including aviation components.
Oceanfront at Twenty-Fourth Street, Virginia Beach
(757) 422-1587
http://www.oldcoastguardstation.com

U.S. Army Transportation Museum on Fort Eustis. Nearly 100 vehicles and aircraft, located both indoors and out, chronicle army transportation from the Revolution to the present day at this museum.
300 Washington Boulevard, Newport News
(757) 878-1115
http://www.eustis.army.mil/

Wright Brothers National Monument. This is a federal government park/monument honoring the first flight at the site of the historic event. A museum/visitors center with interactive displays sits at the base of a 60-foot granite monument. There are also replicas of the 1903 camp buildings on the grounds.
Route 158, Kill Devil Hills, North Carolina
(252) 473-2111
http://www.nps.gov/wrbr/

Virginia Air and Space Center. See page 122 for more information.
600 Settlers Landing Road, Hampton
(757) 727-0900
http://www.vasc.org

Recommended Reading

Evans-Hylton, Patrick. *Hampton Roads: The World War II Years*. Charleston, SC: Arcadia Publishing, 2005.

Mitchell, John B. *The Army Airship Roma*. Hampton, VA.: Syms-Eaton Museum, 1973.

Parramore, Thomas C. *The Gatling Aeroplane of 1873: America's First Airplane*. Murfreesboro, NC: The Murfreesboro Historical Association, Inc., 2003.

Pearcy, Arthur. *A History of U.S. Coast Guard Aviation*. Annapolis, MD: Naval Institute Press, 1989.

Serling, Robert J. *From the Captain to the Colonel: An Informal History of Eastern Airlines*. New York, NY: The Dial Press, 1980.

Yarsinske, Amy Waters. *Mud Flats to Master Jet Base: Fifty Years at NAS Oceana*. Gloucester Point, VA: Hallmark Publishing, 2001.

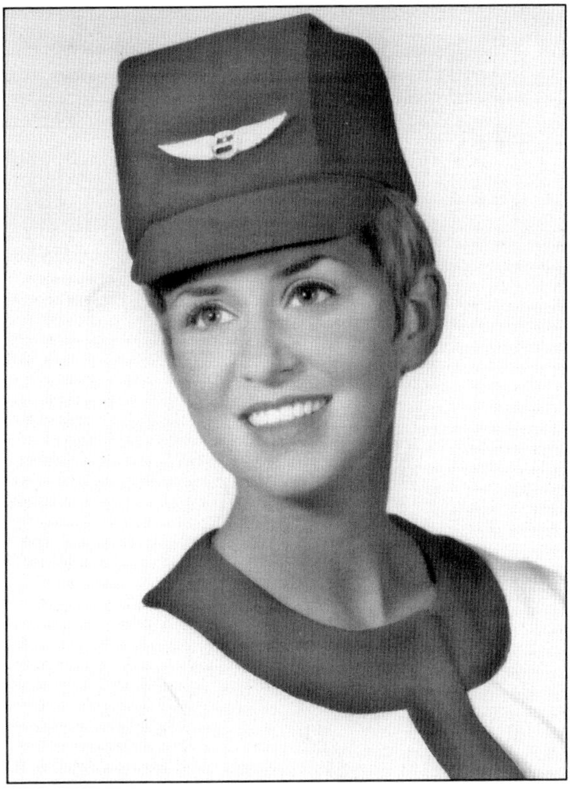

A View from the Top. For 35 years, from 1968 until 2003, the author's aunt, Brenda Evans-Potter, pictured here, was a flight attendant with United Airlines. Her career was the spark for the author's lifelong love of aviation. Over the years, aviation has changed greatly, especially in light of the September 11 terrorist attacks. The golden age of commercial aviation is remembered with two groups, the American Aviation Historical Society (http://www.aahs-online.org/) and Aerofiles (http://www.aerofiles.com/). (PEH.)

BIBLIOGRAPHY

In addition to the publications referenced in the "Recommended Reading" section, the following resources were used in the research of this book.

Norfolk International Airport Web site, July 2004. http://www.norfolkairport.com/
Newport News Airport Web site, July 2004. http://www.nnwairport.com/
Hampton Roads Naval Museum Web site, July 2004. http://www.hrnm.navy.mil/
United States Navy Web site, July 2004. http://www.navy.mil/
United States Air Force Web site, July 2004. http://www.af.mil/
United States Coast Guard Web site, July 2004. http://www.uscg.mil/

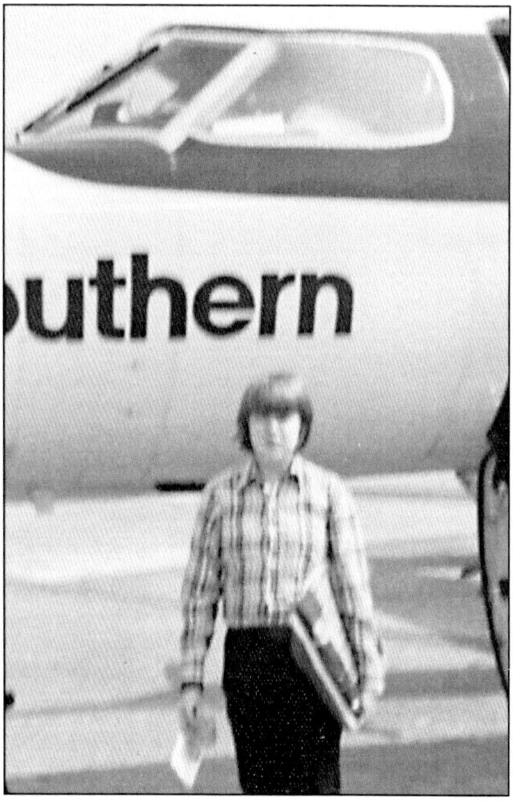

ABOUT THE AUTHOR. Patrick Evans-Hylton has been fascinated with aviation ever since he was a little boy, when he would go to the airport to visit his aunt, who was a flight attendant, between her flights. Often the pilots would take him on the plane, and his love for flying was born. Patrick considers himself a local historian and especially loves the rich heritage of commercial and military aviation found in his adopted southeastern Virginia. He is also the author of *World War II in Hampton Roads* and *Lighthouses and Lifesaving Stations of Virginia*. Patrick, a freelance writer (http://www.evanshyltonink.com) has written for several area publications and is an editor at *Hampton Roads Magazine*, a regional city and lifestyle magazine. He is also a regular contributor to the *Virginian-Pilot* newspaper. (PEH.)